Praise for Patricia Gherovici's
The Puerto Rican Syndrome

"Patricia Gherovici's *The Puerto Rican Syndrome* rescues a suspect label from its racist trappings and turns it into a productive reading of the intricate relationship between history and hysteria; she unveils in what could have been dismissed as yet another case of reckless medication of impotence a powerful political narrative of cultural vindication. By reading the syndrome as a significant return of the largely forgotten psychoanalytic etiology of the hysteric, she enacts a retelling of a seizure as a formidable 'return of the living dead,' where an 'ataque' is not merely a passive reaction to stress, but a strategy, an attack, an act of warfare within the streets of welfare. To see hysteria as resistance is to recapture its Lacanian reading as a political questioning of authority and to effectively restate its power as the originating symptom of psychoanalysis. Gherovici cunningly places the Puerto Rican syndrome at the core of Freud's *The Interpretation of Dreams* by providing a careful reading of his dream of the Spanish-American War that sheds an unexpectedly larger light for the reading of transculturalism as discontent. In this age of facile crossovers and triumphant globalizations of ethnicity, this splendid book will be hard to swallow. It is in itself a powerful symptom for the most disturbing aspects of North American Latinization. There is, after all, a *vida loca* that really kicks ass."
    —Rubén Ríos Ávila
    Professor of Comparative Literature, University of Puerto Rico;
    author of *La raza cómica: del sujeto en Puerto Rico*

"Psychoanalysis is for the elite and hysteria does not exist? Well, just read Patricia Gherovici's book and you will discover why the elite has either never liked psycho-analysis or did not understand it. On top of that, you'll meet a "pur sang" clinician who knows how to write as well."
 —Paul Verhaeghe, Ph.D.
 Professor of Clinical Psychology, Department of Psychoanalysis,
 University of Ghent, Belgium

"In times of a significant increase in the number of Hispanics in the United States, it is worth reading *The Puerto Rican Syndrome* to understand how uncomfortable otherness and difference continue to be for the masters who prefer to pathologize whatever resists homogeneity and silence. Patricia Gherovici's book is an authoritative account on how the colonial other responds to such an attempt, giving an excellent example of how a psychoanalyst can take full responsibility for the human suffering she has been listening to. . . . Gherovici provides powerful insights regarding such a "listening in context" that will be very useful to clinicians in various contexts as she explores the impact of colonial-ism and the place of the Hispanic Other in the United States' political landscape."
 —Alfredo Carrasquillo-Ramírez
 Psychoanalyst, San Juan, Puerto Rico
 Associate Dean for Graduate Studies, University of the Sacred Heart, Puerto Rico

"This groundbreaking study by Patricia Gherovici, a Lacanian psychoanalyst who works with Puerto Rican patients in Philadelphia, provides striking insights into a poorly understood form of hysteria known as the Puerto Rican syndrome, reveals the unique capacities of psychoanalysis to understand and treat the disorder, and in the process provides a fresh articulation of the basic assumptions and strategies of 'the talking cure'. . . . Through an impressive elucidation of the material, social, racial/ethnic, political, cultural, and discursive contexts in which psychological symptoms arise, Gherovici reveals how psychological symptoms and social symptoms interconstitute each other and demonstrates that solutions to problems in either domain must address both the social (and cultural, political, and material) and the psychological forces at play. This is a lesson that urgently needs to be learned by mental health workers, researchers in the human sciences, educators, and policymakers alike, and this book will help them learn it."
 —Mark Bracher
 Editor, *Psychoanalysis, Culture, & Society*

"Patricia Gherovici's *The Puerto Rican Syndrome* is a stunning book: at once a history of psychiatry's crypto-racism, it also offers decisive intervention in discussions of race and colonialism by showing the political situation at the heart of every hysteric's demand for immediate justice or immediate protection."
 —Catherine Liu
 Associate Professor, Department of Cultural Studies and Comparative Literature,
 University of Minnesota

"Patricia Gherovici's book conjugates in a seminal manner the psychoanalytic, sociological, historical, and anthropological discourses in a way that is destined to change American psychiatric discourse. The consequences of her courageous writing will be felt not only in theory and clinical psychoanalysis but in the political field because we witness a concrete denunciation of the mechanism of racism and domination. It is no hyperbole to call this book an essential work."
—Nestor Braunstein, Director of the Masters Program in Psychoanalysis at the Universidad del Claustro de Sor Juana, Mexico

"A short circuit occurs when two currents to be kept apart meet, thus producing an explosive disturbance of the system. Gherovici's book is such a short circuit, bringing together Lacanian psychoanalysis at the highest conceptual level and the concrete experience of social work among Puerto Ricans in Philadelphia. The result is breathtaking: the proof that top theory and engaged social experience need each other. A must for everyone, especially the anemic Cultural Studies academics!"
—Slavoj Žižek, philosopher and psychoanalyst

"Patricia Gherovici in her outstanding book explains how a culturally labeled mental illness, like Puerto Rican syndrome, in a particular way reflects the political, gender, and class divides in today's American society. Never since Freud's *Civilization and Its Discontents* have we encountered such profound understanding of the link between the individual's malaise and the malaise of the civilization. Gherovici's book has to be a must read not only for every psychotherapist working with a multi-ethnic population, but also for anyone who wants to understand how traumas of immigration create new types of neurotic symptoms."
—Renata Salecl, Centennial Professor at London School of Economics, author of *(Per)versions of Love and Hate*

The Puerto Rican Syndrome

CULTURAL STUDIES

A series of books edited by Samir Dayal

The Puerto Rican Syndrome

PATRICIA GHEROVICI

OTHER

Other Press
New York

The cover illustrations are details from a photograph of a community mural at Philadelphia's Taller Puertorriqueño. The public mural stretches around the length of a whole block at Huntington Street and over Fifth Street; it decorates the wall of the Taller Puertorriqueño's Education Building, which includes classrooms, workshop spaces, and a theater. The public mural depicts images chosen by the community as illustrating symbols of cultural identity: the Virgin dressed in the Puerto Rican flag, Taíno drawings, a vejigante (a fantastic carnival character), an open gateway connecting to the island, Roberto Clemente (the famous baseball player), a Grito de Lares flag (the first Puerto Rican flag that carried the inscription "Liberty or Death, Year 1868"), Ramón Emeterio Betances (the leader of the Grito de Lares uprising against the Spaniards), among others. The three women are Maritza de Campos, the granddaughter of the Independentist leader Pedro Albizu Campos, Mariana Bracetti, a Puerto Rican patriot who sewed the Lares flag and was known as Brazo de oro (Arm of Gold), and Julia de Burgos, the distinguished poet. The community was actively involved in the design of the mural, which was executed by artists Danny Polanco, Roldan West, Betsy Casañas, and Dani Torres, students of the Youth Activity Program, and volunteers of all ages from the barrio.

Copyright © 2003 Patricia Gherovici

Production Editor: Robert D. Hack
This book was set in 11 point Berkeley Book by Alpha Graphics of Pittsfield, NH.
ISBN-13: 978-1892746-75-7

Library of Congress Cataloging-in-Publication Data

Gherovici, Patricia.
  The Puerto Rican syndrome / by Patricia Gherovici.
      p. ; cm.
Includes bibliographical references and index.
  ISBN 1-892746-75-1
  1. Puerto Ricans–Mental health.   2. Puerto Ricans–Mental health–United States.   3. Hysteria.   4. Psychoanalysis.
  [DNLM: 1. Hysteria–history–Puerto Rico.   2. Hispanic Americans–Puerto Rico.   3. Mental Disorders–diagnosis–Puerto Rico.   4. Mental Disorders–ethnology–Puerto Rico.   5. Psychoanalytic Theory–Puerto Rico. WM 173 G417p 2003] I. Title.
  RC451.5.P84 G48 2003
  362.2'089'687295–dc21

                                                                    2003004195

Contents

Acknowledgments

Many people have helped me with this book. I feel grateful for the friendship and generous input of Flavia Gutiérrez, Nicolás Buosoño, Pablo Meninato, and Roxana Vogler. I will never forget that the informal meetings of our reading group soon became officially the Philadelphia Lacan Study Group in 1990. Their encouragement back then was instrumental in launching my research on the Puerto Rican syndrome.

Ives Thillet, at the Centro de Servicios para Hispanos, has been an inspirational guidance. I want to honor his memory. I still miss him and his wicked sense of humor.

For reasons of confidentiality I cannot name my patients, but I want to thank them for all I learned with them. Those wonderful hysterics, the *barrio*'s Anna O.s and Emmy von N.s, challenged me and encouraged me to rethink many of psychoanalysis' crucial questions. They confirmed my conviction that psychoanalytic theory derives from its praxis.

I feel incredibly fortunate to have the friendship of Deborah Luepnitz. I benefited appreciably from our stimulating conversations and from her generosity, clinical expertise, and wit. I am grateful for having been able to participate between 1992 and 1994 in the reading group that met in her apartment. There I found a hospitable, stimulating, and congenial place for intellectual discussion. The insights of Vicki Mahaffey, Jo Valente, Craig

Saper, and the late Lynda Hart nurtured my thinking. Thanks to Anabel Salafia and Noberto Ferreira who invited me in 1995 to Argentina to present at the International Conference of the Fundación del Campo Lacaniano. The audience gave helpful feedback to my paper on hysteria and the Puerto Rican syndrome. I am indebted to Veronica Cohen who published that paper in *Estudios sobre la histeria cien años después* (Gherovici 1996d).

I am grateful to Mark Bracher and Marshall Alcorn for publishing my piece "The Puerto Rican Syndrome" in the *Journal for the Psychoanalysis of Culture and Society* in 1996. Special recognition goes to Laura Corbalán Szichman for her warm support in the inaugural stages of this project. The articles published in *Clinical Studies: International Journal of Psychoanalysis* allowed me to test a number of theoretical hypotheses in 1996–1997.

I extend my deepest thanks to Marisa Robert de Ramirez de Arellano, main author of the first study on the Puerto Rican syndrome, who kindly handed me a copy in San Juan, Puerto Rico, of that hard to find unpublished document. Similar appreciation extends to the devoted personnel of the library at the University of Puerto Rico, Recinto de Río Piedras, who helped wholeheartedly with my research, and to Dr. Carlos Avilés Roig at San Juan's Veterans Administration Medical Center for the information provided.

Over the years, I have benefited appreciably from the stimulating discussions and the vibrant atmosphere in the Philadelphia Lacan Study Group and Seminar. Many thanks to Betsy Mossiman, Aldona Middlesworth, Alex Glassman, Lucio Angelo Privitello, Stephen Levine, Chris Lane, Armando Maggi, Gregg Flaxman, Joshua Schuster, Tom Wolman, Radu Turcanu, Caroline Weber, Micaela Farcas, Tom Kelso, and Natalia Rosenfeld. I am particularly grateful to Justine Gudenas for her judicious advice, encouragement, and for opening the doors of her house, allowing me to join the Smedley Writers Group. My warmest thanks to Bernard Stehle for his collaborative ethos, excitement, and precise editing of an earlier version of the manuscript. Thanks a million to the other Writers Group members: Randall Couch, William Gremmel, Daphne Herbert, Larry MacKenzie, Bruce Trinz, and Larry McCarty. I owe them an immensurable debt for helping me shape this project. My work has been challenged and improved by their critical attention and tireless reading.

Kenneth Gergen generously offered me several times the opportunity to present my work to his students at Swarthmore College, which granted me a forum for the discussion of many of this book's ideas.

The careful reading and comments of Suzanne Verderber helped improve this project. Sincere thanks to Judith Feher Gurewich for inviting me twice to present at her Lacan Seminar at Harvard University where I benefited enormously from the scholarly discussion of my work. Her encouragement and obliging enthusiasm for this project has been invaluable and I am grateful for her helpful clinical insights in Chapter 15. *Mil gracias* to Carmen Lamas, who read parts of the manuscript, offering me detailed annotations, insightful suggestions, and helpful critique. I want to acknowledge the many friends and colleagues who offered suggestions, support, and helpful criticism during the various stages of this project: Lisa Ratmansky, Annie Godfrey, Cynthia Schossberger, Raquel Romberg, Kareen Malone, Christine Ware, Joseph Clarke, Charlie Shepherdson, Ligia Ravé Slovic, Alfredo Carrasquillo Ramírez, Silvia Alvárez Curbelo, Iris Zavala Martínez, Lydia Schut, Catherine Liu, Roberto Lewis-Fernández, Peter J. Guarnaccia, Ramón Grosfoguel, Paola Mieli, Diana S. Rabinovich, Nestor Braunstein, Frida Saal, Pablo Kovalosky, Gérard Pommier, and Thomas Bartlett.

I am pleased to acknowledge here the generous contribution of Aaron Levy, who took the cover photographs. His artist's vision made me see the *barrio* in a different light. I am grateful to the two artists who were involved in the community mural reproduced on the cover: Dani Polanco and Roldán West, who gave me a helpful description of the images that appear in Levy's photographs.

Special thanks to Samir Dayal, Other Press' Cultural Studies Series editor, and to my editor at Other Press, Stacy Hague.

I want to express my heartfelt gratitude to Marius and Beba Gherovici for providing moral and logistical support throughout the writing, making possible the completion of this book.

Without the indefatigable support of Jean-Michel Rabaté this book would have not been written: thanks, thanks, thanks.

Series Editor's Introduction

SAMIR DAYAL

The Puerto Rican Syndrome, as the title indicates, brings clinical expertise and theoretical sophistication to bear on the cultural, political, and psychological nexus of the Puerto Rican community in relation to mainstream U.S. culture. The reader will be struck immediately by the interdisciplinary nature of this study. While much has been written in recent years about the alleged disaffection with psychoanalysis, Patricia Gherovici offers compelling evidence of the continuing relevance of the insights of Sigmund Freud and Jacques Lacan.

Indeed, the book takes as a point of departure the moment at which the ancient category of hysteria was falling into disfavor among psychotherapists during the McCarthyite 1950s and when, simultaneously, hysterical symptoms were being observed in Puerto Rican soldiers: hallucinations, amnesia, panic, anxiety, and fear, as well as seizures without traceable somatic etiology. The strangeness of this (non)coincidence is compounded by the fact that these symptoms were being observed not in women but in male soldiers. For hysteria was thought to be a condition that by definition afflicted women, a pathology associated with the "wandering" womb or "hysterus." It is patently impossible to explain these symptoms solely in terms of the rhetoric of traditional Freudian analysis; one cannot understand them except with reference to the social and the political, and Gherovici helps readers make some of these important connections.

The author notes, for instance, that Freud's innovative theory of the workings of the unconscious recognized the centrality of hysteria in conceptualizing some of the links between the individual psyche and wider social phenomena. Lacan, perhaps the most important as well as controversial interpreter of Freud, developed the theory of hysteria by revolutionizing the modern understanding of the complex, and fundamentally "symbolic," nature of subjectivity. Without being too insistent, Gherovici suggests that a Lacanian theorization of hysteria provides a grammar enabling a radical articulation of the "Puerto Rican syndrome" as manifested in the individual with the syndrome as expressed in the minority group.

Gherovici draws lucid but complex connections between the political and the psychic. She focuses our attention specifically on how, in the case of Puerto Ricans, issues of "race," mental illness, national origin, or cultural belonging merge with the problematics of political marginalization and social positioning. Or, to put it differently, the Puerto Rican syndrome derives its particularity from the inscription of the neocolonial status of Puerto Ricans in the U.S. national imagination. This is not to say, of course, that the syndrome is imaginary. Puerto Rico became a colony of the United States in 1899. A governor was appointed in the colony by William McKinley, who was president of the United States at the time. In 1917 Puerto Ricans were made U.S. citizens, conveniently becoming available as soldiers during World War I. The first governor elected by Puerto Ricans came to power in 1948, and a few years later, in 1952, Puerto Rico became an "associated commonwealth" of the United States, and so it remains. This means in part that while Puerto Rico is subject to U.S. military and trade regulations, Puerto Ricans on the island cannot vote for U.S. president and they have no full representation in the U.S. Congress. They pay no federal taxes, but can be drafted. The U.S. military controls vast tracts of Puerto Rico, including over 70 percent of the island of Vieques, which for some time has been subjected to U.S. bombing practice. So while Puerto Ricans nominally identify as members of the U.S. polity, they often find themselves seeking an international audience to lodge complaints about the U.S. government's attitude to Puerto Rico.

Gherovici is always conscious of the anomalous status of Puerto Rico as a "commonwealth"—neither a colony nor a state at the same level as, say, California or Massachusetts. Thus (neo)colonization is protested not only as a feature of life in Puerto Rico but in New York City and elsewhere on the mainland too. The ambivalences of being Puerto Rican result, correspondingly, from their divided loyalties as political subjects. Thus, when Gherovici discusses the way in which Puerto Ricans use the word *país* (country) as an anchor for their identities within the Anglophone mainstream culture of the U.S., the author asks provocatively whether this is an element in the production of a "mental infection," a hysterical fit, and whether there is something unique about this way of conceiving of belonging as a "geopolitics of the psyche."

Gherovici is also able to convey a sense of what it might mean to live as a Puerto Rican in America. The interstitiality or ambivalence of Puerto Ricans may be recognized in the general culture, but this book provides a much more substantive and precise understanding of how this interstitiality is *experienced*. The complexity of understanding how *país* is differently inflected for someone who identifies as a "Nuyorican" and for someone living in Puerto Rico is important. So is the question of how aspirations to assimilate into the mainstream and "make it" in America are thwarted by the recognition that economic success and social acceptance often take divergent trajectories. Gherovici astutely suggests that such calculations not only play a part in conscious identification but also, and differently, work at the level of the unconscious.

The author well understands the class implications of utilizing psychoanalysis as a lens through which to analyze, "diagnose," and treat the Puerto Rican syndrome. One can hardly gloss over the fact that urban Puerto Rican communities in particular disidentify with mainstream "white" or "Anglo" psychoanalysis and psychotherapy, to the extent of refusing medication that is associated with "Anglo" psychotherapy and demanding alternative prescriptions for themselves. Gherovici notes that mental health services available to the Hispanic community are part of a general strategy of "symptom suppression." Is this a form of pacification? As opposed to managed care, she argues, psychoanalysis offers an "ethical model that is not utilitarian." Indeed the successes of *barrio* psychotherapy point, in Gherovici's estimation, to alternative approaches made available by what might be termed hybridized or refracted psychoanalytic epistemologies. Among the project's most distinctive features is the articulation of the ethnographic and the clinical psychoanalytic accounts. Gherovici retains both the theoretical complexity of a psychoanalytic understanding of hysteria and the cultural/historical (colonial and neocolonial) contexts of the *ataque*, in all their specificity.

What emerges in these pages, then, is a complex picture of a community from the inside, an internal critique in two senses. First, this book offers a perspective that is adumbrated by but unavailable in the annals of postcolonial critique produced from within metropolitan space. Second, it also elaborates the perspective of someone who is herself a "native informant," of sorts. After all, the syndrome emerges in response to what is effectively the last imperial power of the contemporary period. While psychoanalysis provides a framework for understanding the "syndrome," the author emphasizes the importance of recognizing that praxis guides theory and not the other way round. The study is grounded in the author's work with patients and in her close analysis of the history of Puerto Ricans in the U.S.

The book is crafted with the precision of someone steeped in the discipline of clinically guided psychoanalysis. And it is driven by a passionate concern for and investment in those she takes as her subject. This exemplary work in cultural studies offers the general reader an adroit negotiation between an "expert" voice and the voice of someone who works for and with real-world problems of the Puerto Rican community.

The New Other America

It was early on a sunny Tuesday. I got off the Market-Frankford elevated subway line at the North Philadelphia Somerset station. All the subway stations in North Philadelphia were being rebuilt. Descending into the cavernous darkness under the high rail structure, I passed a labyrinth of yellow tape lines. Once I had clambered down the stairs into the street underneath, instead of being met by the usual denizens of the street corner—drug-dealers, bodies lying on the ground sleeping off a drug overdose, crack-prostitutes—I was surprised by the uncommonly intense level of activity. Trucks parked all over the place were moving what looked like construction material. Teams of workers were daubing the graffiti-encrusted walls with white paint. Stylized publicity posters were being pasted over the freshly painted walls. Store fronts were washed clean. The abandoned washing machines and refrigerators piling up on the sidewalk had been carted away. A new sign hung on the corner shop. Crowds of awed neighbors watched, mesmerized. Finally, gentrification has caught up with the *barrio*, I thought. On a second look, I noticed here and there projectors and lighting equipment. As I reached the mental health clinic where I worked, just half a block down the street, I was told what was *really* happening.

Everyone was thrilled. Among the excited comments, I heard the word "Hollywood." Hollywood? What would Hollywood have to do with neighborhood development? *"Están filmando una gran película."* Indeed, they were shooting a big budget film with well-known movie stars—Bruce Willis, Madeleine Stowe, and Brad Pitt. I learned that the movie takes place in an imaginary future when humanity has been eradicated from the face of the Earth. In *Twelve Monkeys*, the film that was in progress, a few survivors inhabit a desolate underground netherworld because the planet's surface remains lethal. Precisely, Kensington Avenue had been chosen as the setting for one scene of the futuristic drama. This drab *barrio* street was selected to portray how the planet would look after a deadly virus has eliminated all human life and only lions and giraffes are seen ambling around Philadelphia's City Hall. What I had mistaken naïvely for a sign of urban cleanup pointed to an even more disquieting truth: the *barrio* setting had to be cleaned up to look post-Apocalyptic!

What was I doing in this inauspicious environment that soon would swallow the gaudy posters and the fresh paint in a new wave of urban detritus? I was working at a bilingual mental-health outpatient clinic. During my six years of clinical work in the field of so-called mental health, within the Latino, primarily Puerto Rican, community of North Philadelphia, I experienced a reversed version of the American dream. Puerto Ricans comprise the city's most impoverished group in Philadelphia.[1] Inner-city realities introduce the Third World at the core of the U.S. mainland. The neighborhood is vividly described by Kristin Koptiuch (1997) as a "dilapidated, drug-infested, trash-strewn, graffiti-riddled Puerto Rican barrio in the *urban* jungle of North Philadelphia" a "third world" at home (p. 235).

> Oxymoronically then, Philadelphia, the nation's oldest city, city of the Liberty Bell and the signing of the U.S. Constitution, has become the site of a largely uncolonized imperial frontier situated at a transnational intersection of language, labor and everyday life. But it is by no way unique. Instead, it simply manifests a process of "third worlding" that in the last fifteen to twenty years has become apparent throughout the United States. [p. 235]

---

1. Puerto Ricans with comparable education levels earn, on average, only 82 percent of what African Americans earn, and only 66 percent of the salaries and wages of white workers in Philadelphia.

My daily commute to work can serve as an example of the language/social demarcation that defines the invisible boundaries of the ghetto. A fifteen-minute bus ride would take me from a middle-class center-city district (a busy commercial and business area) through postindustrial decay of abandoned factories, to housing "projects," symbols of a collapsing welfare state, and finally to a cluster of stagnating sociolinguistic islands. Coming from a developing Latin-American culture myself, I was hoping to find in a big U.S. city an improvement in lifestyle and health. Because of my training in clinical psychology in Argentina and the scarcity of Spanish-speaking professionals, I had no problem finding employment in the Puerto Rican community of North Philadelphia. Feeling disenfranchised as a minority, since after all I was a Lacanian psychoanalyst, I found myself working in the middle of a much more disenfranchised community. Lacan, for many critics in North American circles, is known as the "French Freud" and considered to be elitist; his take on psychoanalysis is seen as an abstract intellectual pursuit closer to literary theory than to clinical practice. Anyone with such training may look like an unlikely candidate to offer any useful clinical contribution, especially given the practical concerns raised by "ghettoized" Latino populations. My clinical work in the *barrio* has led me to conclude that psychoanalytic practice itself has been "ghettoized." Indeed, being a Lacanian today in the United States means being a minority within a minority. However, what did I exactly mean by calling myself "a Lacanian"?

In the North American context, the first definition that comes to mind is that to be a Lacanian means above all to be a Freudian. To explain a little more, being a Lacanian today means being part of a minority in expansion of clinicians and academicians who, if they are not "bringing the plague," as Freud famously said he brought with him to the United States when he visited and lectured in 1909, are at least offering a new form of psychoanalytic outlook. In the United States, Lacan's clinical relevance is slowly taking its place next to Carl Jung's, Wilfred Bion's, or Melanie Klein's. Thus far, it has encountered a lot of resistance. Lacan's prose appears too poetic for a "scientist of the psyche." For most readers, professional or not, Lacan's style has been found to be obscure, baroque, almost unreadable. However, a growing number of analysts and academics in the United States have taken upon themselves the task of explaining key Lacanian theses, insisting upon the fact that his contributions are not only literary or philosophical but apply above all to clinical practice. This trend is also linked with a Lacan-inspired rereading of Freud that integrates social conditions with individual psychology—his subject is, after all, one whose unconscious is "structured like a language." Lacan's notion of the "subject" posits a human entity that has become social when subjected to language—this is, produced and alienated by culture. While pointing to an irreducible discontent in speaking subjects, Lacan radically opposes any adaptationist therapy.

In the 1950s, Lacan proclaimed a "Return to Freud." For Lacan, Freudianism, although dominant in American culture, had become severely distorted. American psychoanalysis is geared toward the adaptation to "reality" and places strongly optimistic hopes in an ego that would be reinforced by therapy and endowed with better coping skills. This American optimism could not be more opposed to Freud's pessimism about irremediable unconscious determinations. Freud rebuffed any attempt at salvation, whether religious, political, or therapeutic. Freud remained skeptical of James Putnam, who fervently recommended psychoanalysis to his co-nationals while transforming it into a form of Protestantism, enforcing an implicit return to William James and his psychologization of religious experience. Thus, American psychoanalysts embraced an "impossible" reconstruction that was successfully disseminated. Psychoanalysis would provide a universal ethical conception and emerge as a submedical specialty. While Freudian psychoanalysis in France and Latin America opened the path for Lacanian psychoanalysis, in the United States ego psychology Americanized Freud by transforming psychoanalysis into adaptive techniques. A second chance at the American dream was provided by the works of Erik Erikson, who emphasized development and a vital cycle directed toward ideals of maturity and by Heinz Kohut, who pledged for an optimistic self, fortified, able to overcome conflict.[2] Was the greatly popular American Freudianism of the 1950s psychoanalysis or a hybridized by-product closer to behaviorism?

Even though one may claim that the Freudian spirit was lost in the translation, today in the United States the capacity of Freud to elicit unrest remains undiminished. The antagonism to a recent Library of Congress exhibit in his honor is indicative. The Freudian unconscious is still stirring passionate reactions.

Early in the planning stage, Freud's exhibit raised a heated controversy among opposed intellectual groups. As a result, it was postponed for

---

2. For more on the "American Freud," see Turkle 1992, pp. xiii–xxiii.

a couple of years, finally opening in Washington, DC, in October 1998 under the title "Sigmund Freud: Conflict and Culture." The show traveled internationally, from the United States to Brazil and Austria, closing in Israel in September 2002. To erase the initial uneasiness and calm aroused passions, the exhibition became a compromise formation—flaunting its culturalist ideology, it exhibited the very symptom of what American culture represses and magnifies.

The Library of Congress exhibit contained various objects and fragments of film, cartoons, and TV shows, each one supporting the only claim the organizers could safely make: Freud has been and will continue to be part of American culture, even though many disagree with his ideas. The exhibit effectively reduced Freud to a cultural phenomenon; he became a star or an idol, comparable to Andy Warhol or John F. Kennedy. However, conflict crept back into the items exhibited, subtly and silently, at least through quotes of followers and detractors. Their comments, spread over the walls, appeared to have been chosen for their timidity rather than for brash condemnations or lavish praise. Thus in this context it was a surprise to discover Lacan's famous last phrase, from the 1980 Caracas conference, a little more than a year before his death: *"C'est à vous d'être lacanien, moi je suis freudien."* ("It is up to you to be Lacanian; as for myself I am a Freudian.") Among the exhibit's misfires and parapraxes, one reads after Lacan's quote, ominously: "no date." In the eternal present of a symptomatic suspension, Lacan's presence is acknowledged but left outside history.

The exhibit appeared as a symptomatic compromise formation and so provides keys for a solution. Any solution had to be found in "culture" and in the possibilities of transformation within psychoanalysis itself. Whether brought about by Lacan or by an internal logical evolution, here was a way of suggesting that psychoanalysis reflects and challenges its own cultural environment. As we know, in the United States that cultural environment is changing very fast. Just as one can now find drinkable coffee, luxury wines, edible croissants, and nice outdoor cafés in most American downtowns, one might expect to find good psychoanalysis as an attendant phenomenon. Mike Davis (2000) maintains, "To be Latino in the United States is rather to participate in an unique process of cultural syncretism that may become a transformative template for the whole society" (p. 15). This complex cultural transformation derives less from the globalization of culture, which is a general occurrence, than from what I have called elsewhere the Hispanization of American culture—a development that some see looming out with some terror or suspicion, but to which I wholeheartedly subscribe (see Gherovici 1996a, 2001).

American culture seems more and more infatuated with things Latin—"Latin is hot." Mexican salsa sells more than ketchup, and a taco-selling Chihuahua is a national icon. Demographic data show that the U.S., which used to think of itself along the old dichotomy of white or black, will no longer be either. In New York City, so-called Hispanics make up 27 percent of the population. In only one decade, the Hispanic population in the United States has increased by 58 percent, from 22.4 million in 1990 to 35.3 million in 2000 (and these numbers do not include undocumented immigrants who may not have participated in the Census.)[3] Thus Hispanics cause panic: they have become the "first" (that is, most numerous) minority group and by 2050 they will account for nearly one quarter of the total population.[4] Already the large numbers of Hispanics living in the U.S. have transformed this country into the fifth largest Latin American "nation" in the continent. In less that half a century the U.S. will be third only to Brazil and Mexico.[5] Given this projection, "It is not hyperbole to suggest that the future of the nation and its economy depend on the well-being of Latinos," states *Latinos: Remaking America* (Brown and Yu 2002, p. 251), the recent book produced by Harvard's Rockefeller Center for Latin American Studies. Today, moreover, the word "bilingual" in the U.S. only means one thing: Spanish/English. Sensing this shift, both presidential candidates in the last election tried to lure voters by addressing them in Spanish.

In this fast-moving context, being a Lacanian in the United States implies foreseeing a quite different future but also analyzing the present with different tools, perhaps also a more critical eye. What an approach influenced by Lacanian psychoanalysis can bring will also apply to current social issues of global pathology, developments of a fluctuating minority group with permeable borders. In the dead-end manifested by the

---

3. The statistics found regarding the Hispanic population of the United States do not incude the population of the Commonwealth of Puerto Rico; only Puerto Ricans residing in the United States are included.

4. See U.S. Census Bureau 2000, 2001 (www.census.gov: "Race" and "Hispanic"); also Therrien and Ramírez 2000.

5. Demographic studies estimate that the U.S. Latino population will be as high as 100 million by 2040.

Hispanic experiences, the reality of the unconscious insists; it stubbornly reminds us that despite the demographics, there is no social rapport. Hispanics embody the contradictions of a country that does not think of itself as "colonial" but has colonies (Puerto Rico being one of its most painful examples), that is proud of becoming a "melting pot" but divides its population into ethnic groups like cloistered units, that maintains "third world" (or "fourth world") inner city enclaves within a "first world" country. As for sexuality, the anomie of a heterogeneous group, almost invisible if not by the salience of worrying symptoms, forces Americans to revise their notions about the unconscious. As for me, being Lacanian today means to be reading a "French Freud" but in an English spiced with a Spanish accent.

A GOLD-PAVED PATH TO THE UNCONSCIOUS

This book has emerged from my six-year clinical experience as a psychotherapist and clinical director with the so-called Hispanic community of North Philadelphia. There, in my consultation room in the *Bloque de Oro* (Golden Block), the main street whose sidewalks have been painted yellow to wink at the American dream of gold-paved success, now tarnished with the disillusionment caused by a drab reality, I met for the first time the Puerto Rican syndrome. This diagnosis was coined during the 1950s. At that time, U.S. Army doctors reported strange symptoms among distressed Puerto Rican soldiers, mostly Korean War veterans. Their symptoms ranged from sudden outbursts of verbal hostility to destructive physical assault, from wildly infantile behavior to catatonia, from forgetfulness to suicidal gestures, from a state of frenzy to lack of interest in physical appearance, from partial loss of consciousness to seizures followed by amnesia. Although there were no specific recurrent or single symptoms found in each case, some patterns suggested serious neurological conditions. Physical examination, however, showed no sign of any organic disease. This group of varied manifestations has also been described as "hyperkinetic seizure," *nervios* (nerves), *mal de pelea* (disease of fighting), and *ataque de nervios* (which means *attacks* and *nerves*, respectively, and could be translated as nervous breakdown).

What is remarkable about this syndrome? Not only is it a mode of disease labeled as uniquely Puerto Rican, thus linking nationality, cultural phenomena, and psychiatric disease, but it is strikingly similar to the extravagant behavior of classical hysterics who rendered the invention of psychoanalysis possible. The reappearance of such noteworthy, almost "old fashioned" forms of hysteria is even more surprising at a time when the mere use of the word "hysteria" in clinical practice seems an anachronism.[6] Although hysteria has its place of honor in the history of psychoanalysis, the diagnosis quickly disappeared from the standard psychiatric nomenclature during the 1950s. Ironically, the semantic suppression of the diagnosis of hysteria happened at the time that the Puerto Rican syndrome was identified.

I understand the Puerto Rican syndrome as a mode of hysteria, and define hysteria in the extended sense given to it by Lacan. For Lacan, hysteria is a neurosis but also a mode of discourse whose ultimate function is to tighten particular social links. I consider the Puerto Rican syndrome less a neurosis than a social phenomenon producing knowledge and creating want. The apparent contradiction between virulent hysteria as conceived in the classical clinical image and the social link that it generates can be resolved if hysteria is conceived as *normal*. As Lacan (1998a) indicates in Seminar 5, hysteria is a universal condition for the speaking subject. He evokes the "world of hysteria, manifest or latent, that is the essential hysteria of the human subject insofar as s/he wonders (or interrogates the Other) about her or his desire" (pp. 466–467).[7] In this "Puerto Rican" hysteria, society, class, race, nationality, and language all converge dramatically and symptomatically.

Since the Puerto Rican syndrome is at once a clinical and political problem, my contention is that the paroxysmic exhibition of "nerves" (*nervios*) that I will describe at length throughout the book can only find adequate explanation when seen from a point of view that allies the empirical observations of clinical experience and Lacanian theory. This supposes a close rereading of Freud, which is why I review the Puerto Rican syndrome operating under the hypothesis that it is a hysteria. From there, I will move to a process that can be described as a hysterization of the Puerto Rican syndrome. My aim is to explore how the Puerto Rican syndrome as a "hysteric discourse" can produce some form of knowledge.

Lacanian and post-Lacanian psychoanalysis addresses hysteria as the paradigmatic example of the relationship of subjects to the so-called Mas-

---

6. See Slavney (1990); Micale (1995), especially Introduction, Chapters 1 and 2.
7. Unless otherwise specified, all translations from French and Spanish are my own.

ter. The hysteric produces a powerful Other while attempting to depose it again and again. However, the power at stake is never recaptured, because once a Master has fallen from the position of authority, the hysteric always manages to find a new Master. Since hysteria not only implies but institutes or "makes" the Other, hysteria is in a privileged position to explore what is the inscription of the discourse of the Other.

In one of Lacan's latest elaborations, he contends that hysteria is coming back today in the social field, more precisely as a social symptom. The idea of a displacement of hysteria onto the social field finds a precursor in one key figure of hysteria's gaudy history. Thomas Sydenham, the great seventeenth-century English doctor, ascribed to culture an important factor in the genesis of hysteria. He noted that hysterical symptoms "imitate" the culture in which they were produced. Thus, the Puerto Rican syndrome is a "symptom" not only for those suffering it but for those identifying it and diagnosing it—it is a cultural barometer. To understand this complex cultural construct in its whole dimension, I review the appearance of the diagnosis of Puerto Rican syndrome in the literature and interpret its sociopolitical implications. I will explore the clinical field by analyzing the ways in which it is treated in current mental health practices. Quite often, practitioners and insurance companies rule out psychoanalysis as an option for the poor, which implies absurdly that the poor cannot afford to have an unconscious.

Whenever I talk about applying psychoanalytic techniques to people living in economically deprived areas like the *barrio*, I trigger doubt, dismay, or dismissal. American psychoanalysis tends to shun Lacan's clinical contributions to the Freudian field. Such resistance to Lacanian psychoanalysis, however, in the long run may turn out to be beneficial. As Bruce Fink (2000) contends, cultural skepticism about psychoanalysis may make patients less open to suggestions and thus better candidates for true analytic treatment. It does not really matter if patients attribute greater or lesser value to Freud's and Lacan's theories, or even if they know about them at all. The important relationship that needs to be established is between the analysand and his or her unconscious. By its extreme and theatrical violence and its resistance to being domesticated by behavioral approaches, the Puerto Rican syndrome effectively questions current mental health services.

2

HYSTERIA IN THE *BARRIO*

It was the police who brought Anita to the emergency room of the hospital. Wrapped in a blanket, soaked in rain, she was screaming, biting, and
fighting. She was experiencing an *ataque*. Around her, total chaos made
her very utterances incomprehensible: nobody understood her mixture of
Spanish and English broken by cries and grunts. She thrashed around so
violently that the whole waiting room had turned into a battlefield. The
sign that carried "*Favor de mostrar un Tarjeta Medical*" ("Please show one
medical card") to all incoming patients finally crashed. A nurse came and
wiped her foaming mouth, preventing her from biting her tongue. Anita's
body convulsed in an epileptic crisis. She had a last spasm and lost consciousness. In a few minutes, she had run the whole gamut of dramatically spectacular symptoms leading to some sort of seizure. Earlier that
night, the police had found her roaming in North Philadelphia's Juniata
Park; she was stark naked, totally disoriented, and had no memory of
why she was there.

Here is the long answer Anita gave to my question, "Why are you here
today and how do you think I may help you?" when I was assessing her
during her initial intake session at the *barrio*'s clinic. She had been discharged from the hospital and referred to outpatient psychotherapy; this

is how Anita introduced me to her life and to the Puerto Rican syndrome. Everything had begun when she was 19; she had run away from her family in Puerto Rico because of frequent brawls and disputes with her mother and one of her sisters. She explained that her mother, her brother Teddy, two aunts, Margarita and Yvette, and her brother Filberto were suffering regularly from *ataques*. In the hospital, the psychiatrist described her symptoms as an "atypical psychosis" that was later diagnosed as "Puerto Rican syndrome." In order to explain how I was able to help her, which I did finally and in a certain measure, it is necessary to make a detour so as to understand the full context in which such clinical entities can be met.

In subsequent treatments of other patients coming from the North Philadelphia Spanish-speaking ghetto, I encountered more often the striking manifestations that are the subject of this book. I must insist upon the context. Philadelphia has the third largest Puerto Rican population outside the island, after New York and Chicago (U.S. Census Bureau 2001). Those patients identify themselves primarily as belonging to "the Puerto Rican race" or to "*La Raza*" rather than as Hispanic or Latino. The term "Hispanic" is itself already a problematic construct conflating categories of language (a Spaniard, for example, is not Hispanic), of race (there is no unique ethnic group identifiable solely as Spanish-speaking), and of class (a rich Hispanic, away from the ghetto, loses most of the characteristics associated with being Hispanic). Behind a common language, Hispanics are not a homogeneous group—they come from more than twenty different countries with distinct histories, customs, and specific blends of European, African, and native populations.

Even if we may call them the more politically correctly "Latino," those subjects and their experiences of oppression, like other populations belonging to so-called minorities, will continue to be negated, seen as part of a crowd that becomes one undifferentiated body. Hispanics or Latinos are presented by mainstream discursive practices as a host of frozen images in which any trace of individuality or class, cultural, and gender differences is erased. This is why the notion of "race" has shaped Latino identities. The racialization of such a diverse group of individuals with distinctive Latin American roots is, at least, problematic. Often the use of "race" serves to conceal the social conditions experienced by marginalized groups and "naturalize" historical conditions, becoming a legitimate tool of exclusion. Is there a better term to categorize this varied group? This issue is likely to remain unresolved. For half a century the U.S. Census has struggled to find an all-encompassing category for this ethnic group with fluid borders. In the 1930 census Mexicans were considered a race, but not in the 1940 census. A decade later, the U.S. Census tried a language criterion with the category "Person of Spanish Mother Tongue," which was used in 1950, and employed lineage as a designation in 1960 with the category "Spanish Surname." In this statistical universe these tools were abandoned because of their unreliability, and the designers of the U.S. Census finally took on the term "Hispanic"—a category that was adopted by the Nixon administration in the 1970s and first deployed in 1980 (Davis 2001). The Census 2000 data on the Hispanic or Latino population was derived from answers to a question that was asked to all; people were required to identify their origin as Spanish, Hispanic, or Latino independently from the "usual" categories of race. For the first time, respondents were allowed to choose more than one skin color in identifying themselves. According to the U.S. Census Bureau, "Hispanics may be of any race."[1]

The usage of the term "Hispanic" has been eloquently criticized by Juan Flores (1993) for its bureaucratic shallowness and invidiousness. "Hispanic" evokes a link with "Hispania" (Spain), thus emphasizing a common Spanish-language heritage as a meta-ethnicity disregarding structural inequalities of class and race. Furthermore, Neil Foley (1997) contends that the term "Hispanic" entails a Faustian pact with "whiteness": "Hispanic identity thus implies a kind of 'separate but equal' whiteness with a twist of salsa, enough to make one ethnically flavorful and culturally exotic without, however, compromising one's racial privilege as a White person" (p. 53).

As scholars attempt to move away from "Hispanic"—a term that negates that the New World population had not only Iberian roots but also a strong African and aboriginal component—the label "Latino" comes to the forefront as an identification strategy for grassroot initiatives. Paradoxically, both the concept of "Latinity" and "Hispanicity" were intro-

---

1. In the Census 2000, people classified themselves as Spanish, Hispanic, or Latino according to the categories "Mexican, Mexican Am., Chicano," "Puerto Rican," "Cuban," and "other Spanish/Hispanic/Latino." Persons indicating that they are "other Spanish/ Hispanic/Latino" included those whose origins are from Spain and the Spanish-speaking countries of Central or South America. People identifying themselves generally as Spanish, Spanish-American, Hispanic, Latino, and so on were labeled as "Hispanics or Latinos." For tallies that show race categories for Hispanics and non-Hispanics separately, see U.S. Census Bureau 2000.

duced in the nineteenth century to legitimize European imperialist claims. In the 1860s ideas of "Latinity" were invoked by the France of Napoleon III to justify the presence of a French emperor in Mexico, while claims of "Hispanicity" were used by Spain in its reconquest of Santo Domingo. There is no doubt that both terms are inextricably linked to ideology. Nevertheless, Ramón Grosfoguel and Chloe S. Georas (2000) observe that in recent times the rubric "Latino" has been employed as a less "colonial" alternative to "Hispanic." "Latino" has been made use of productively in order to build coalitions among diverse Latin American and Latino Caribbean groups to support bilingual education, cultural and immigration rights, and to oppose police brutality. Grosfoguel and Georas contend that although "Latino" is a useful political term, it nevertheless collapses important differences that obscure the complex and diverse histories of oppression of these groups. They propose instead the use of three categories: "colonial/racial subjects," "colonial immigrants," and "immigrants." They contend that these categories offer a useful framework to better address the social position of "racialized" immigrant groups in the U.S. By using a notion of "coloniality of power," they reconceptualize the construction of Puerto Ricans as a colonial racialized minority in the Euro-American imaginary. This process of "racialization" accounts for the fact that some minorities in the U.S. succeed economically while others remain impoverished. They argue that Puerto Ricans form what has been called an "underclass" that they prefer to describe as a "redundant colonial/racialized labor force," which can explain why in the New York metropolitan area Dominicans became "PuertoRicanized" and ended up at the bottom of the labor market ladder while Cuban migrants became "colonial immigrants" and improved their situation, independent of their socioeconomic background or labor skills.

For the purpose of exposing its contradictions and symptomatic function, I avoid the use of "Latino" as a "gentler" alternative while retaining throughout the book the word "Hispanic," keeping in mind that it is a loaded political term that is used as a segregation device to lump together people who fail to be seen as subjects in mainstream discourses. I also employ the category "Puerto Rican," noting that this notion, as Grosfoguel and Georas (2000) argue, implies a racialization of Puerto Ricans and other oppressed groups and can only be understood considering their history of colonial subjection: "Although Puerto Ricans form a phenotypically variable group, they have become a new 'race' in the United States" (p. 24). I will further discuss the process of "racialization" of Puerto Ricans in Chapter 12.

These questions will return with all the explosive force of a Freudian repressed in view of the current Latinization of the United States. The multiethnic Hispanic presence suggests the radical transformation of the nation and recalls the changes that the United States underwent a century earlier with Irish, Italian, and Jewish immigrants. Hispanics are the "new immigration" that is bringing about the most dramatic transformation of a country that triggered wave after wave of immigration for the purpose of economical benefits and neocolonialist exploitation. For a country that likes to think of itself as the worldwide defender of freedom, the United States has a regrettable history of military interventions and economic opportunism at the expense of the locals. It would take too long to list all the countries like Chile and Venezuela in which a friendly interest in economic welfare barely hides political interventionism. It has also kept one of the last existing colonies with Puerto Rico, an American possession with an anomalous status that has created deep social, economic, and national instability for Puerto Ricans.

Puerto Ricans as a group dramatically illustrate the situation of the so-called Hispanic population at large. Puerto Ricans occupy a paradoxical position for they are U.S. citizens, a fact that remains largely ignored by the non-Hispanic American population. Puerto Ricans constitute a special group among the so-called Hispanics: they are neither foreign nor completely alien to mainstream American culture, nor are they fully enfranchised U.S. citizens. They cannot vote for president unless they are on the mainland, but are subjected to wartime draft. Puerto Ricans are legal American citizens; thus they cannot be called immigrants, as they are often considered. Puerto Ricans' ambiguous "in-between" position appears condensed and exposed by the regionalisms of the eastern United States: "NuyoRican" or "Porto Yorker." This ambiguity is reinforced by a constant migration between the American mainland and Puerto Rico. Their plight has earned Puerto Ricans the denomination of "commuter-nation" (Torre et al. 1994).

The choices and opportunities are obviously not the same for all socioeconomic groups. The middle class that "commutes" often blends in with the other middle classes of American society. Once in the U.S., the majority of those belonging to the poorer classes live within the closed frontiers of the ghetto, where language establishes an insurmountable limit. Many obstinately resist the passage into the dominant American culture, living in the U.S. for decades without speaking a word of English. For these disenfranchised citizens, language creates an uncrossable divide that becomes the frontier of the ghetto's territory. This is a community for which language is mainly oral (the rate of illiteracy is very high in both Spanish and English) and where bilingualism has created "Spanglish."[2] The United States will soon have the second largest Spanish-speaking population in the world—after Mexico. The trials and tribulations of the Puerto Ricans are illustrative of those of the Spanish-speaking population at large. Exploring those experiences, it is possible to draw surprising conclusions about the whole country and what is projected onto its margins, applicable now and in times to come.

Lost in the margins, questioning the Master's discourse, we find the remainders and reminders of the ineffable: the Puerto Rican syndrome also known as *ataque*—an attack that counterattacks from one of the most overdetermined areas of today's American society, the Hispanic ghettos. The very fact that the set of manifestations already described has been called the "Puerto Rican syndrome" by the official medical discourse of the United States suggests that a whole community can act as an hysteric in front of a Master—a Master who articulates the political discourse of the majority—whereas the hysterics produce a distinctive symptom formation in response to the dominant discourse. One may object to the idea of a "community of hysterics," as David Metzger (1995–1996) did when he claimed that "the theoretical promise of a community of hysterics" can only be made when "analysis is not taken far enough or when it is taken too far" (p. 24). Indeed, when one faces a whole community, one needs to move from a purely analytic position to a position that takes into account issues more often dealt with by the sociologist, the historian, the pedagogue, or the political reformer. Metzger argues that

> the notion of a community of hysterics may be contradictory insofar as
> "communal hysterics" would not be hysterics at all. At their best, these
> "communal hysterics" would be enlightened masters: it is only after the
> revolution that the masters, now endowed with the knowledge of slaves,
> might wonder; "if only I knew then (as a master) what I know now (as
> a slave)." At their worst, these "communal hysterics" would be psychotic:
> having recognized that there is no way for them to guarantee that their

---

2. In my experience in North Philadelphia, Spanish-dominant speakers usually integrate phonologically and morphologically English loanwords into their native system. Whether this happens because of their very limited access to English phonology and morphology or because their mother tongue prevails should be determined by a linguist.

position in the Other has a name except as "rigid designation/destination," psychotics must live instead of the name-of-the-father, as the symptom itself. [p. 25]

Metzger seems reluctant to take into account the possibility of mass hysteria. He also dismisses the fact that hysteria conceived of as a discourse is a form of social link for hysterics and nonhysterics alike. In his latest elaboration on hysteria given at a conference that took place in Brussels in February of 1977, "A Few Words on Hysteria," Lacan (1977a) stressed that hysteria was returning as a social symptom. This displacement of hysteria onto the social realm provides me with a central thesis to rethink the Puerto Rican syndrome.

Since my thesis in this book is based upon clinical experience, it relies on a psychoanalytically oriented practice that is grounded on the particularity of each case. However, what is specific about the Puerto Rican syndrome is that individual subjects are forcibly reminded of their belonging to a group by what sounds like a *quasi* racist terminology. Did the military doctors hit upon the truth of the symptom? All seems to suggest that the particular structure of the Puerto Rican syndrome makes each individual case of *ataque* an unwilling allegory of a collective situation. They are also being reminded of a history they often ignore, but that weighs on them like a ghost, a hangover of a painful past. This is why they "suffer from reminiscences" and repeat symptoms already manifested by Parisian or Viennese patients in the nineteenth century. They belong to a "present" blasted out by historical continuity. As Homi Bhabha (1994) puts it,

> Transnational capitalism and the impoverishment of the Third World certainly create the chains of circumstance that incarcerate the Salvadorean or the Filipino/a. In their cultural passage, hither and thither, as migrant workers, part of the massive economic and political diaspora of the modern world, they embody the Benjaminian "present": that moment blasted out of the continuum of history. [p. 8]

In a similar key, André Michels (2001) links Walter Benjamin's original formulation of messianic time with the hysterical urgency of the "Now." He argues that this is how the political context can take on a clinical connotation, capturing the subjectivity of a given period while bringing to the fore the urgency of time. "The present time (*Jetztzeit*), the model for messianic time, intervenes as a 'foreign body' condensing the whole of history, the history of humanity, all the while transmitting its subversive germination" (p. 41). Michels notes that the hysterical urgency of the present is the same tense that Freud identified as the grammatical time of dreams. For Freud this present tense is the temporal form (*Zeitform*) that embodies the realization of desire. Hysteria's temporal structure, a "Now" that cannot be reduced to chronology, manifests desire both as realized and as unfulfilled, hovering between present and future.

Starting from the curious temporality of a symptom that appears frozen more in the present than in the past, this book tackles the issue of the collective production of such social manifestations. These symptoms emerge from a population that is still caught up in a colonial situation while waking up to the age of multiculturalism and globalization. Even though my observations are restricted to the particularities of each case treated, one may say that the sharp opposition between individual and collective psychology softens when examined more closely. In the opening thesis of *Group Psychology and the Analysis of the Ego*, Freud (1921) argues that "someone else" is always integrated in the individual's mental life "as a model, as an object, as a helper, as an opponent; and so from the very first individual psychology, in this extended but entirely justifiable sense of the words, is at the same time social psychology as well" (p. 69). Freud also observes, "The relations of an individual to his parents and to his brothers and sisters, to the object of his love, and to his physician—in fact all the relations which have hitherto been the chief subject of psychoanalytic research—may claim to be considered as *social phenomena*" (p. 69, italics mine). The "other" that Freud identifies as the hinge between individual psychology and social psychology, "the model, the object, the helper, the opponent," overlaps with the Lacanian Other. For Lacan, the Other is the signifying treasure, the reservoir of language, human laws, and culture, which is, obviously, social. Lacan also defines the unconscious as the discourse of the Other. This does not mean that the unconscious is a collective unconscious. Lacan's conceptualization of an unconscious "structured like a language" does not mean that the common elements of language are arranged in the same way for everyone. Each subject will have a particular history that has been written on the body as the first signifiers, the first marks (that Lacan calls S1, or Signifier One) that require other signifiers to generate a history.[3] Those

---

3. The unconscious is made up of signifiers (S2) that exclude the S1 or first marks. The S2s keep on talking about the S1, which is written in the body. Words, symptoms, acts (S2s) give an account of the original marks (S1).

original marks stand for points of identification with a specific trait (*trait unaire*) of the Other. This identification to the Other's traits is not imaginary and anchors the subject in an order that transcends him or her—this is why it is called by Lacan (1977b) "the birth of possibility" (p. 306). Then the subject can be fixed in his or her particularity to a point in the Other from which he or she can become somebody.

In the same text on collective formations, Freud devotes a whole chapter to identification in order to point out how it occurs in the structure of a neurotic symptom. Freud differentiates between three types of identification: one is the earliest expression of an emotional tie with another person; it is based on the incorporation of the love object. The model is cannibalistic—we devour those we are fond of. The second type is identification with a trait of the other (*einziger Zug*). Freud gives the example of a girl who develops the same symptom as her mother, and of an hysterical patient (Dora) who imitates her father's cough. Identification appears instead of object-choice or object-choice regresses to identification. Lacan's elaboration of the function of the specific trait (S1) that I have mentioned above corresponds to this second type of identification described by Freud. For the third type of identification, which takes place independent of any libidinal attitude with respect to the person copied, Freud gives the example of a young girl in a boarding school who receives a diffident letter from someone with whom she is secretly in love. She experiences jealousy and reacts to it with an attack, a fit of hysterics. Then, by contagion, hysteria spreads: many of her friends who know about her attack also catch it, as Freud says, by "mental infection." It would be wrong to suppose that they take on the symptom out of sympathy. Freud (1921) explains the "infection" as an ego-identification. One ego has perceived a significant analogy with another upon one point, and under the influence of the pathogenic situation that point of analogy is displaced onto the symptom produced. "The identification by means of the symptom has thus become the mark of a point of coincidence between two egos which has to be kept repressed" (Lacan 1977b, p. 107). Lacan (1961–1962) would say that this is an identification to the other mediated by desire, an "identification from desire to desire."[4] This third type of identification, Freud says, is what creates the tie between members of a group. An "identification from desire to desire" lies at the bottom of the libidi-

---

4. Unpublished; Class of November 13, 1961, and June 20, 1962.

nal organization of groups—they have a common desire because they find their desire in the other.

Freud's opening remarks about the invariable presence of an "other" in our mental life relates to a characteristic seen in patients diagnosed with Puerto Rican syndrome: their syndrome is an appeal to the other. This feature was identified by Freud as a foundational element of the structure of hysteria. He wrote in Letter 52 to Fliess: "Attacks . . . are aimed at *another person*—but above all the prehistoric, unforgettable other person whom no one coming after can equal" (1954, p. 239). The Puerto Rican syndrome, also known as *ataque* (attack), is fundamentally aimed at the Freudian other and at the Lacanian Other. This Other is an idealized image, a privileged Other that usually occupies a position of prestige or authority in society. Within this perspective, it supports the desire for an agent of the paternal Law and acknowledges that it requires an Other as an addressee. Thus, it offers a paradigmatic example of the radically ambiguous relationship between the subject and the so-called Master in response to whom the subject's identity is constituted. Lacan (1991b) sees hysteria as the model of the subject's attempt to create a relationship with the Other, thereby pointing to its determination by unconscious desire.[5] The Puerto Rican syndrome both creates and questions the Other.

The Puerto Rican syndrome, like any hysteria, forces itself on us as an enigma that poses a question addressed to the Other. This question makes us aware of our impotence facing issues of gender, class, race, nationality, and language while leading us to challenge them. In the example of the boarding school episode showing a contagious hysterical attack, Freud argues that a symptom can become a point of coincidence between egos; the symptom thus functions as an identity matrix. What is the function of the Puerto Rican syndrome in the construction of identity? Nancy Morris (1995) traced the elusive concept of national identity among Puerto Ricans in the twentieth century. Her extensive research leads her to conclude that Puerto Rican national identity is not just complex, it is even more symptomatic. The respondents she surveyed unequivocally identified themselves as "Puerto Rican," using language as the most consistent element cited to define "Puerto Ricanness" (p. 82). Morris notes that Puerto Ricans use

---

5. Lacan (1991b) defines the unconscious as "the discourse of the Other." This Other introduces at the core of subjectivity the register of language, the symbolic function, the complexity of the human order (pp. 89–90).

the word "*país*," meaning country, when they talk about the island (p. 3). This creates an equivocal situation because Puerto Rico is not an independent political entity. The fact that this psychiatric "syndrome" is called "Puerto Rican" would suggest that nationalities are engraved in the human psyche. The Puerto Rican syndrome raises issues of identity, cultural meaning, and political behavior.

In the *barrio* one finds all the hurdles one can expect when dealing with marginalized groups: urban poverty, alcoholism, drug addiction, disintegrating families, and the most extreme violence, encountered on a daily basis and manifesting itself in the most aberrant forms. This community provides a privileged context to explore how the American community mental health model can apply. In most cases, the mental health services available to the Hispanic community are geared toward simple symptom suppression. This model is functionalist, based on the idea of correcting symptoms with the goal of helping—or even forcing—the patient to comply with the model of capitalist productivity.

In North Philadelphia poverty is extreme, with three generations of unemployment often present in a family (Ericksen 1986). While Philadelphia has been experiencing a continuous increase in employment opportunities in the professional and middle classes, in the last 25 years it has gone through an overall 28 percent decline in jobs. Of those Philadelphia Puerto Ricans still with jobs, most are employed in the lowest rungs of the labor market—blue collar and service jobs—the sector with the least job security and little hope of upward mobility. The biggest concentration of employment lost is to be found in the North Philadelphia community where most Hispanics live. This is evident in the *barrio's* postindustrial scene—abandoned and decaying factories everywhere. Before this decline, from the 1940s to the 1960s, the Puerto Rican women's labor participation rate was among the highest in the country. But ready access to jobs that required few skills soon disappeared—between the 1950s and 1960s the Northeast region alone lost nearly 40 percent of the manufacturing jobs that employed large numbers of Puerto Rican women. The result was dire—by 1960 half of all Puerto Rican families were on some form of public assistance (Glazer and Moynihan 1986). Since then, welfare recipience among Puerto Ricans has risen steeply. L.H. Gann and Peter Duignan (1986) note that historically, Puerto Ricans "were the first immigrant group who unwittingly moved into what became . . . a welfare economy with a powerful and intrusive commitment for social planning" (p. 80).

The unemployment rate among Hispanic Philadelphians is two times larger than the nationwide percentage,[6] this not counting the underemployment rate that among the local Hispanics is estimated between 20 to 30 percent. Nationally, Puerto Ricans have the highest unemployment rate, the lowest median income, and the highest percentage of families and children living in poverty of any other Hispanic group. Since the majority of Hispanics in Philadelphia are Puerto Rican, this is important data to consider.

A majority of Philadelphia's *barrio* population is unemployed and there is little likelihood that they will become part of the productive segment of the U.S. population (Ericksen et al. 1986). The educational challenges faced by the city's Hispanic population should be taken into consideration in the community's cycle of poverty. Much of the growth in the local economy has occurred in the high-skilled service sector for which a large proportion of the Hispanic community is not prepared. In Philadelphia, Hispanic students have the highest dropout rates in the city and an overall low educational achievement level. A greater part of those over the age of 25 have not graduated from high school.[7]

This is a community haunted by poverty and death. In addition to the highest school dropout rates in the city, Latino youth have a death rate four times the city's yearly rate and twelve times the national norm. Drugs, violence, poverty, lack of education, insufficient health care, high rates of unemployment and scarce job opportunities, together with no access to recreational and cultural activities, jeopardize youth survival in Philadelphia. According to Ericksen and colleagues (1986), "Puerto Ricans are much worse off than Blacks, Whites, or other Hispanics" (p. ii). Some 48 percent of Puerto Rican males and 54 percent of Puerto Rican females live in pov-

---

6. The unemployment rate for Hispanics in Philadelphia City/County in 2001 was 11.6 percent. This estimate, from the Current Population Survey (CPS), is published in "Geographic Profile of Employment and Unemployment," and is available online at http://stats.bls.gov. As of March 2003, the nationwide rate was estimated at 5.8 percent (Bureau of Labor Statistics 2003).

7. "In Pennsylvania, Latinos are at the bottom of the educational ladder with increasing drop-out rates, academic underachievement, and very few of our young people going on to higher education." Latinos have "one of the highest drop-out rates in the Commonwealth—40 percent statewide and over 70 percent in some areas" (Pennsylvania Governor's Advisory Commission on Latino Affairs 1991, pp. 6–8). For those in Philadelphia schools, "Average test scores for schools with a Latino majority were much lower than City averages" (Philadelphia Commission on Human Relations 1991, p. 13). A rate of 70 percent of Philadelphia Puerto Ricans of age 25 or over had not graduated from high school (Ericksen et al. 1986).

erty. Statistics predict a gloomy future—nationwide 40 percent of Puerto Rican children live in poverty.

Here, the concept of "productivity" has an ironic ring that naturalizes the drab reality of class boundaries. Yet, in the North Philadelphia community this concept of productivity acquires a new dimension—in consideration of the location of so-called Hispanics within the power structure of wider society: instead of being encouraged to produce goods they are expected to produce symptoms.

The normative modalities of mental health practices can be read as symptoms of deep contradictions within American society. In the case of Hispanic mental health services, we can see how today's practice of normalization responds to the needs for productive labor in the present postindustrial society. Community mental health centers can and do actually operate as a site for social control. This social control has crucial political implications not only at a clinical but also at a cultural level. Currently, we witness the imposition of cost-saving strategies that have been called "managed care"—which means that medical costs are no longer refunded after the fact but "managed" in advance by an agreement with the insurer. This entails that the leading health insurance companies decide in advance a policy in which a given set of symptoms will determine a diagnosis and a specific treatment within a limited time frame. This standardized strategy does not take into account the eventuality that not all patients respond in the same exact way to a given treatment. It also privileges a psychopharmacological and behavioral treatment as the only efficient therapeutic modality, medically treating the psyche as if it were a sick organ.

The sad truth is that if there has been any reduction in mental healthcare expenses in recent years, it is not because the speediest and most cost-efficient treatments were chosen but because the insurance systems of managed care cut mental health and substance abuse benefits by more than half since 1987.[8] We all agree that mental health care saves money and lives; however, it is indisputable that mental health benefits

---

8. Where the value of general healthcare benefits has declined 7 percent (from $2,326.86 per covered individual in 1988 to $2,155.60 in 1997), the value of behavioral healthcare benefits has declined 54 percent (from $154.08 in 1988 to $69.61 in 1997). Behavioral health as a percent of the total healthcare benefit has plummeted 50 percent in 10 years (dropping from 6.2 percent in 1988 to 3.1 percent in 1997) (Hay Group Study 1987–1997). To access a complete copy of the Hay Group report on the erosion of behavioral health care benefits and an Employer's Checklist to help businesses evaluate their own behavioral health benefits, visit http://www.nami.org/pressroom/keyfind.html.

have been aggressively reduced by managed health care in the 1990s. Mental health benefits costs in 10 years (1988–1997) were cut 67 percent *more* than general healthcare benefit costs (Hay Group Study 1987–1997). This trend raises worrisome problems for the estimated 5 to 7 percent of adults in the U.S. who are estimated to suffer from severe mental illnesses and seem destined to endure them without appropriate coverage or treatment.

The limited care funded by the health insurance industry has a strong preference for a pharmaceutical approach primarily because it seems to promise cost-effectiveness. However, the statistics that support these claims come straight from the very profitable pharmaceutical laboratories. Despite all the media hype, one may wonder about the actual benefits of drug therapy. It is quite startling to see that the mechanism of action of FDA-approved psychotropic drugs has not been entirely demonstrated: for instance, no evidence has been found yet on how most drugs used for mental disorders really work. One just needs to read the small print in the information accompanying medications to see that pharmaceutical companies lack this data on the medications they market. Let us take, for instance, the prescribing information given by Eli Lilly and Co. for its Zyprexa (Olanzapina), a psychotropic agent of the thienobenzodiazepine class prescribed for schizophrenia. In the clinical pharmacological section it states, "The mechanism of action of olanzapine, as with other drugs having efficacy in schizophrenia, is unknown." Behind an allure of scientific authority, very often uncertainty reigns. Psychopharmacology is a domain in which we are still at an early stage of experimentation and speculation. For less serious conditions like depression, it is not even clear whether popular antidepressants like Prozac, Paxil, and other SSRIs that hit the market 15 years ago work "chemically" or by cultural contagion (Slingsby 2002). For example, "biochemical imbalance" is a catch phrase that has not been sustained by any systematic evidence. The aggressive advertising of mood-altering drugs has given rise to a burgeoning market and has created a legal drug culture. The antidepressants themselves have become celebrities. Prozac is a good example of a drug that has been on TV and on the covers of major magazines, has been discussed on talk shows and at cocktails parties, has been the subject of numerous books, and finally has reached its pinnacle of glory by becoming the theme of a few movies.[9] Smart publicity can spark a cultural contagion that becomes

---

9. See Gherovici 1997b, 1999a, 1999b, 2000.

an epidemic: recent research shows that sugar pills or "dummy pills" are as effective as popular antidepressant drugs. "Chemical" results are presumably due to a placebo effect. Appropriately, Roger Greenberg calls the inclination for a "quick-fix" treatment a "fast-mood mentality" (see Greenberg 1989, 1997). It might well be that the secret behind the so-called revolution in the treatment of depression is a very intelligent marketing strategy. In any case, the miraculous cure is not a real "cure" but rather a transitory reduction of the symptoms.

At the exact opposite end of the spectrum, psychoanalysis offers an ethical model that is not utilitarian. Psychoanalysis, rather than adapting, addresses and confronts the subject with some of the most unbearable aspects of reality. Instead of forcing patients to "normalize" their symptoms, psychoanalysis makes symptoms "productive" by allowing patients to find subjective meaning in them. Since it cannot avoid being caught up in the capitalist mode of production, psychoanalysis is, in Lacan's view, the very "symptom of capitalism," insofar as it encourages the symptom to produce meaning rather than commodities. Indeed, when patients recognize that their subjectivity has been expressed in symptoms, we witness the sense that there has been a moment of productive discovery, like the birth of a singular truth allowing for a new sense of agency. The analyst's discourse can impact individuals and society alike if it effectively releases changes in subjective positions brought about by the emergence of unconscious knowledge.

Here we should keep in mind the existing connections between medical discourse and late capitalist ideology in a society in which Hispanics occupy a position of otherness, facing the Other played by the dominant American culture. There are certain dynamics at stake through which society at large imposes a peripheral role on some groups. This dynamic pertains to the core of subjectivity as well as of social organization. The symptoms produced by these "subjected" hysterics point to the emergence of a concealed truth. Lacan (1975) famously claimed, "One has to look for the origins of the notion of symptom not in Hippocrates, but in Marx" (p. 106). If Marx "invented the symptom" in general, did he also invent the Puerto Rican syndrome? We will see later how Freud had dreamed this symptom in advance when he had his "castle by the sea dream," a dream about the Spanish-American War, the very war that ended with the annexation of Puerto Rico to the U.S. territory. This crucial historical incident in the history of the Puerto Rican syndrome appears in *The Interpretation of Dreams* (1900) in an intriguing dream that shows how Freud's unconscious resonates with echoes of imperialist wars (see Chapter 11, this volume). Taken together, Marx's "invention" and Freud's "castle dream" suggest that hysteria works with the drive as well, and calls upon violence, rage, and war. Our society is unavoidably at war for, says Lacan (1977b), "war is proving more and more to be the inevitable and necessary midwife of all progress in our civilization" (p. 27). This progress is the progress of a subject who "constitutes its world by its suicide" (p. 28). Hysteria, as Juliet Mitchell (2000) contends, can only be fully understood in relation to Freud's death drive and Lacan's concept of *jouissance*—that traumatizing, excessive, horrifying, forbidden pleasure beyond law and speech.

A Lacanian reading of the Puerto Rican syndrome begins if one does not simply equate it with classical hysteria, as I suggested earlier; it requests that one observe how the hysteric's discourse gives birth to a liberating process instead of merely generating crippling neuroses. In the discourse of the hysteric, subjective division takes a position of dominance. The subtle differences in which hysterics organize the *jouissance* involved by their symptoms can and must be mobilized. Then the resilience, the protest, and the complaint conveyed by the Puerto Rican syndrome will find an expression that effectively undermines oppressive structures and reaches from the individual to the social level. Psychoanalysis, as Joan Copjec (1994) has argued, is the precarious anathema of capitalism. Lacan similarly envisioned psychoanalysis as the only rational way out of the impasses of late capitalism. This derouting implies that one should analyze the desire at stake in the production of the Puerto Rican syndrome. Then, perhaps, it will appear as more than a demand for successful social sublimation: it will be seen as a scrawled letter made up of half-readable graffiti on a wall that the hysterics of the *barrio*, whom we can call the "Hyspanics," address to an elusive Other.

3

What Is the Puerto Rican Syndrome?

William Grace (1959) provided a compelling description of an episode of Puerto Rican syndrome in New York:

> The episode begins quite suddenly, without warning either to specta-
> tors or without any warning from the patient; there may be a short
> cry or scream before the patient falls. Usually the presenting symp-
> tom is falling to the ground or sliding off a chair. In doing so the pa-
> tients often injure themselves. . . . Shortly after the fall to the ground,
> or at the same moment, the patient begins moving arms and legs,
> usually both arms doing the same thing and both legs doing the same
> thing. These movements are often purposeful, such as beating fists on
> the floor, striking out at persons nearby or banging his head on the
> floor. Foaming at the mouth is common, but no instance of inconti-
> nence or biting of the tongue was seen. The attack usually ceases
> abruptly, the individual then resuming whatever he was doing before
> without ill effect. The usual *ataque* lasts for 5 to 10 minutes but it may
> go on for hours, and I have seen one patient continue this for four
> days. [p. 12]

Here is Charcot in Paris, almost a century earlier, as he was producing his famous systematization of the hysterical attack:[1]

> The patient loses consciousness and the paroxysm begins. It is divided into four periods . . . first, the patient executes certain epileptiform convulsive movements. Then comes the period of great gestures of salutation which are of extreme violence, interrupted from time to time by an arching of the body which is absolutely characteristic. . . . Then comes the third period, called the period of passional attitudes during which the patient utters words and cries in relation with the sad delirium and terrifying visions which pursue him . . . the delirium and hallucinations still continue for some time . . . the attack is over, although is generally sure to be repeated a few minutes later . . . never during the course of these crises has he bitten his tongue or wet his bed. [Riley and Roy 1982, p. 7]

Lacan (1977a), playing on the famous trope of *ubi sunt?* asked (with a hint of nostalgia) about the changed fate of those extravagant hysterics of Freud's time:

> Where have they gone, the hysterics of the olden days, these wonderful women—the Anna O.s, or the Emmy von N.s. . . . ? They not only played a certain social role but when Freud started to listen to them, they allowed for the birth of psychoanalysis. By listening to them Freud inaugurated an entirely new mode of human relations. What has replaced the former hysterical symptoms today? Has hysteria not been displaced to the social field? [p. 5]

One may answer that the hysterics of a glorious *fin-de-siècle* heyday are alive and well. They simply moved to America and have been spotted out and about Spanish-speaking ghettos. But *what* exactly is this phenomenon that vanishes and reemerges? And how can we account for hysteria's displacement from the clinical sphere to the social field? In other words, what is the Puerto Rican syndrome?

---

1. Charcot's systematization of the hysterical attack recognized a logic behind the seemingly chaotic manifestations. In his search for general laws of hysteria, he attempted to eradicate the speculation that hysteria was disparate, fragmented, and uncoordinated. Charcot believed that hysteric fits happened according to rules common to all countries, times, and races.

PERIPATETIC HYSTORY

In the 1950s, U.S. medical officers examining Puerto Rican soldiers—mostly involved with the Korean War—were puzzled by an inexplicable mystery. They observed patients with paroxysms of anxiety, rage, psychotic symptoms, and unpremeditated suicidal attempts, followed with depression and often amnesia about the spectacular crises. Thinking they had discovered a manifestation uniquely Puerto Rican, the armed forces psychiatrists labeled the startling set of symptoms "Puerto Rican syndrome." This set of symptoms that was considered to be uniquely Puerto Rican, and thus meriting the invention of a new diagnosis, is identical to the most famous form of hysteria that some hundred years earlier helped Freud invent a revolutionary cure—psychoanalysis—and showed him the path to the unconscious. This is a strange coincidence.

In the late nineteenth century, hysteria—an infamously resilient somatic illness without organic lesions and indifferent to medical interventions, with a history that goes back more than 40 centuries—truly became "the great neurosis," awaking vast medical interest and developing a prominent cultural presence. And the specialist on hysteria, the French neurologist Jean-Martin Charcot, became the most famous doctor of his time with his celebrated Salpêtrière lecture-demonstrations.[2] This literal repetition of a particular somatic grammar of hysteria suggests resonant parallels between the context of the theatrical clinical manifestations of Charcot's Parisian Tuesday lectures and the social conditions under which these same symptoms reappear with eerie exactitude in Puerto Rican soldiers admitted to military hospitals, almost a hundred years later. Indeed, this repetition is all the more compelling because, this time, the *grandes hystériques* were not frail, suggestible females brought to confront the formidable Charcot, but courageous, macho soldiers who performed their dramatic range of symptoms in front of bewildered U.S. armed forces medical officers. Besides, these startling hysterical manifestations did not die out in the 1950s. Today, over a century and a half later, in the heart of the Philadelphia Hispanic ghetto, the flamboyant hysteria of yesteryear continues to

---

2. At the height of Charcot's fame, during hysteria's heyday, Freud spent four months in Paris (between October 1885 and February 1886) studying with the so-called "Master of Hysteria." The hospital of La Salpêtrière was then the biggest in the world. Charcot's Tuesday-night lessons transfixed his audience of doctors and the Parisian intellectual and artistic elite.

manifest itself indifferent to the passage of time, spiced up by a *Spanglish* accent.

According to Elaine Showalter (1993),

> Above all the hysteric is someone who has a story, an *histoire*, and whose story is told by science. Hysteria is no longer a question of the wandering womb; it is a question of the wandering story, and of whether that story belongs to the hysteric, the doctor, the historian, or the critic. The stories of race and gender in hysteria still remain to be told. [p. 335]

One may say with Showalter and Lacan that hysteria needs to be understood as a "hystory"—conflating the proximity in spelling of hysteria and history, and pointing at the coupling between the two. In the case of the Puerto Rican syndrome, the same wandering *hystory* is being told over and over again. It is told by hysterics, by U.S. armed forces medical officers, by anthropologists, and by social workers. At least one hopes that this hystory, which operates like a fundamental fantasy, will return to the hysteric (as knowledge from which the hysteric is no longer alienated) through the intervention of the psychoanalyst.

A first step in this process of restitution of knowledge should be to attempt to understand how classic hysteria has been preserved in a time capsule, as it were, with the Puerto Rican syndrome. A rapid overview of the existing literature on the Puerto Rican syndrome indicates contradictorily that it is hysteria (Badillo Ghali 1975), schizophrenia (Freeman et al. 1975), hysterical psychosis (not just psychosis) (Pies 1994), and even more, cross-cultural hysterical psychosis (Hirsh and Hollander 1968, Langness 1967). The Puerto Rican syndrome is described as resulting from common folk beliefs that could at the same time be part of a delusional system (Martínez 1986), as a sudden homicidal impulse or "suicidal fit" (Langness 1967), as a multiple personality disorder (Steinberg 1990), and as a manipulative "reaction" pattern for hysterical personalities (Rubio et al. 1955). It is also understood as an indication of a higher rate of organic brain disorder among Puerto Ricans (Robert de Ramirez de Arellano et al. 1954). The syndrome's distinctive symptoms include it among culture-specific syndromes equivalent to "geographically restricted mental disorders such as *Hsieh-Ping* of Formosa, *Koro* of Malaya, and *Arctic Hysteria*, a schizophrenic disorder suffered only by Eskimos and natives of Siberia" (Maldonado-Sierra and Trent 1960, p. 239). *Koro* is the Malay name for a syndrome according to which men become extremely anxious, convinced that their penises are shrinking into their bodies. In their despair they may end up committing suicide. *Arctic Hysteria*, or *pibloktoq*, is known as a combination of anxiety and depression reaching a climax in abrupt convulsive seizures and coma. During the attack, affected individuals may tear off their clothing, break objects, shout, eat feces, act out, and endanger their lives. Culture-bound syndrome is a category of psychiatric illness standing for mental disorders whose pathology is induced not organically but by a specific culture. While reopening the old debate of nature versus culture, these syndromes are often contagious and occasionally trigger social epidemics.

This is why even if the Puerto Rican syndrome's symptoms are quite striking and look like clear signs of severe pathology for observers, the syndrome taken globally is often described as a "normal" reaction within Hispanic culture (Ruiz 1982). Although considered specific only to migrant Puerto Ricans, the syndrome is also thought to be typical for most Puerto Ricans on the island, and more specifically, as a culturally prescribed behavior in some rural areas of Puerto Rico (LaRuffa 1971). But here again, a measure of confusion reigns: one study contemplates the possibility that the Puerto Rican syndrome may not occur exclusively among Puerto Ricans (Jones 1991)[3] and another concludes unhesitatingly that the Puerto Rican syndrome is not even Puerto Rican (Guarnaccia et al. 1989). The Puerto Rican syndrome has been repeatedly described as capable of simulating other illnesses, especially neurological ones. Such an ability to imitate other diseases appears as a predominant feature, and it can mislead whoever proposes a definition of the Puerto Rican syndrome, thus perpetuating the syndrome's riddle.

In its productive "hystory," it looks as if everything and its contrary had already been said about the Puerto Rican syndrome. This chameleonlike nature of the Puerto Rican syndrome is a legendary feature of hysteria. Hysteria in its four thousand years of history has incited innumerable, often extravagant, interpretations, undermining the dominant scientific paradigm in various epochs.[4] This crucial aspect of hysteria can be seen amply documented in our rapid review of the Puerto Rican syndrome, which in half a century has inspired a host of definitions with their array of demarcations

---

3. This study uses a sample of 118 young Hispanics suffering Puerto Rican syndrome's symptoms; 101 are Puerto Rican, the rest are predominantly Mexican or Panamanian.
   4. For a history of hysteria, see Micale 1995, Trillat 1986, and Veith 1965.

and blurred or overlapping boundaries. The interpretations of the poly-
morphous manifestations of the syndrome are wildly divergent and often
directly contradictory. Their glaring discrepancies suggest either that the
Puerto Rican syndrome is an organic brain disorder or that it has no organic cause at all, that it is a culturally acceptable idiom of distress, the
bodily manifestation of deep social problems, a universal pathology, and a
cultural oddity. The syndome's paradox lies in its being exceptional and
normal, natural and cultural at the same time.

THE RISE AND FALL OF A STRATEGIC SYNDROME

To answer the initial question "What is the Puerto Rican syndrome?" and
avoid proposing yet another theory doomed to fail, we need to search for
a genealogy of the *ataque* as well, since the Puerto Rican syndrome is also
known as "hyperkinetic seizure," *nervios* (nerves), *mal de pelea* (disease of
fighting), and *ataque de nervios* (which means *attacks* and *nerves*, respectively, and could be translated as nervous breakdown). The Puerto Rican
syndrome not only refers to striking psychological symptoms; it also describes symptoms caused by the traps of universalistic biomedical psychiatry
while telling us a great deal about the degree to which U.S. colonialism
has permeated mental health practice. As noted by Foucault (1965), psychiatry is located in a treacherous bordering region often used by the state
to exercise power by pursuing social control through medical and public
health channels. Precisely, to start unearthing the different elements involved in the Puerto Rican syndrome's wandering "hystory," we must explore the wider sociohistorical context of its invention. Let us, then, examine closely the first two documents in which the Puerto Rican syndrome
initially appears in order to produce an archaeology of the problematic label,
excavating the hidden assumptions that govern it.

The first document that we will analyze carries the title "'Ataques,'
Hyperkinetic Type: The So-Called Puerto Rican Syndrome. Its Medical, Psychological, and Social Implications." This piece results from a multidisciplinary research and was presented (Robert de Ramírez de Arellano 1954)
at the Annual Meeting of the Puerto Rico Medical Association. We may
note that in such an early study, the title suggests that the Puerto Rican
syndrome is a synonym of the more commonly known *ataques*.

This inceptive study should be located within the then emerging generation of multidisciplinary research. It is the outcome of an exhaustive

survey that combines the findings of neurologists, psychiatrists, psychologists, and social workers wishing to determine the precipitating factors of hyperkinetic manifestations (*ataques*) and attempting to find out more about the newly coined Puerto Rican syndrome. For this inaugural study on the Puerto Rican syndrome, a group of patients presenting seizures of non-traumatic origin was selected from a total of 2,436 veterans examined at the Neuropsychiatric Unit of the V.A. Center. These patients were all males ranging in age from 19 to 45 years, with a preponderance of Korean War veterans.

PSYCHIATRIC DIAGNOSES AND WAR

It is quite important to keep in mind the power dynamics at stake. The Puerto Rican syndrome was first identified among inducted Puerto Rican soldiers; Veterans Administration centers received distressed Puerto Rican recruits presenting what was diagnosed by U.S. armed forces doctors as severe psychopathological reactions. This study was conducted under military auspices but its findings transcend military objectives (exploring the emotional and social reasons for breakdowns and inefficiency in soldiers rejected or separated from service), encroaching onto psychiatric notions of normalcy and pathology. Furthermore, that the "Puerto Rican syndrome" was coined by military psychiatrists is crucial, for it highlights the fact that a substantial number of terms in use in the current psychiatric nomenclature were developed by either the U. S. Army or the Veterans Administration. The American psychiatric taxonomy, in general, and the standardized classification systems, like the *International Classification of Diseases* and its offspring, the APA *Diagnostic and Statistical Manuals* (*DSM*) in particular, have been extremely influenced by military psychiatry—many wartime mental disorders expanded the classification systems.

The first manual that marked the beginning of the still prevailing trend of standardized psychiatric terminology was the 1932 *Standard Classified Nomenclature of Disease* (*SCND*). When most of the symptoms that World War II servicemen and veterans experienced could not be found in the *SCND* classifications, a major revision took place. LaBruzza and Mendez-Villarrubia (1994) note that at the time a staggering 90 percent of the cases treated by military psychiatrists could not be classified. The stress induced by the war produced new manifestations not defined in standard diagnoses; thus it is safe to assert that the psychic states of soldiers returning from battlefields challenged previous limitations of psychiatric nomenclature. The U.S. Navy in 1944 and the U.S. Army in 1945 dramatically expanded the nosology, adding the myriad presentations that they identified among servicemen. And in 1946, the Veterans Administration developed its own standardized nomenclature for mental disorders that was taken as the basis for the 1948 World Health Organization's *International Classification of Diseases-6* (now in its tenth version—*ICD-10*). For the *ICD-6*, the Veterans Adminstration contributed 26 diagnostic categories.[5] The first edition of the *Diagnostic and Statistical Manual of Mental Disorders* (*DSM-I*) (American Psychiatric Association 1952), produced by the American Psychiatric Association's Committee on Nomenclature and Statistics, was nothing but a variation of the *ICD-6*, whose nomenclature was profoundly influenced by the Veterans Administration's classification and whose main objective was to describe more accurately outpatient presentations of war servicemen and veterans (American Psychiatric Association 2000).

"'Ataques,' Hyperkinetic Type: The So-Called Puerto Rican Syndrome" is the first and groundbreaking study on the Puerto Rican syndrome, and it remains a landmark. It was conducted at the Veterans Administration Medical Center in San Juan, Puerto Rico, which was then serving a war-veteran population of approximately 95,000. This first study took place between November 1953 and October 1954, immediately following the resolution of two years of negotiations and laborious peace discussions regarding the war in Korea. Whereas an armistice was signed on June 6, 1953, ensuing discussions were fruitless, and the hostility did not end until July 27, 1953. This comprehensive research was started only four months after the actual implementation of the armistice.

This foundational study of the Puerto Rican syndrome has become the syndrome's inaugural document and is often quoted in the bibliography; however, what is remarkable is that it has never been published. Neither was it issued as a Veterans Administration report, as many sources claim, nor is there any copy currently available in any library in the United States or Puerto Rico. How, then, could I obtain a copy of such a nonexistent original publication? I had to ask for a photocopy of a typed version of the whole report from the main author herself, Marisa Robert de Ramírez de Arellano, whom I contacted personally in Puerto Rico in 1996, and to whom I am greatly indebted. But since this study was never published,

---

5. For the *ICD-6*, the Veterans Administration contributed 10 categories for psychoses, 9 for psychoneurosis, and 7 for disorders of character, behavior, and intelligence.

the syndrome's nosological origins have receded forever into an almost mythical past. This has established a peculiar intertextual relationship, creating a tradition of interpretation supported by contradictory data based or not even based on actual evidence.

Notably, the study records that "hyperkinetic manifestations in the Puerto Rican soldier" become a problem when observed by continental medical officers stationed in Puerto Rico and Panama not well acquainted with either the symptoms or with the frequency of occurrence among the Puerto Rican troops. The authors state: "This phenomenon of 'ataques' is nothing new to any of you who has practiced medicine here in Puerto Rico" (Robert de Ramirez de Arellano 1954, p. 1). Geographical location seems crucial in order to determine the strangeness of the manifestations and the severity of its repercussions. In a similar manner, William Grace (1959), a New York-based physician, has observed that "when it [the *ataque*] occurs in Puerto Rico, it is a phenomenon of every day life; when it occurs on Fourteenth Street, it is likely to be considered a major catastrophe" (p. 12).

For the Puerto Rican practitioners, authors of this initial study, who, as they themselves admitted, "have all been called to see Doña Fulana,[6] who is having another '*ataque*,'" the *ataque* was viewed as a normative experience that was neither exceptional nor exotic. In contrast, the denomination of Puerto Rican syndrome superficially stereotyped an entire national group and transformed a customary experience into a serious mental health problem with an eccentric location. Thus the Puerto Rican syndrome was coined as a new illness category for an otherwise culturally accepted normal manifestation.

In medical practice, a diagnostic category may appear as an objective description of a clinical fact that only affects those who experience health problems. However, the clinician is not only implicated in understanding and engaging the patient; since the clinician provides an account of the disease, he or she is not just an observer but also a participant. This mutual implication is made more evident in the case of the Puerto Rican syndrome. Let us think about the armed forces American psychiatrists who labeled the syndrome: puzzled by a set of strange manifestations, their medical sectarianism and scientific nationalism betrayed themselves when they chose to describe patients' clinical conditions by characterizing them

---

6. The name "Doña Fulana" is a colloquial expression used to refer to anyone and to no one in particular, like the English expression "She was a Jane Doe."

with a pejorative classification. Why? Guarnaccia and colleagues (1989) argue that the label of Puerto Rican syndrome denotes

> the need for physicians to distance themselves from patients and phenomena which appear "bizarre" to them. It appears "bizarre" because the presentation does not fit into their medical culture's categories; because the symptoms do not respond to treatment in the expected ways; and because the patients come from a different social class, speak another language and employ unfamiliar expressions of distress. [p. 49]

While it is clear that in the 1950s the *ataques* were nothing new to doctors practicing in Puerto Rico, one may wonder why Puerto Rican physicians needed to distance themselves from a well-known phenomenon in their culture, whose presentation fitted well with their culture's categories, whose symptoms did not even surprise them. Indeed, the multidiscipline team involved in Robert de Ramírez de Arellano and colleagues' study on the Puerto Rican syndrome appears in a curious position—accepting the scientific validity of an "imported" diagnosis for a "domestic" manifestation. They readily adopted a new diagnosis that rendered pathological an experience that was socially normative and personally normal. Why did they embrace a perspective that was at variance with their clinical experience and cultural knowledge? One wonders if they identified with mainstream American culture as many other middle-class educated Puerto Ricans have done and still do.

For the patients who presented hyperkinetic seizures of the "Puerto Rican syndrome type,"[7] involving periodic bouts of hyperactivity, partial or total loss of consciousness, amnesia for those periods, and whose paroxysm included "assaultive and destructive behavior, self-inflicted injuries, and thrashing about" (Robert de Ramírez de Arellano 1954, p. 3), the psychiatric investigations mention one very revealing socioeconomical factor. The Veterans Administration awards compensation benefits for illnesses contracted during service and pension benefits for illnesses appearing at other times. Service-connected cases receive higher financial benefits and privileges. Some veterans involved in this survey were already receiving compensation but most of them, who were veterans from the Korean War,

---

7. Many war veterans who complain of *ataques*, but who on further exploration are also found to be suffering from what we may describe as signs of intense anxiety (headaches, shaking, palpitations, and fears), are excluded from the study.

were still in the process of examinations verifying eligibility for compensation benefits.

All these veterans claimed that they did not have any symptom prior to their entry into the service; they stated that if they had been ill then, they would have been rejected at the time of induction, during their physical examination. They insisted that their symptoms were directly related to the stress of service and

> . . . usually began during or shortly after such situations as combat, handling dangerous weapons, performance of menial jobs as K.P., while superiors were criticizing or threatening the individual, while in the hospital awaiting, or after surgical procedures, while sleeping in crowded quarters, and similar situations from which the individual could not get away. The main motive in seeking help was the fact that they could not perform their previous jobs, and therefore could not meet their financial responsibilities. Many were concerned about the possibility of producing serious injuries to others, especially relatives, or to themselves. Many stated that they were considered crazy by members of the community because of their unpredictable behavior, and therefore lived in relative isolation. [Robert de Ramírez de Arellano et al. 1954, p. 7]

The researchers recorded that these veterans felt that "the experiences in the service produced a deficiency in their nervous system which was not there before" (p. 8). They also observed that the general feeling of these patients was one of irritability and anger, which they could not direct to a definite object. Remarkably, the psychological report included in the study was curiously named in a militaristic fashion "Operation Ataques." It concludes that among the subjects in the "psychogenic group" (those who showed no signs of neurological problems in the psychological tests), hostility toward the environment was outstanding, whereas among the "organic cases" hostility was rather an insignificant factor. A prevalent trait observed throughout the study was marked hostility either directed at the environment or turned against the self. In almost all cases, the onset was experienced during combat; most patients used the word "explosion" at some time during the interview while describing the development of their ailments. Let us keep in mind that irritability, anger, and hostility appear as predominant features; we shall return to these salient aspects in Chapter 7.

From a sociological perspective, in all cases there was an important recurrent feature—all the patients suffering "*ataques*" had joined the army in the hope of escaping from a difficult economic situation to find financial security. Of the 20 cases featured in the sociopsychiatric preliminary report of the study, there are only three cases in which the authors considered that the subjects studied had a relatively healthy family background; the other 17—that is, 85 percent of the cases analyzed in this section— had "overprotective, immature, alcoholic, domineering, and high-strung . . . parents and close relatives" (p. 16). This segment of the study also noted a "history of neurotic traits and inadequate interpersonal relationships" in about 70 percent of the veterans involved in the research. The study ends with no clear-cut conclusion and recommends further study of the so-called Puerto Rican syndrome; the authors manifest a measure of healthy skepticism and agree that "the term 'Puerto Rican syndrome' probably has its origin in initial impressions without the benefit of complete neuropsychiatric work-up" (p. 16).

Even though the authors I have examined were all aware that *ataque* was a common phenomenon that was culturally accepted, their perspective seems patterned by the reliance on the American scientific model that overemphasized the validity of the foreign diagnostic category and underestimated the interpretations of their own culture. The implicit assumption is that the observations of U.S. army psychiatrists were granted scientific validity and were immune to cultural or political influences. Or that doctors may not be aware of the power conveyed by their scientific authority. As Foucault (1965) notes, the power inherent in medical, and particularly psychiatric, practice is based on the "myth of scientific objectivity" (p. 276) and is often forgotten or downplayed. Those who thought they could measure and justify the Puerto Rican syndrome through the invention of the label must justify themselves before it; the Puerto Rican syndrome expresses a sociopolitical beyond by the very excess of symptoms that, however, do not seem to justify the designation any longer.

4

Private Agony Gone Public

One should approach the first published account of the Puerto Rican syndrome with caution. It is clear from the outset that this article is politicized although it carries an illusion of scientific "neutrality." The strategic value of the Puerto Rican syndrome becomes apparent: it appeared one year after the end of the Korean War in the *U.S. Armed Forces Medical Journal*; it was authored by Mauricio Rubio, Mario Urdaneta, and John Doyle (1955); a Major, MC USAR, a Captain, MSC USAR, and a First Lieutenant, MC USAR, respectively; it carried the title "Psychopathologic Reaction Patterns in the Antilles Command." The data survey began just two months after Robert de Ramirez de Arellano and colleagues' study; in fact both were conducted almost simultaneously. The article describes five "patterns of reaction" of "hysterical personality type" observed in military personnel (recruits) from the island of Puerto Rico. The explicit purpose of the study is to avoid diagnostic confusions stemming from the resemblance of these manifestations to more serious conditions like schizophrenia or epilepsy. They observed the outpatients and medically evacuated inpatients from Puerto Rican personnel of the Antilles Command at the Rodriguez U.S. Army Hospital in New York—a total of 998 patients—from January 1 to

December 31, 1954.[1] The authors surveyed five striking "reaction patterns of the hysterical personality type" precipitated by minor stress. As the sources of "minor stress" they listed:

> induction into the Armed Forces; transfer from induction center to basic training camp; experiences in basic training, particularly with weapon familiarization, infiltration, and combat courses; prolonged hikes; stand-by details that prevent going home on pass; minor reprimands from officers and non-commissioned officers; and alerts for overseas shipment and routine overseas duty. [Rubio et al. 1955, p. 1769]

The "reactions" lasted from a few hours to several days and were accompanied by secondary gains, special privileges, and removal from the source of stress. The first and most outstanding "reaction pattern" was characterized by

> a transient state of partial loss of consciousness, most frequently accompanied by convulsive movements, hyperventilation, moaning and groaning, profuse salivation, and aggressiveness to self or others in the form of biting, scratching, or striking; and of sudden onset and termination. . . . The crises are quite spectacular, and when they take place in the company area or at home they cause great alarm and confusion to those around the patient. [p. 1767]

The paroxysm may look quite dramatic, but the authors noted that the degree of dissociation from the environment was never complete since serious injury was avoided. They also saw a "cathartic effect" in the attack since after the crisis patients looked better and expressed a sense of relief.[2]

A second "reaction pattern" was identified as "*mal de pelea*" (fighting disease) and consisted of "sudden outbursts of verbal and physical hostility, with destructiveness, assaultiveness, and expressions of some persecutory trends." During these episodes the patients were markedly hyperactive and noisy but discriminatory in the type of property they destroyed

---

1. Of the total 998 patients participating, 517 are of insular origin.

2. "The patient, especially when he believes that he is not being observed, is also careful to avoid sustaining serious injury, and at the onset of a crisis finds a bed or falls gradually to the ground. Upon the termination of the crisis he claims complete amnesia, for he often appears more alert than prior to it, and expresses a sense of relief, as though he had experienced an emotional catharsis" (p. 1768).

and the persons they attacked. Some of these patients also claimed complete amnesia after the outburst, particularly those who faced disciplinary action as a result. A third reaction was manifested by "a behavior pattern of infantile regression" providing a general impression of "mental deficiency." This clinical picture tended to disappear overnight, leaving patients with a feeling of relief and well-being. The fourth modality was a type of dramatic "pseudosuicidal attempt."

> Superficial scratches on the anterior aspects of the wrist, forearm, and chest, carefully inflicted with razor blades, fountain pens, or pins, are the commonest means of self-injury. The ingestion of rat poison or disinfectants mixed with drinks and attempts at hanging are also frequent. [p. 1768]

The fifth and least striking "reaction pattern" was identified as "mild dissociation": an inability to concentrate, forgetfulness, loss of interest in personal appearance, preoccupation, flat affect. This "reaction" was usually brief and lasted one to two days.

Overall, this piece appeared to be written to alert inexperienced physicians about a treacherous symptom cluster. The authors used this text as a prophylactic measure to warn the unaware doctor, thus preventing the practitioner unfamiliar with the syndrome from being fooled by it. They cautioned the reader about the display of spectacular "reaction patterns," which could "often simulate more serious psychiatric entities, particularly when the persons concerned are examined from the viewpoint of a different culture and language" (p. 1772). However, in all likelihood, doctors could be easily misled not so much by the ability of the patients to perform dramatic symptoms but by their own ignorance—especially if physicians did not know the patients' culture or speak their language. On the whole, those observed come across as talented manipulators in this account: they may use tactics of deception or respond with anger, temper tantrums, suicidal histrionic gestures, crying spells, or convulsive seizures. Ultimately, the text offers precise guidelines for practitioners on how to handle these cases.

Most of all, the symptoms point to unruliness and lack of discipline, two characteristics that are totally unacceptable for a soldier. To make things clearer, the symptoms have been regrouped in five separate "reaction patterns." Thus, order and coherence are given to the seemingly chaotic manifestations; in the future, other colleagues will make more accurate diagnoses and anticipate strategies for success. No longer disorganized, the Puerto Rican syndrome has been reduced to a series of uniform reaction patterns; the disorderly conduct becomes an "orderly disorder." In this piece, the attack (identified as first reaction pattern) is predominant but not central to the disorder. Curiously, the second reaction pattern, or "*mal de pelea*" (fighting disease), seems to present a caricature of what a good soldier should be: physically hostile, destructive, assaultive, markedly hyperactive, noisy but discriminatory in the type of property he destroys and the persons he attacks. Let us note in passing that the hostility displayed by these soldiers is explosive but not blind; it can discriminate quite well along levels of authority and items of value in the objects destroyed. The syndrome looks crazy but is not illogical.

Notably, the prevailing sentiment that comes across throughout the authors' descriptions of those suffering from the "pathological reactions" is one of hostility. One may wonder how the ingestion of rat poison or disinfectants mixed with drinks, how attempts at hanging, how cuts inflicted with razor blades and pins, may be taken by Rubio and colleagues as purely theatrical gestures deemed not worthy of serious consideration. The doctors' contempt may be a reaction to the fierce determination of soldiers ready to fight but whose aggressivity turns against themselves. The authors appear to minimize the power struggle at play while overstressing the histrionic features of suicidal gestures presented as a mere *mise en scène* aimed at deceiving an all too naive medico-military audience.

As we have seen, hysteria has a chameleonlike ability to reflect its environments. If the symptoms are socially determined, what does this specific form of hysteria tell us about these hysterics in this time and place? Given the severity of what is described as "minor stress" (in time of war), the crises seem to be the outcome of an unbearable situation, and may ultimately function as a form of passive resistance when facing an all but impossible predicament. Who would need to make use of such a desperate move? According to this study, those suffering the manifestations are "basic overly dependent, emotionally unstable personality" types. Rubio and colleagues (1955) note certain "remarkable similarities in the genetics and dynamic of their personalities" (p. 1769): a strong attachment to and dependence on the mother, noticing that the patients often say that they would never marry as long as the mother is living because "Mother always comes first." They also observe "a lack of proper identification with the father or with an adequate masculine figure" and little influence from U.S. "highly competitive culture"—they live "on a very small income" (p. 1769).

"Exceptionally these reaction patterns have been observed in persons of the social middle class whose strong maternal attachment and weak masculine identifications were prominent" (p. 1770). The psychodynamic factors identified (a strong attachment to the mother and a weak father figure) do not all have the same effects across class boundaries—it may seem obvious, according to these data at least, that the real cause for these psychopathological reactions may be poverty.

It is interesting to note that the prospect of discharge from the service at the completion of a tour of duty and the consequent return to smaller incomes and lower living standards are mentioned as important precipitating factors for the syndrome. The authors stress how the patients *profit* from symptoms that "bring considerable attention and special privileges to the patient" (p. 1769). The authors contend that "the greater the secondary gains, the longer it lasts" (p. 1769). The desperate "flight to illness" allows the soldiers to resist prescribed roles, thus moving from the battlefield to the hospital. They try to escape and at the same time expose an impossible situation. The syndrome appears as a product and indictment of a concrete historical setting. Ultimately, the symptom looks like a return in inverted form of the message received by soldiers during their training. Both a failed revolt of soldiers forced to fight for a country that is not theirs and a declaration of defeat, the symptom spells out a realization that there is no other way out.

Overall, the main concern of the first published piece is to identify the "psychopathologic reaction patterns" because they cause severe "problems in the management" of the affected soldiers. The authors mention that during their hospitalization the patients do not want to return to duty and believe that they "'should be cured' or given a pension" as they complain that they will "never be the same again" (p. 1770). Rubio and colleagues use the loaded term "reaction patterns." Of course we cannot disregard the fact that these observations take place in military settings, with the inherent complexities of power hierarchies. Patients who refuse to return to duty are often caught up in a proverbial Catch 22: refusing to fight out of fear means that the person is sane and therefore qualifies for action, while only someone insane would accept too willingly the idea of going to war and run the risk of being killed. Should they be simply branded as traitors? Are they perceived as mischievous in their mental warfare—like an enemy who renders inefficient their diagnostic psychiatric weapons? To make things worse, the patients seem to enjoy too much the secondary gains of their "bizarre" condition—the symptoms subside when they are separated from the service. The authors' final advice is that "these patients with baffling symptoms and severe language barriers should be evacuated to Puerto Rico for final disposition." The possibility of treatment, or anything resembling a cure, is totally dismissed. In consequence, the study's concluding recommendation is drastic: "Attempts to rehabilitate patients with these character disorders are impeded by their extreme dependence, needs, and the secondary gains they derive from their illness. Administrative separation from the service is usually indicated" (p. 1772).

A SYMPTOMATOLOGY OF VIOLENCE

It is possible that the soldiers presenting the "psychopathological reactions" were aware that the scenario they played involved some level of deception. They may have laid false traces and implicated themselves in a deliberate deception of their interpellators. On the other hand, they may also have betrayed the very premise of deception because their enactment was based in a disbelief or mistrust in their superiors. The symptoms were bizarre, desperate, unpredictable. They appropriated the irrationality of a national diagnosis and played it out so as to undermine the authority of the Other as medical and military power and to produce a point of rupture in an impossible situation.

We should not neglect the social variables at play. In both articles discussed so far, socioeconomic problems are identified as the main precipitating factor for these exuberant reactions. These two studies mark a predominance of military psychiatric reports in the literature on the Puerto Rican syndrome. Tracing the Puerto Rican syndrome to its origins, early evidence of its existence is found in military medical documentation, as if it had some strategic, bellicose connotation, perhaps defensive, possibly a mode of *ataque* needing to be prevented. This suggests a strategic or logistic interest in such hyperkinetic seizures. But are the studies of the Puerto Rican syndrome a way to understand how such a "peaceful" and "tolerant" society as the Puerto Rican could produce a symptomatology of violence (issues that will be treated in detail in Chapter 9)? Could the sociopolitical conditions that surrounded the invention of the Puerto Rican syndrome more than fifty years ago still shape today's manifestations? If the manifestations have changed, have the beliefs as to etiology and methods of treatment evolved accordingly?

To start answering these questions we must now bridge a chronological gap in our "hystorical" exploration and examine a few recent representative interpretations chosen from the existing scientific literature. This can be done with little risk of error because these examples are paradigmatic. Marlene Steinberg (1990), a research psychiatrist at the Yale University School of Medicine, writes:

> *Ataque de nervios*, "nervous attack," or "Puerto Rican Syndrome" is characterized by a variety of transient symptoms including partial loss of consciousness, convulsive movements of psychogenic origin, assaultive hyperactivity, childlike behavior, and/or psychosis, and may also include impulsive suicidal or homicidal acts. [p. 31]

Steinberg notes the diagnostic difficulties created by a syndrome that seems to appear under every possible guise:

> While not well understood, this syndrome has been described in varying ways in the psychiatric literature. . . . The *ataque* has been hypothesized to be an acute dissociative reaction which can occur within a variety of psychiatric disorders, particularly hysterical syndromes, and it is thought to be a culturally acceptable reaction to stress within the Hispanic community. [p. 31]

Despite her awareness that the symptom has been described in varying, and often divergent, *hypothetical* ways, Steinberg does not question whether, objectively, the diagnosis of the Puerto Rican syndrome corresponds to any actual entity. She believes in its existence without questioning its clinical validity, and even attempts to offer a new diagnosis, recommending "that the diagnosis of Multiple Personality Disorder be considered in Hispanics with histories of ataque" (p. 31). This attitude shows how the syndrome remains a riddle and cannot be fully mastered by any definition even though it is seen as part of a culturally acceptable reaction in the Hispanic community. Its otherness is redoubled when an apparent lack of rationality transforms it into the pure symptom of alienation, the distinctive mark of a segregated group.

Thus attitudes continue diverging. "The Puerto Rican syndrome is a term that has been used not in the official nosology but rather as a curiosity," contends, on the one hand, Mario Rendón (1984, p. 305). On the other hand, Sonia Badillo Ghalli (1977) asserts that "The Puerto Rican syndrome has become so well known that there is a reference to it in Alfred M. Freed-man, Harold Kaplan, and Benjamin Sadock's *A Comprehensive Textbook of Psychiatry*. Unfortunately, it does not present the accurate version" (p. 463). As we have seen, the Puerto Rican syndrome, a label for a nationality-specific syndrome, has not been well understood in standard medical and, espe-cially, in psychiatric diagnostic systems. In addition, it is a designation for symptoms that continue changing in their clinical presentations, thus chal-lenging their very interpretation. The Puerto Rican syndrome varies in characteristics, incidence, prevalence, geographical location of occurrence, prognosis, severity, and risk factors. Each observer seems to have a par-ticular perspective about it. Since the disparity of the descriptions makes it harder to produce a comparative evaluation that would provide clues to its cause, no generalization can be safely proposed about it.

The Puerto Rican syndrome's symptoms not only affect the bodies and souls of the patients who suffer from it. The multisymptomatic manifesta-tions of the "disease" powerfully subvert the possibility of making a definite medical diagnosis. They cause diagnostic "anomalies" that challenge not only the existence of the entity designated by the diagnosis, but also, and most importantly, the usefulness of the existing psychiatric clinical categories. The cumulative effect of diagnostic discrepancies in the literature on the Puerto Rican syndrome calls into question the diagnostic procedure itself.

Let us put aside momentarily the general ethical problems that psy-chiatric diagnoses raise. Their influence goes beyond their purported util-ity in helping decide the most adequate treatment. One of the many pos-sible adverse consequences of psychiatric labeling is that it can condition negatively a person's sense of identity by becoming a lifetime marker of stigma. The example of homosexuality (which until 1973 was considered a "mental illness" by the American Psychiatric Association and was finally taken out of its famous diagnostic manual only 15 years later, that is, in 1987) illustrates how psychiatric practice has been abused in the hands of experts intent on dogmatic conformism and social control. Let us also postpone an examination of the relationship between popular illness cat-egories and psychiatric disorders. We will delay assessing how culturally dependent psychiatric diagnoses are, and whether or not a cluster of symp-toms can be considered a psychiatric illness in one culture and a normal occurrence in another, which leads us to interrogate the reliability and validity of cross-cultural psychiatric diagnoses—these are questions that will be addressed later. We need to focus exclusively on the Puerto Rican syndrome before assessing whether the lessons we derive can be generalized to other diagnoses of "mental illness."

LOOKING DIFFERENT

The symptoms described under the name Puerto Rican syndrome are indeed "symptomatic" in the sense that they obey the logic of overdetermination in which antagonistic ideas coexist. In the clinical example of an *ataque* that follows, which Braulio Montalvo (1974) sees as a reaction to stress caused by insensitivity to cultural particularities, a typical manifestation of Puerto Rican syndrome is triggered by a confrontration with differential social relationships. It is a young woman (13 years old) who finds in crisis the means to resolve the dilemma of being an "other" and makes oppositional ideas concur. Montalvo evocatively calls his case "María, the different-looking girl." María was a young student who wore long dresses. Her drama was unleashed when her teacher asked her to wear revealing clothes and some lipstick for her part in a school play. Although enthusiastic about the play, María was reluctant to wear makeup and a shorter dress. Suspecting María's parents' disapproval, the teacher contacted them. The parents were not very moved by the evocation of María's talents and felt threatened by the idea of her traveling with the drama group. The teacher, who herself wore a mini-skirt during her interview with the parents, did not know that María's plain long dresses were the ones preferred by her family; they were Pentecostal members of a Puerto Rican church praising humble, unadorned demeanor in women. Caught between the contradictory expectations of her teacher and her family, María developed a convulsive *ataque* three days before the play. "The *ataque* has left her with a hoarse voice and so weak that all she could do was drag herself to church with her family" (p. 105). She was rushed to a psychiatrist, who could not find any clue for her pseudoepileptic seizure.

In his interpretation of the case, Montalvo does not think that one should look for a "level of psychosexual regression being recapitulated" or "ego functions gone amiss while defending against the breakthrough of infantile rage." He rather recommends exploring the girl's broader circumstances; there one might find what he calls "secondary gains." "In this case, the gains were in the actions which the girl wanted to elicit from people in the family and the school so as to change her situation" (p. 105). Montalvo admits that the school meant well but was not aware of the cultural nuances that produced the unfortunate result. If the teacher had known about the parents' Pentecostal beliefs, she would have probably worn a longer skirt, would have stressed adult supervision, and thus achieved much better results. Montalvo's analysis described the "dramatic convulsive *ataque*" as a manipulative, albeit desperate, attempt at mastering an impossible situation. "It is a culturally expected reaction and an ordinary occurrence. It is most often used as a means to control. It may occur regularly, for example, when a teen-age son gets out of hand or when a husband is going out to drink," states Badillo Ghali (1977, p. 463).

One cannot help seeing in the circumstances surrounding the dramatic *ataque* that María, the different-looking girl, experienced classical elements of the hysterical symptoms as they were described by Freud (1908). Freud writes that "the hysterical symptom arises as a compromise between two opposing affects or instinctual trends" (p. 164). María managed to reconcile antithetical impulses and found a way out of a seemingly impossible situation. By losing her voice she expressed the inexpressible conflict that was resolved via her *ataque*. The contradiction between her family's wishes and her teacher's request finds expression in a compromise solution. As Freud noted, the hysterical attack is substitute gratification and María wisely deflected the tension by solving an irreconcilable difference. Let us resist the temptation to establish a general rule applying to all cases; in a true psychoanalytic treatment one could explore the meaning of María's symptoms and the unconscious dynamics at work. The material of her case, however, confirms once more that María's *ataque* is a classic repetition of hysterical attack *à la* Freud.

THE TEACHINGS OF HYSTERIA

The very name of "Puerto Rican syndrome" reveals that the diagnosis is geographically bound, which may lead to the conclusion that the validity of the diagnosis is discredited because of its limitative, almost derogative nature. But before criticizing and rejecting the ideological implications of the "invention" of the Puerto Rican syndrome, we need to take into account its cultural, symbolic, and political meanings. As with any form of hysteria, the syndrome is underpinned by a history of social conflict. Showalter has explained, as we have seen in Chapter 3, that the hysteric is fundamentally someone whose story gets unstuck, unmoored, adrift in a wandering History, or *histoire*. We no longer see hysteria in terms of wandering wombs but of wandering stories; here is a *hystory* of race, gender, and madness told by hysterics, doctors, historians, and finally critics.

By its very elusive nature, hysteria poses key questions about class, gender, politics, and ideology. Its *hystory* operates as a force propelling the production of knowledge. We have already met some of these characters caught up in insane dilemmas, exhibiting their theatrical symptoms, foaming at the mouth, screaming, biting, kicking, crying uncontrollably, shaking in seizures, finally fainting. When they force the physician in the emergency room to witness such extreme pain, their suffering also urges the doctor to give a name to the illness. And then the physician answers with the diagnosis of "Puerto Rican syndrome." Having recovered in a matter of hours, the hysteric harshly criticizes the doctor: She is not cured at all, the illness persists; but this time the pain has moved: a leg and an arm are paralyzed, leaving the patient unable to walk. And it goes on. . . . Wajeman (1986) analyzes this interaction in the following way: "the hysteric starts out with her 'I am what you say' and ends with her 'All of what I am you cannot say' bringing about the disjunction between knowledge and object"[3] (p. 19).

In this interaction, hysteria exposes the structure of language—the $S1 \rightarrow S2$ that constitutes the chain of signifiers (the Other), and, at the same time, is pointing out the fact that the Other (the treasure of signifiers) is always deficient (there is at least one signifier missing). As we have seen in the exchange with the doctor in María's example, the hysteric's strategy throws light on an Other, the Other that does not and cannot have all the answers; thus the Other is lacking, even inconsistent. Wajeman deduces from this typical hysterical mode of rapport a structural affinity between hysteria and psychoanalysis. "While Freud took hysteria to be the nucleus of all neurotic disorders, Lacan has revealed the speaking subject as fundamentally hysterical: the only subject of psychoanalysis is the barred, hysterical subject." Thus, Wajeman, following Lacan, elevates hysteria to the status of "*the* fact of language if we admit that anyone who speaks is hysterical" (p. 20).

The hysteric's demand that something be said about her symptoms almost inevitably produces some form of knowledge. This movement has inspired extensive knowledge—medical knowledge (from ancient wander-

---

3. This is the notation that Lacan proposes: <a>//S2.

ing wombs to contemporary panic attacks) and religious knowledge (from demonic possession to miraculous sanctity) and even psychoanalysis (from a missing organic lesion to Freud's discovery of the unconscious truth concealed in bodily symptoms). Yet, as Wajeman notes, the hysteric's role regarding knowledge is ambiguous. On the one hand, the hysteric "sells" symptoms, soliciting knowledge by offering elusive symptoms as a com-pelling object (making someone desire this object they have no need of, in order to push them to demand it). No matter how accurate that knowl-edge may be, however, it fails to fully account for hysteria. Nonetheless, as we have seen, the failure perpetually fuels the riddle, and with it, the pro-duction of knowledge.

We have seen how the Puerto Rican syndrome has guided us, inspir-ing us to produce, page after page, some knowledge. This characteristic of hysteria—eliciting knowledge, a knowledge that is destined to fail in mas-tering its object but never relents in its attempts to seize it, corresponds to the structure that Lacan identified as the hysteric's discourse. For him, hysteria is not only a form of neurosis but more globally a mode of dis-course whose function is to tighten particular social links. In Lacan's theory, hysteria creates a particular relationship with the Other: It compels the Other to produce a knowledge destined to fail in its rationale. This failure, however, makes the mystery even more appealing and invigorates the pro-duction of knowledge. Hysteria presses for an answer and generates more knowledge. As Wajeman (1986) observes, "While knowledge cannot ar-ticulate the hysteric, the hysteric ushers the articulation of knowledge" (p. 3). In order to abstain from producing just another spurious definition of the Puerto Rican syndrome, let us take a closer look at its dynamics and at the structure underlying it.

In its pathological dislocation, the Puerto Rican syndrome performs a scene; it acts out something in a performance addressed to a spectator, an other. This enactment, at times threatening, at other times fascinating, poses a question that turns into a riddle. The other who acknowledges that a question is posed and attempts to answer it is soon raised to the position of Other: the master of a knowledge he or she is supposed to have about the enigma. This question constitutes a demand.[4] Whoever accepts the challenge by trying to articulate an answer will become this Other. This demand produces speech and also implies a surrender of power and a trans-

---

4. Lacan (1977b) opposes demand and desire (demand is always address to the Other).

fer to the Other. The question addressed to the Other becomes: "Tell me who am I, I'll be whatever you say I am." This circular movement exemplifies the structure of a performative language in action in which we may find the elementary conditions for a symbolic dependence of the subject from the Other. The initial question starts with an "I" and presents intriguing symptoms addressed to the Other—any Army doctor, priest, anthropologist, social worker, *espiritista* will do. In fact, while the question appears incarnated in the body of the hysteric, the answer begins in the Other who produces speech. This answer is sent back to the hysteric who then becomes indeed whatever the Other says. Since one always receives one's own message from the other in an inverted form, when those who are in the position of Other tell the hysteric what he or she (the hysteric) "is," this answer then comes back to the Other as well. Thus the inverted message returns to say more about the speaker (the Other) than it may say about the addressee (the hysteric).

THE PUERTO RICAN SYNDROME DEFIES DEFINITION

Most of hysteria's medical interpreters agree to define it as undefinable. Is hysteria one illness or many? Has a definite causal mechanism for hysteria been established beyond doubt? Can a single pathogen be identified for hysteria? As Wajeman (1986) indicates, "There doesn't seem to be anything medicine has not said about hysteria: it is multiple, it is one, it is nothing; it is an entity, a malfunction, an illusion; it is true and deceptive; organic or perhaps mental; it exists, it does not exist" (p. 1). Let us emphasize that the general nosological frustration that the multiple mutations of hysteria have been eliciting for centuries reveals one of its most interesting aspects and helps explain why psychoanalysis is so indebted to hysteria. Hysteria has left an indelible imprint on the evolution of the health sciences. From the very beginning of medicine we have had a hysteric, her symptoms, and a doctor.[5] What has always been important is how these three elements are articulated. Inevitably—and this has become more evident with contemporary medical practice—medical knowledge erases sub-

---

5. This suggests, as Bronfen (1998, p. 102) notes, an interesting relationship, a "romance" between medicine and hysteria in which hysteria and the medical discourse about hysteria are mutually constitutive.

jectivity by reducing subjects to a set of organs, symptoms, and clearly ascertainable complaints. Hysteria, however, appeals to the subject's most entrenched resistance to all these coercive systems. This resistance takes effect by actively baffling or provoking the dominant medical knowledge. The manifestations are so numerous and contradictory that they expose all the faultlines and blind spots of medical knowledge. In this struggle, what prevails in the end is subjectivity: hysteria presents us with the idiosyncrasies of intractable subjectivity.

This chameleonlike quality of hysteria exposes the confines of the anatomo-clinical method, which, as Foucault (1975) noted, is used by the medical sciences to articulate space, body, language, and death. Hysterical symptoms are unconditionally faithful to the cultural mandates in place at any given time. Certain symptoms appear only at a particular period, in accordance with its prevailing medical knowledge. This openness to medical discourse shapes hysterical symptoms: the hysteric shows what the physician "wants" to see, while at the same time revealing the limits of this gaze. Hysterical manifestations seem to confirm medical knowledge, only to challenge it in the end, reducing the practitioner to a position of impotence. Hysteria is fundamentally culture-specific; its manifestations are based on the dominant theories of disease for each culture and are syntonic with the rest of the cultural beliefs. Hysterical symptoms come and go with the fashions. Like other aspects of human culture, hysteria is constantly changing. It is because hysteria is permeable to collective formations that certain modalities of hysteria will be produced only in particular cultures and in specific time periods. This articulation of bodies and time, of medical knowledge and cultural mandates, is at the basis of the political and transformative power of hysteria and this is particularly true of the Puerto Rican syndrome.

As we have seen, the symptoms identified and classified as a new disease that was supposed to be uniquely Puerto Rican repeated in uncanny detail the epileptiform agitation, the *grands mouvements*, the passional attitudes and delirious withdrawal of the hysterical paroxysm observed in the public performances conducted by Charcot at the end of hysteria's golden age. In the clinical presentations at the Parisian Salpêtrière Hospital, Freud confronted the theater of hysteria. Back in Vienna, he continued working with hysterical patients and produced one of the most important cultural revolutions of modern times—psychoanalysis. Now the fact that psychoanalysis owes its "invention" to hysteria should highlight its position outside a purely medical field. Psychoanalysis, being the science of the particular aiming at uncovering singular configurations exhibited through a subject's symptoms, should be uniquely adapted to lending a new type of hearing taking in these unaccountable pathologies. It was by treating hysteric patients that Freud developed a new method of treatment that provided him with the foundations for psychoanalysis.

It is not a coincidence that hysteria led to the creation of a *talking* cure, because this complicated entity exposes how subjectivity is constituted as a discursive effect, as an effect of the signifier. Hysteria helps us discern the constitution of the subject as what Lacan calls *parlêtre*, "speaking-being," a word coined to stress the fact that for humans, being is constituted in and through language. Let us, for example, think about the dualism of body and mind that is resolved by hysteria. Pierre Janet (1901) discovered that hysterical anesthesias take the shape of a jacket sleeve, a leg of lamb, a wristband. Conversion symptoms do not follow anatomy but popular ideas about the body. Freud (1893) noted that the hysterical symptom "takes the organs in the ordinary, popular sense of the names they bear: the leg is the leg as far as its insertion into the hip, the arm is the upper limb as it is visible under the clothing" (p. 169). Nothing corresponds to the pathways and topography of nerve branches.

What Charcot revealed with his precise distinction between epilepsy and hysteria, above all, was that the hysteric's body is imaginary, as Lacan has noted. With hysterical symptoms, the psychical becomes physiological, following an imaginary anatomy that depends on language. In hysteria, we can see the human body as something that belongs to another's logic: an *Other*'s logic, the logic of the signifier. Hysterical anesthesias challenge the biological organization of the body, following instead a given culture's popular understanding about the function of organs. This very fact gives us interesting insights into the primacy of the signifier for the "speaking-being." It is also illuminating in regard to how culture is articulated in the body. The body not being just a collection of organs, culture inscribes itself onto the body. This result of such inscription we may call subjectivity.

We have also seen how much the sociocultural environment permeates hysteria—hysteria readily changes its manifestations according to mandates of time and culture. This intimate connection of hysteria to its milieu tells us a lot about hysteria while revealing its sociohistorical context. Hysteria allows us to see how at any given time culture writes its specific discontents on the body while reminding us constantly that human bodies are subjected to the effects of signifiers. The hysteric body in pain writes on its flesh the psychic discontent and anguish brought about by culture. Hysteric symptoms show us how culture writes on the body and through the body. Hysteric symptoms articulate the resulting desire attributable to a mythical encounter of biology, psyche, and culture. The hysterical body educates us by showing that the human body is not simply a body made of flesh and blood but a network of signifiers. Hysteria puts the body on center stage, and with it, sexuality and desire. Since this hysterical body speaks, language introduces an alienation that makes the body experience *jouissance*. And because it is thus traversed by language, the body is radically transformed, fragmented, and exploded.

Hysteria has always been with us. Every era understood it differently, weaved it into the social fabric with a new and fashionable pattern. It is commonly assumed that in our own time, conversion symptoms and theatrical attacks "à la Salpêtrière" have not simply become rare but have disappeared altogether. Yet, the Puerto Rican syndrome haunts us by fits and starts, preserving in the *barrio*'s incubator hundred-year-old manifestations of a four-thousand-year-old disease.[6] This form of hysteria is not limited to the consultation room; it comes to light in the social field. No longer restricted to dealings with God or the Devil, the doctor or the analyst, hysteria expresses loud and clear "what is not working" for human beings. Hysteria exposes the irremediable conflict and discontent that culture creates when it imposes a "civilized" life. Hysteria symptomatically denounces the failures of the law of the father, and reveals the alienation and precariousness of identity while challenging the absurdity of social bonds. One of Freud's claims was to bridge the gap between the patients' individual life stories and a vaster history of culture, disclosing a "wandering story" written in uncanny collaboration by the hysteric and the doctor. As with hysteria, the Puerto Rican syndrome's stories of race and gender remain to be told.

---

6. The world's most ancient surviving medical document, the *Kahun Papyrus* (named for the Egyptian city in whose ruins it was found) dates from about 1900 B.C., and its principal topic is a definition of hysteria conceived of as a disease of the womb.

5

The Pathology of Otherness

In recent years it has become a rather common practice both on the Island of Puerto Rico, in areas of the Continental United States such as New York City where there are large concentrations of Puerto Rican patients, and in the Armed Services where Puerto Rican troops are frequently seen medically, for physicians to make a diagnosis of Puerto Rican syndrome or "ataque."

Capt. Robert D. Mehlman (1961, p. 328)

What factors motivated the invention of a "Puerto Rican" syndrome? A first answer might be found in an awareness of cultural diversity; however, it looks more likely that the invention of the Puerto Rican syndrome is due to a patronizing gesture hiding a real intolerance for otherness. The fact is that when inexplicable symptoms were observed among Puerto Rican soldiers such as sudden attacks of anger, eccentric seizures with no organic origin, anxiety and fear in a choleric battle with an imaginary enemy, suicidal gestures, hallucinations, and amnesia, military physicians were at a loss before a seemingly incoherent set of symptoms. They responded by inventing a name for the set of symptoms that then entered medical records as "a group of striking psychopathological reaction patterns, precipitated by minor stress" (Rubio et al. 1955, p. 1767). Thus, U.S. Army psychiatrists translated the customarily called *ataque* into a *"Puerto Rican* syndrome." This classification did not bring new details in the rendering of the manifestations nor did it offer reliable or valid clinical guidelines. Therefore, from the very beginning the Puerto Rican syndrome was irrelevant as a medical category; it was not a discrete entity, like diabetes. There was no clear-cut brain pathology or dysfunction associated with it and the cause of the disorder remained unknown. Neither the *ataque de nervios* nor the Puerto Rican syndrome can be taken as a psychiatric category because the symptoms do not fit in any traditional psychiatric classification system. Migdalia Rivera-Arzola and Julia Ramos-Greniers (1997) observe that "Diagnostically speaking, the *ataque de nervios* is an anomaly" (pp. 126–127). A nosological anomaly for a normal condition, given that some specialists contend that the *ataque* is not even pathological since most Puerto Ricans on the island and on the mainland perceive it as a "normal," expectable, cultural occurrence (DeLaCancela et al. 1986, Grace 1959, Guarnaccia et al. 1989).

Why did military psychiatrists feel the need to expand the psychiatric nosology in use in the United States by adding a new diagnosis for a disruptive behavior among Puerto Rican servicemen that had been culturally sanctioned, thus almost "normal"? Unaware of their ethnocentric biases and of the political implications of their gesture, these doctors were forced to explore the limits of a psychiatric practice of universalistic and decontextualized diagnoses; this essentialism can be traced to what Juan Mezzich and colleagues (1996) call use of categories taken as "platonic nosological entities" (p. xvii). Evaluating patients from a different culture, they were faced with the challenge of recognizing differences of language, religion, race, traditions, and, internally, of social locality. In response to a puzzling manifestation located between the realms of psyche and soma and between two cultures, mainstream American and Puerto Rican, the U.S. Army diagnosis tended to obliterate the patients' personal experiences and the cultural references these were buttressed by, thus essentializing difference in terms of nationality and race.

The diagnosis of the Puerto Rican syndrome appears as a series of contradictory and racially and ethnically charged statements, which can be arranged chronologically and treated as history.[1] Whereas previously

---

1. A quick chronological review can follow Foucault's (1972) agenda, that is, remain aware "of discontinuity, of series, of limits, of unities, of specific orders, and differentiated

we examined in detail the first two documents on the syndrome, we will need to move forward in the "hystorical" chronology by addressing several paradigmatic contemporary analyses. To avoid repetition, we will focus on representations of the main interpretative trends that reveal the evolution of historical and cultural contexts; thus we will assess the Puerto Rican syndrome's development, obsolescence, and alleged disappearance.

We saw that in the first (though never published) written contribution to the topic, Robert de Ramirez de Arellano and colleagues (1954) pose crucial questions. Are the syndrome's seizures organic or psychogenic in origin? What is the psychology of the patients who suffer the syndrome, considering the social aspects in play? The authors focus on the manifestations of the syndrome and look for common factors behind the seizures. They also speculate about the increased accuracy of the diagnosis if aided by proper psychological evaluation. Despite their efforts, however, the puzzling syndrome continued to baffle the researchers, which is why this groundbreaking study concluded with a call for "further study of the so-called Puerto Rican syndrome." From its inception, the truth about the Puerto Rican syndrome remains inaccessible. The answers sought are never found. In fact, the study opens new questions that call for further studies, thus pushing for a new production of knowledge.

As the reader may have noticed, U.S. armed forces medical officers only observed the syndrome among soldiers. That is why Rubio and colleagues' interest in the Puerto Rican syndrome was purely practical: they were Army psychiatrists examining the disposition of armed forces recruits. The similarity to more severe conditions such as schizophrenia and epilepsy presented not only a medical problem but also an administrative one, especially for the psychiatrists who did not speak the same language or were unaware of the cultural particularities of Puerto Ricans. The idea of this foundational 1955 article was mostly to expose a malingering syndrome and alert physicians unaware of its multiple tricks. To this strategy, Fernández Marina responded in 1961 by wondering why English-speaking Army psychiatrists believed in the existence of a "classical" set of symptoms that was strictly "Puerto Rican." Fernández Marina assumed that their view resulted from the presumption that Puerto Ricans were inferior beings. Nonetheless, while eloquently exposing the prejudice behind the invention of the syndrome, Fernández Marina did not fully reject it, offer-

---

autonomies and dependencies," with the ultimate aim of "conceiv[ing] the *Other* in the time of our own thought" (p. 12).

ing instead an interpretation of the positive functions of the hyperkinetic episode of the Puerto Rican syndrome from an ego-psychology perspective. Noting the absence in Puerto Rico of extremely regressed and low-functioning patients like those often found in mainland psychiatric institutions, patients who need to be tube fed or are totally incontinent, he attributed the improved condition of schizophrenic patients in Puerto Rico precisely to the Puerto Rican syndrome. For Fernández Marina, "such hysterical attacks can also function as basic ego defenses against psychotic breaks, or as limits to extreme regression or total disorganization of the ego" (p. 79).

It was also in 1961 that Robert Mehlman defined the Puerto Rican syndrome within the parameters of hysteria as an "acute dissociative reaction of a hysterical sort" (p. 332). In his view, however, patients should not be diagnosed with the Puerto Rican syndrome since for him the diagnosis remained an inapplicable designation—it was not a disease entity but a "superficial" entity, a "misnomer" in the nomenclature, the mere deformation of insights that would otherwise be helpful for social psychiatry. Mehlman warned against the danger of a social psychology that, when applied to clinical practice, was all too ready to erase the patients' idiosyncrasies and miss important clinical factors. He considered the Puerto Rican syndrome "a collection of various disease processes that tend to be superficially deceivingly similar in a particular culture" (p. 332). While assessing its clinical importance, Mehlman makes a plea for further investigation of cultural phenomena and for the understanding of their impact upon psychiatric diseases. His opinion is categorical: he observes that during his extensive clinical experience with Puerto Ricans he *never* felt any clinical justification for the use of the diagnosis of Puerto Rican syndrome.

While it appears that there is no real clinical validation for the use of the diagnosis, let us take a closer look at the term "syndrome" involved in the construction of the label. Semantically, "syndrome" denotes a group of concurrent signs and symptoms that usually form an identifiable pattern but not a separate disease entity. As Rothenberg (1964) observes while reviewing the existing literature on the Puerto Rican syndrome, "the term 'syndrome' has never, in a time honored medical sense, referred to anything else but a symptom complex rather than a disease entity" (p. 962). Given the variations in presentation and uncertainties about its essential elements, the Puerto Rican syndrome cannot even be regarded as a unique disease. While Rothenberg questions the specificity of the diagnosis, the appeal to "culture" seems to override clinical reason. He notes that the fact that a group of symptoms had enough affinity to be labeled by different observers as specifically Puerto Rican may reveal nonetheless something important about this particular culture. This group of concurrent signs and symptoms qualified as uniquely "Puerto Rican" offers a cultural specificity that is highly questionable. In a landmark anthropological study published in 1952 on Puerto Rican cultural norms and behaviors (based on how children grow within three different class groupings—rural farmers, sugar workers, and the middle class of a small rural town), Kathleen Wolf concludes that "there is not such a thing as one uniform Puerto Rican personality type, in spite of the fairly uniform cultural tradition" (p. 401). According to Wolf's research, socioeconomic class demarcation determines different ways of life and varying levels of permeability to the United States cultural model for each Puerto Rican "subculture." Then, if the cultural validity of the diagnosis is questionable and its clinical relevancy is unconvincing, we may wonder, once more, what is the actual use of the diagnosis of Puerto Rican syndrome. Wolf's observation that cultural differences are dependent on class calls to mind Antonio Gramsci's (1971) contention that "political [economic] questions are often disguised as cultural ones, and as such become insoluble" (p. 149). Is class difference being evaded and concealed under "Puerto Rican syndrome," an exotic "regional" psychiatric diagnosis?

A COLD WAR PRODUCT

Against a backdrop of colonial relations, of political and economic domination that produce inequalities and subordinate cultural groups, we must consider the power relations at stake in the creation of the Puerto Rican syndrome. Guarnaccia and colleagues (1989) argue that the "'Puerto Rican syndrome' does not describe the symptoms of a particular individual; it is a label arising from the power relationship of American army psychiatrists over Puerto Rican inductees at a particular historical time" (p. 49). Then, in order to understand better the wider historical circumstances surrounding the invention of the label, we should keep in mind that the original commentaries on the Puerto Rican syndrome were produced at a peculiar moment in the history of the United States. Why invoke history and social conflict when talking about the Puerto Rican syndrome, which we have already defined as a form of hysteria? Because the Puerto Rican syndrome, as a form of hysteria, reveals social conflicts while it challenges the static temporality of history. As noted before, once a set of symptoms is properly identified and classified, hysteria surmounts established definitions and produces new and disconcerting symptoms. Thus, hysteria is never out of fashion; what is outdated is merely the attempt at seizing it, never hysteria itself. Hysteria, in its endless renewal, continues to send researchers to a new beginning in a circular chronology of returns. Hysteria is commanded by the Lacanian Real, that is, that which does not work, by that which does not fit, but which returns always to the same place. Since the hysteric always manages to present the humiliating truth that "this does not work," that "this does not fit," we may wonder what type of social conflict is at the core of the Puerto Rican syndrome and to which the symptoms send us back over and over again. Let us then explore the particular historical and material circumstances of the invention of the label.

In 1947 President Truman started a program that aimed at identifying any "infiltration of disloyal persons."[2] This led to the Cold War era of McCarthysm, a witch-hunt for Communists everywhere. Later, Truman would complain about "a great wave of hysteria" sweeping the nation (Zinn 1980, p. 420), underlining in effect the notorious semantic slippage of the term from the clinical field to the political realm. As seen before, 1952 marks a crucial year both in Puerto Rican history and in the history of hysteria in American psychiatry. Hysteria was excluded from psychiatric discourse as it seemed to have exhausted its potential as a medical diagnosis, but concomitantly receded from the medical to the social and political arena. Once more, hysteria had adjusted to the times and symptomatically voiced its discontent.

Meanwhile, American psychiatry was undergoing a major transformation and the elimination of the diagnosis of hysteria was only one of its manifestations. In 1961, Thomas Szasz published *The Myth of Mental Illness*, a book that courageously questioned the validity of the idea of mental *illness*. Its impact was aided by Ken Kesey's 1962 popular novel *One Flew Over the Cuckoo's Nest*. Thus through fiction and polemic, the general public was exposed to the aberrations of institutional psychiatric practice. Issues of freedom and responsibility were raised. The antipsychiatry movement of the 1960s brought to light the dehumanizing aspects of institutional psychiatry while blurring the distinction between mental health and mental illness—anyone could develop a mental disorder under

---

2. Executive Order 9835, March 22, 1947.

certain conditions. Antipsychiatry denounced the way society used psychiatry to control and alienate people by labeling behavior as deviant; and radical deviancy led to repressive confinement in mental institutions seen by many as prisons. The integrity of the practice of psychiatry was severely questioned and psychoanalysis was lumped with social strategies of repressive confinement.

However, the political implications of lay psychoanalysis soon appeared as being closer to the postulates of antipsychiatry, since on the whole, social adaptation seems at odds with Freud's (Freud and Breuer 1895) description of the analytic cure, which aims at transforming "misery into common unhappiness" (p. 305). But whereas in France and South America, psychoanalysis was looked at as an alternative to repressive institutionalization, the situation was quite different in the United States. As Freud himself had observed with wry disapproval, in the U.S. psychoanalysis became a medical, psychiatric, even corporate practice geared to preserving the money-making framework. A later critic, Sherry Turkle (1992), describes how "antipsychiatric stances that challenged the status quo of institutional psychology have tended to imply antipsychoanalytic ones" (p. 8).

In the context of the then emerging field of mental health in the United States, a series of programs of psychosocial rehabilitation were put into practice in the 1960s and 1970s. This project of social reform working as therapeutic poultices merely plastering over social problems corresponds exactly to the policy that Lacan strongly criticized, claiming that its adaptive naiveté was hiding a repressive spirit. The project of therapeutic social reform had many drawbacks: the expectations were unrealistic, and the solutions proposed contradictory. In recent decades the sociocultural conditions of the chronic mentally ill have only worsened. The treatment continues to be ineffective, housing problems have increased, and the social disenfranchisement, isolation, and victimization of discharged psychiatric patients have become more acute (Estroff 1981). Another victim of this largely failed project was psychiatry itself. By 1977, Alan Stone, then president of the American Psychiatric Association, warned that the interest of psychiatry in social issues and comprehensive human well-being risked leading to the extinction of psychiatry. The loss of a clear demarcation between mental health and mental illness brought about by the antipsychiatric movement originated a serious problem for psychiatry: If mental illness was no longer an organic disease but a social problem, where was the specificity and the legitimacy of medical psychiatry? In order to narrow its focus and restore validity to the field, psychiatry realigned itself with traditional medicine. Thus, the "psychosocial" model that proposed a "humanization" of psychiatry while pursuing a domestication of individual maladjustment as the key to social justice could not last very long. By the late 1970s, insurance companies were reducing steadily the extent of psychiatric treatment covered. Another economic pressure was the growing development of the psychopharmacological industry with its enormous financial power. With the advent of the first antipsychotic drugs, the practice of psychiatry took a dramatic new turn.

CROSSING CULTURES

We have seen that, during the 1960s, cross-cultural[3] psychiatry, initially social psychiatry influenced by the theoretical movement of antipsychiatry, did change the views on the Puerto Rican syndrome. Psychiatrists looked to the community for answers to the problems of mental illness. Thus, the interest was turned outward from the individual patient to the family, the community, and the cultural scene. The emerging field of cross-cultural psychiatry was generated by uncertainties regarding assessment and treatment of patients from different cultural backgrounds. Many historical factors contributed to this new multicultural situation: the immigration waves after World War II, the emerging field of social work, and internal migration patterns. In the particular case of Puerto Rico, in 1952 more than 52,000 people moved to the mainland after Puerto Rico acquired its new Commonwealth status (Rodriguez et al. 1984). And in 1953, Puerto Rican migration to New York reached its peak when more than 70,000 people left the island. Some estimates determine that more than one million Puerto Ricans migrated during the decade that followed Puerto Rico's 1952 change of status. Already by 1964, the Puerto Rican community made up 9.3 percent of the total New York City population.

In a recent historical analysis, Grosfoguel and Georas (2000) state that this trend was encouraged by agreements between the Truman administration and the Puerto Rican government. The main idea was to showcase Puerto Rico as a model of American capitalist development at a time when

---

3. It is interesting to note that currently the term "cross-cultural" is employed in fact to simply mean non-American.

the Third World was tempted by communist models and the help of the Soviet Union. In order to transform San Juan into the desired paradigm of success and prosperity, it was vital to solve the problem of poverty quickly, while at the same time providing the U.S. with cheap labor. Therefore, airfare costs were significantly reduced in order to foster mass migration (Grosfoguel 1992).

Increasing immigration waves intensified cultural diversity; the fluid diaspora of legal and illegal immigrants, exiles, and refugees provided a fertile ground for the germination of the ideas of the new field of social psychiatry, which spread rapidly in the late 1950s and early 1960s. Psychiatric and psychological concepts were put to use outside the clinical setting and the promotion of mental health in the community at large was pursued. Mental health and illness were no longer thought of as individual concerns but as stemming from wider social problems. Anthropologists and mental health workers were brought into different programs in the newly created community mental health centers. The relation of social conditions to mental health was approached with a dose of naive optimism that precluded any political interpretation. Whereas the antipsychiatric movement provided a ground of skepticism and political suspicion, in the late 1950s and early 1960s what permeated the ideology of programs promoting social improvement was in fact, as Charles Morris (1984) has observed, the earlier pragmatic idealism of John Dewey. In a remarkable historical moment, the combined influence of the liberal humanitarian ideals of the antipsychiatry movement, of the development and increasing use of psychotropic medications, and of conservative financial considerations, resulted in the closure of state mental hospitals and in a deinstitutionalization of the care of the mentally ill.

PSYCHIC WARFARE

In the early 1960s, Michael Harrington awakened the upper middle class from its American dream of prosperity with his book *The Other America* (1963). Harrington shocked affluent American society by revealing that one of the wealthiest countries in the world had 40 to 50 million people living in poverty—U.S. citizens lacking proper nutrition, housing, medical care, and education. The reprisal did not make itself wait—in 1965 President Lyndon Johnson's "Great Society" declared a "War on Poverty." The belief was that research could provide the facts to teach how to make people healthier, friendlier, and more industrious. The War on Poverty assumed that access to housing, jobs, and health services could grant equality to all. Morris notes that there was a spread conviction that the advances of social science could modify the physical environment and psychological disposition of the poor. As a result, the poor would act "middle-class." This approach to social change was sustained by the belief that educational, mental, and physical deficiencies could simply be overcome with adequate treatment. Therefore, Morris concludes, the "War on Poverty" needed to be fought in the minds of the poor. The psychological "warfare" was waged by the Joint Commission on Mental Illness and Health created in 1957, which recommended the creation of a system of community mental health centers in the belief that drug therapy would make confinement in asylums unnecessary (in the 1950s, mental hospital beds were the fastest growing medical sector and the living conditions in those hospitals were horrendous). These recommendations were embodied in the Community Mental Health Act of 1962. The dream of social reform relied on outpatient mental health care (Morris 1984). By 1965, amendments to the Social Security Act provided access to Medicaid and Medicare healthcare coverage. With the new programs of education in mental health matters and hopes of achieving increased social adaptation, poverty could no longer be tolerated in good faith.

For the first time, immigrants in urban centers such as New York, Chicago, and Philadelphia had access to free mental health services in their communities. This new situation made even more pertinent the contributions of social psychiatry. The impact of the constant flow of immigrants from all over the world forced psychiatrists to return to one of Freud's favorite quotes, Terence's *Homo sum humani nihil a me alienum puto* (I am a human being and nothing human is alien to me). Anthropology, economics, psychology, psychiatry, public health, and sociology started to be considered part of the complex fabric of social psychiatry.[4] The cultural diversity of those seeking mental health care created a new form of social disparity between patients and mental health workers. Adding the problem of cultural barriers to the existing class differences, the increasing cultural diversity of psychiatric symptoms undermined the practitioner's confidence in being equipped to give final and exhaustive answers. In particular, psychiatrists trying to make diagnoses were fraught with doubts

---

4. For early work on Social Psychiatry, see Rennie 1956 or Redlich and Pepper 1960.

about whether to consider a culturally acceptable belief as a delusion, or on the contrary, to dismiss a severe perturbation that might have been concealed because of language and other cultural barriers.[5] Unfortunately, the new expanding field of well-wishing social psychiatry, rather than raising the awareness and respect of cultural differences, soon got swamped in generalizations, simplifications, and reductionism.

Paradoxically, this attention to "culture," instead of expanding the scope and training of the practitioner, produced an increased human—too human perhaps—sensitivity to cultural diversity, creating an artificial slicing of the whole without thoroughly questioning the unavoidable cultural bias of the observers themselves. This is the trend that has led to a bias one observes today in the *DSM-IV*.[6]

AN OUTDATED COMMODITY

Since the 1980s, Western psychiatry has turned to biology when looking for a model of scientific validation. The biological model assumes a neurological root for mental illnesses. Accordingly, any depression is thought of as the result of a neurological malfunction, of a chemical imbalance (e.g., a deficiency in serotonin levels in the brain). The advantages of this model are its universality and equanimity: in the same way that all over the world one finds people who develop pneumonia, some people happen to get depressed. However, the universalism of the model soon meets obvious limits. For instance, not all cultures experience depression in the same way, and there are even cultures that do not know the concept of depression. Nonetheless, this biological model has allowed psychiatry to align itself with the hard sciences and regain some of the credibility it lost in the 1960s. Mental "illness" is thus conceived as a medical problem that will be treated most effectively with drug therapies.

By a strange paradox, the revolutionary blurring of the distinctions between normalcy and pathology brought about by the antipsychiatry movement of the 1960s was not in contradiction with the postulates of

---

5. See Kesselman 1973, Marcos 1975, Marcos et al. 1973, and Westermeyer 1987.

6. Kleinman (1977) pioneered interdisciplinary research integrating anthropology and psychiatry. See his review of the first decade of developments in cultural psychopathology (Kleinman 1988 and Guarnaccia and colleagues 2000) for the 1988–2000 period.

pharmacotherapy, which believed in restoring mental health through chemical interventions. For the idea of reversing a condition by reestablishing a missing chemical balance posited a continuity between normalcy and pathology—the cause of the illness was considered organic instead of social, and there was a continuity between illness and health since anyone could develop a mental "illness" under certain conditions. Thus, responsibility for mental disorders was shifted from society to the individual. Today, causes for mental illness are mostly considered as organic, therefore "real," rather than functional or "illusory," which entails that their social components tend to be obliterated. With the increasing popularity of psychopharmacotherapy, psychiatry has returned to a biological model that medicalizes the practice—the mind has become purely an organ. Let us take a look at the American Psychiatric Association's diagnostic manual—a book of almost 900 pages involving more than seven years of work by more than a thousand authors—which is an exemplary paradigm of current psychiatric practice. What is most astonishing about it is that the *DSM* diagnostic standards are empirical and atheoretical, true to a style that closely imitates Emil Kraepelin's nineteenth-century model, which presupposes underlying brain pathology for every mental disorder. Within today's neo-Kraepelian framework, etiology and psychodynamics are no longer taken into account. Following this paradigm, psychiatrists behave in their interventions like technicians who simply collect data from their patients, follow a checklist, and then medicate with the drug of the moment (one could speak of the Thorazine, Valium, or Prozac ages, according to "the" drug in fashion at a given time). Tanya M. Luhrmann (2001) observes that the combination of socioeconomic forces and ideology has driven psychotherapy out of psychiatry. After doing extensive participant–observer studies of American psychiatry and the socialization of psychiatrists, she concludes that although it is well known that new drugs perform no better than old-style "talk therapy" in alleviating mental health symptoms, and that for most disorders psychopharmacology works best in combination with psychotherapy, the pressure to cut costs or rather to increase profits in the new managed care system is eliminating psychotherapy, along with distorting the way we think about the psyche. The debate between psychoanalysis and psychopharmacology has been superseded by the imposition of managed care that sees mental illness as a disease best treated with drugs.

Given this state of things, one can question the place occupied in our days by the diagnosis of the Puerto Rican syndrome. What purpose can it serve if it does not precisely assign treatment or prescribe medicine? How can neo-Kraepelian psychiatry make sense of a mental disorder induced primarily by culture, not bodily pathology? How sensitive can today's psychiatric practice be to social and cultural questions if the mind has become an isolated and purely biological organ that has to be treated chemically? And how can this kind of practice be aware of its political implications if it considers itself scientific, objective, and universal?

Strictly speaking, the arcane and exotic diagnosis of the Puerto Rican syndrome dating from the fifties is not used often today and is clearly absent from recent psychiatric discussions. Indeed, the psychiatric literature specifically focused on this topic has been rather scarce, after an initial bout of interest in the late 1950s and early 1960s. One could assume that the current biologization and mechanization of clinical care in mental health renders the Puerto Rican syndrome obsolete. It looks as if the Puerto Rican syndrome was an outdated commodity surpassed by newer and more sophisticated technologies, a discarded typewriter replaced by a personal computer. Still, one may wonder whether it can totally lose its currency when concerns for the Spanish-speaking population and identity politics have drawn again the attention to anything that is specifically "Puerto-Rican." This belated timeliness is provided by globalization and the ever increasing "Hispanization" of the United States.[7] Given the demographic data, fifty years after its invention, the number of patients suffering the Puerto Rican syndrome should be skyrocketing. Still, the Puerto Rican syndrome's etiology remains virtually unknown and its treatments are mostly ineffective—in part because clinicians and researchers have focused on describing the pathology or on identifying the conscious, cognitive effects of social processes at play without reaching their causes. Nevertheless the cluster of symptoms comprising the Puerto Rican syndrome is listed as a separate diagnosis in the diagnostic tool most widely used in the U.S.: the American Psychiatric Association's *Diagnostic and Statistical Manual of Mental Disorders* (*DSM-IV* and *DSM-IV TR* versions). The multiple implications of this unprecedented inclusion are the subject of the next chapter.

---

7. In 2003 the Hispanic population in the United States surpassed 37 million, while blacks numbered about 36.2 million.

6

Geopolitics of the Psyche

Where cultural difference is represented as natural and immutable, then it has all the qualities signified by the notion of biological difference, with the result that the distinction between racism and nationalism seems to have been dissolved.

Robert Miles (1993, p. 100)

What I discovered as the Puerto Rican syndrome became clear to me first when I was able to conceptualize it via Freud's theory of hysteria revised by Lacan, but soon I realized that the clarity of certain abstract models risked again being blurred when the Puerto Rican syndrome started dissolving into the broader category of the *ataques*. People would use interchangeably the term of *ataque* to talk about the paroxysm itself, *nervios* to mean a general state of emotional distress, or the idiom *ataques* to refer to their common combination as *ataque de nervios*.

In recent years, there has been a vigorous resurgence of interest in the folk category corresponding to the cluster of symptoms collected under the label "Puerto Rican syndrome" in the psychosocial, sociocultural, and anthropological discussion of nerves, *nervios*, and *ataque de nervios* as experienced by the increasing number of Hispanics currently residing in the United States. Whereas early publications focus mostly on the clinical manifestations of the Puerto Rican syndrome and the pathology it generates, the most recent articles on *ataque* and *nervios* describe their cultural meaning and identify possible social determinants that trigger attacks. The scholarship originates from a variety of fields of inquiry—medicine, psychiatry, anthropology. Thus, in the last decades, there has been an interesting development of studies devoted to the varied interpretations of *ataque* and *nervios*, as if advances in the study and criticism (and, often, even rejection of previous interpretive efforts) were interdependent. Yet rather than allowing for an accumulation of linear knowledge, these efforts often seem to send researchers back to a new beginning.

One should not disregard the ability of the Puerto Rican syndrome to reinvent itself based on the recent profusion of literature on the topic in new fields; this ability renders testimony to its prolific nature and to the endless production of theories it triggers. It resists definition; no explanation seems to be able ever to settle the account, once and for all.

As we have seen, what goes by the name of Puerto Rican syndrome is an endless succession of discrepant statements and conflicting propositions. The literature on the subject asserts everything and its contrary. This diagnosis with an unlikely name reveals and imitates the discourse that tries to seize it, as Margarite Fernández Olmos (Fernández Olmos and Paravisini-Gebert 2001) notes: the "Puerto Rican syndrome is a malady that varies in description depending on one's medical/anthropological/political perspective and/or agenda" (p. 12). Even the very existence of the syndrome is at times questioned by those who contend that it is not a disease. What is then perpetuated? My thesis is that the symptoms grouped under the label Puerto Rican syndrome produce antagonistic and inappropriate classifications because they do not constitute coherent symptom sets. In fact, the invention of the Puerto Rican syndrome has been purely ideological. As Rendón (1984) states,

> In summary, a social force, ethnocentrism, has utilized—through mechanisms similar to displacement and condensation—an old semiological unit which refers to a natural disorder—syndrome—to construct a modern myth. The myth of the Puerto Rican Syndrome, however, even though naturalizing the problem by including it in the class of syndromes, evokes the social conflict in its very name. [p. 308]

I will further argue that the social conflict evoked by Rendón has not been resolved but rather reemerges in the current denomination *"ataque de nervios."* The Puerto Rican syndrome returns disguised under a different name that manages to diffuse the prejudice of the earlier designation. Thus, unquestioned in its ideological content, the Puerto Rican syndrome made its way into the most widely used diagnostic tool, the *Diagnostic and Statistical Manual* of the American Psychiatric Association.

In its most recent editions, the *DSM-IV* mentions both *nervios* and the *ataque de nervios* in its "Culture-Bound Syndromes Appendix," ascribing them to Latinos from the Caribbean and Latinos in the United States. The year 2000 revision of the *DSM-IV* maintained the ambiguous label "Latin Mediterranean groups" (American Psychiatric Association 2000) for Latinos from the Caribbean and the United States. This is how *ataques* and *nervios* are characterized:

> **Ataque de nervios** An idiom of distress. . . . Commonly reported symptoms include uncontrollable shouting, attacks of crying, trembling, heat in the chest rising into the head, and verbal or physical aggression. Dissociative experiences, seizurelike or fainting episodes, and suicidal gestures are prominent in some ataques but absent in others. A general feature of an ataque de nervios is a sense of being out of control. Ataques de nervios frequently occur as a direct result of a stressful event relating to the family (e.g., news of the death of a close relative, a separation or divorce from a spouse, conflicts with a spouse or children, or witnessing an accident involving a family member). People may experience amnesia for what occurred during the ataque de nervios, but they otherwise return rapidly to their usual level of functioning. [American Psychiatric Association 1994, p. 845]

> **Nervios** A common idiom of distress. . . . Nervios refers both to a general state of vulnerability to stressful life experiences and to a syndrome brought on by difficult life circumstances. The term *nervios* includes a wide range of symptoms of emotional distress, somatic disturbance, and inability to function. Common symptoms include headaches and "brain aches," irritability, stomach disturbances, sleep difficulties, nervousness, easy tearfulness, inability to concentrate, trembling, tingling sensations, and *mareos* (dizziness with occasional vertigo-like exacerbations). [Ibid, p. 847]

This incorporation of *ataque de nervios* and *nervios* into the *DSM-IV* as culture-bound syndrome is unprecedented. According to the appendix, "culture-bound syndromes" refer to "recurrent, locally specific patterns of aberrant behavior and troubling experience that may or may not be linked to a particular *DSM-IV* diagnostic category." Even though "presentations conforming to the major *DSM-IV* categories can be found through the world," that is, they are universal, "culture-bound syndromes are generally limited to specific societies or culture areas and are localized, folk, diagnostic categories that frame coherent meanings for certain repetitive, patterned, and troubling set of experiences and observations" (Ibid, p. 844).

The inclusion of *ataques* and *nervios* in the "Glossary of Culture-Bound Syndromes" is quite problematic.[1] Already the mere existence of a separated appendix makes clear that so-called culture-bound syndromes cannot be equated to standard psychiatric categories contradicting *de facto* the claim that the *DSM-IV* taxonomy is universal. Still, one can debate the breadth of recognition of the culture-bound syndrome within the cultural group. "For many years, windigo psychosis was cited in the literature on the mental health of American Indians until Marano demonstrated that windigo psychosis never existed,"[2] observe Guarnaccia and Rogler (1999). "In the case of the ataque de nervios, 30 years of articles in the psychiatric and anthropological literature are available, although the syndrome is often mislabeled pejoratively as the 'Puerto Rican syndrome.'" Indeed, the salience of the *ataque de nervios* has been doubted until an epidemiological study of adult mental health in Puerto Rico (Guarnaccia et al. 1993) directly queried whether the respondents had suffered an *ataque de nervios* and what the experience was like. This epidemiological study proved the salience of the *ataque de nervios* in Puerto Rican mental health, specifying that it is quite frequent in the Puerto Rican community and particularly predominent among Hispanic clients of mental health. Roberto Lewis-Fernández (1996)

---

1. Jewell's (1952) case is a classic example of a diagnosis of schizophrenia resulting from the staff's unfamiliarity with Navaho behavior rather than due to demonstrable psychopathology.

2. Marano (1982) argues that although Windigo psychosis was used as a standard example of culture-bound psychopathology for almost half a century, his five-year field experience among Algonkian-speaking Indians of northeastern Canada, extensive archival research, and a critical examination of the literature show that there probably never were any windigo psychotics in an etic/behavioral sense. When the windigo phenomenon is examined from the point of view of group sociodynamics, the crucial issue is not what makes a person become a cannibalistic maniac, but under what circumstances a Northern Algonkian is likely to be accused of having become a cannibalistic maniac and thus risk being put to death. Marano argues that those so killed were victims of the kind of witch-hunt that appears in societies under stress. He concludes that the term "psychosis" is an artifact of research imposed on the phenomenon by outsiders.

argues that "*Ataques de nervios* are very prevalent expressions of emotional distress and psychopathology among Puerto Ricans; their prevalence in Puerto Rico has recently been established at nearly 14%" (p. 159). According to the U.S. Census data published in 2001, Puerto Ricans total 3.8 million on the island. Lewis-Fernández's findings translate into an average of roughly 53,200 people on the island who suffer from *ataque de nervios*. This does not take into account a number of potential cases that is almost as important given that in the U.S. the Puerto Rican population is 3 million. In the case of mental health patients, *ataques* occur with an astonishing frequency—recent studies suggest that two thirds of Latino mental health patients experience *ataques*. Clinical researchers in Boston and New York mental health clinics questioned the patients about their experience with *ataques* and found out that 75 percent of Latino mental health patients had at least experienced one *ataque de nervios* (Guarnaccia and Rogler 1999).

Although "mislabeled pejoratively," the Puerto Rican syndrome is quite predominant within the prescribed culture; its prevalence and wide recognition therefore seem to justify its inclusion in the American Psychiatric Association diagnostic manual. Since the *DSM-IV* is a manual that classifies and standardizes mental pathology, how can we know what a culture-bound syndrome means within the culture in which it appears? Is the *ataque* considered an illness within the community? No. The literature reviewed suggests that *nervios* and *ataques* are not considered abnormal behavior in Puerto Rico. In an earlier contribution, Guarnaccia and colleagues (1989) establish that the *ataque de nervios* is an exacerbated condition of *nervios*, which is viewed as an expectable state of being for anyone under stress. These authors confirm that *ataques de nervios* and *nervios* are idioms of distress that are not viewed as illnesses by Hispanics themselves.

Let us keep in mind that illness categories reflect cultural principles. It is important then to recognize that a diagnosis is a cultural phenomenon, and that the perspective of those defining symptoms and treatment for psychiatric conditions is affected by their culture—this bias becomes more evident for conditions occurring in "exotic" places and affecting "special" groups. Then, an important question rises: How can a cultural prototype, which is applied clinically as a diagnosis, be empirically related, if at all, to psychiatric disorders? Hughes and colleagues (1997) convincingly argue that

> the phenomena of culture-bound syndromes do not constitute discrete, bounded entities that can be directly translated into conventional Western categories. Rather, when examined at a primary level, they inter-

> penetrate established diagnostic entities with symptoms that flood across
> numerous parts of the *DSM* nosological structure. [quoted in Guarnaccia
> and Rogler 1999, p. 1326]

Thus, like other so-called culture-bound syndromes, the Puerto Rican syndrome cannot be equated to any standard Western psychiatric category because its symptoms span several categories. Consequently, let us repeat that
the Puerto Rican syndrome is not and cannot be a psychiatric diagnosis.

The debate about symptom clusters unique to particular cultural
groups and their relation with psychiatric categories has been extensive in
recent years.[3] Setha Low (1985) questions altogether the utility of the classification of "culture-bound syndromes" and proposes instead the concept
of "culturally interpreted symptoms." The multiple character of the symptoms calls for interpretation:

> Symptoms are culturally expressed through the body as a symbol sys-
> tem; symptoms are culturally received, sorted and identified within
> the theory of disease and cultural rules of etiology; and symptoms are
> given sociocultural meaning based on values and the social system.
> [pp. 187–188]

Thus, Low attributes to *nervios* different meanings in different circumstances: anger, family problems, social distress (poverty). Reevaluating her
earlier research on *nervios* in Costa Rica, which led her to conclude that
"*nervios* is an effective and culturally acceptable manifestation and communication of a socially unacceptable reality" (1981, p. 42), Low (1985)
argues that the classification "nerves" cannot be categorized as culture-
bound syndrome because it does not appear in one specific cultural group
but in various groups, and with similar symptoms. The status Low ascribes
to symptoms is close to a Freudian and Lacanian position: symptoms are
signifying—they produce meaning.

Pamela Dunk (1989) agrees with Low that one should not overlook the
meaning of the symptoms comprised in illness categories. In the case of nerves,
Dunk underlines the importance of class, ethnicity, and gender in both the
causation and the meaning of the symptoms. Via a preliminary analysis of
data from an ethnomedical survey of 100 families belonging to first genera-

---

3. See the first issue of Volume 11 (1987) of *Culture, Medicine and Psychiatry* devoted to the discussion of culture-bound syndromes. See also Mezzich et al. 1996.

tion Greek immigrants in Montreal, she contends that nerves (*nevra*) is a phenomenon produced by poor working conditions, low wages, and gender relations. Dunk suggests that cross-cultural comparisons with other groups in similar oppressive situations may help to interpret the symptoms' meaning. Margaret Lock (1989) emphasizes the link between the experience of oppression and "poor nerves" and views nerves as an "awakening of political consciousness" often regarded as nonsense by those in authority (p. 86).

PATHOLOGIZING DIFFERENCE

As we have seen, the cluster of symptoms identified under the label of Puerto Rican syndrome is not a provisional definition for a disease category that has a consistent pathology for which, because of a long-standing cross-cultural gap, traditional Western classification cannot account. While it is true that the Puerto Rican syndrome as such cannot be equated to one specific standard psychiatric category, still we may wonder why once the practitioners identify the main presenting symptoms in each particular case, they would not use any other *DSM-IV* diagnoses such as Panic Attack, Somatoform, Anxiety, or Depressive Disorders, among others, which can be successfully applied. Besides, as Guarnaccia and Rogler (1999) note, while culture-bound syndromes often coexist within a range of psychiatric disorders, this is also true for many psychiatric disorders. The segregation of *ataque* and *nervios* to the "culture-bound" appendix firstly questions the efficacy and scope of Western standard psychiatric classifications, and, secondly, betrays something shocking about the politics of the American Psychiatric Association's manual.

The aspiration to universality that appears as the rationale of the *DSM-IV* taxonomy obliterates an evident bias that emerges conspicuously in the section devoted to culturally bound syndromes. One cannot help contending that the standard Western psychiatric classification system has to be also equally influenced by local cultural factors; that is, it is as culture-bound as the Puerto Rican syndrome's manifestations may be. Obviously, this "culture-bound syndromes" section is "culture-bound"—it takes American mainstream culture as the universal norm and considers the rest of the world as the exception. Anorexia is a blatant example of how the influence of culture and ethnicity is not acknowledged when the culture in question is Western—anorexia is not included in the glossary of culture-bound syndromes. Nevertheless, anorexia is also a culture-bound syndrome that does not occur in Asia (except in the "Westernized" upper-middle class of Japan).

How universal, objective, and rational can psychiatry be from a cultural point of view? The *DSM-IV* diagnostic criteria rely on the utilization of Western Euro-American conventions about illness, behavior, and social standards as if they were in fact culturally free and universally applicable. Arthur Kleinman (1977) calls importing diagnostic categories from one culture to another without substantiating their validity for that culture a "category fallacy."

To bring out another paradox, let us note that the *DSM-IV* "Culture-Bound Glossary Appendix" advises to take into account the influence of the individual's cultural background, the role of the cultural context in the evaluation, and so on. Its aim is mainly to provide American clinicians with cultural information in evaluating symptoms according to a given cultural context. It lists syndromes from Laos, Philippines, Papua New Guinea, Malaysia, Polynesia, West Africa, Tahiti, Sri Lanka, Korea, Thailand, Siberia, Cape Verde, Haiti, Puerto Rico, Mexico, Ethiopia, Somalia, Egypt, Sudan, Iran, and the Southern United States. The sociopolitical location of these countries where the syndromes originate (with the curious annexation of the Southern United States to the list) suggests that only developing countries qualify as providers of "exotic" culture-bound syndromes. The ideological connotations of such a gesture hardly need to be underlined.

Culture-bound syndromes are not just eccentric; they are also controversial. They question the universality of Western psychiatry. Examining the unprecedented inclusion of culture-bound syndromes in the *DSM-IV*, Guarnaccia and Rogler (1999) strongly recommend further research to understand their complexity, observing that a systematic research of culture-bound syndromes had been called for more than 20 years earlier:

> Whether or not there are new psychiatric illnesses to be found in folk cultures or nonmetropolitan populations is a question that first requires semantic solution. Undoubtedly there are in certain cultures clinical manifestations quite unlike these described in standard psychiatric textbooks, which historically are based on the experiences of Western psychiatrists. In this sense, illnesses presenting so strangely may be regarded as new. However, each of the same textbooks also espouses a system of disease classification that by its own logic is meant to be final and exhaustive. From this point of view, no more new illnesses are to be discovered, and any strange clinical condition can only be a variation of something already described. Two problems arise: firstly, how much do we know about the culture-bound syndromes for us to be able to fit them into standard classification; and secondly, whether such a stan-

dard and exhaustive classification in fact exists. [Yap 1974, quoted in Guarnaccia and Rogler 1999, p. 1323]

As Guarnaccia and Rogler observe, such a needed programmatic study is still missing. One can wonder if it could ever be produced. Also, it is lacking a consideration of the political consequences of these denominations.

Is it because the *DSM-IV* is a diagnostic tool with such a considerable degree of inaccuracy that this section attempts to remedy its shortcomings? Or is this diagnostic manual a Procrustean system of segregation ready to label otherness as pathology? The apparently inconsequential fact that the syndromes listed in the appendix are not included in the multiaxial model of this manual has enormous consequences. One very important and detrimental consequence is economic. Many American health insurance companies will refuse to pay for the costs of treatments included in the appendix. Most major health insurance carriers will only agree to pay for the expenses of a treatment that has a standard *DSM-IV* diagnosis.

An enormous problem is opened here, since paradoxically this appendix is explicitly an attempt at making the diagnostician aware of cultural differences, raising the sensitivity to diversity. Disguised in the language of order, rationality, and the irrefutability of scientific observations, this section demonstrates that prejudice coexists with arguments supporting cultural diversity. From this perspective, the American Psychiatric Association's ideology is not far from the bias of the Army doctors who invented the Puerto Rican syndrome half a century ago. An examination of the underlying logic for the inclusion of *ataque de nervios* and *nervios* in a separate *culture-bound* appendix of the *DSM-IV* reveals astonishing exclusionary standards.

CULTURES IN CONFLICT

The APA's *DSM-IV* "Outline for Cultural Formulations" and "Glossary of Culture-Bound Syndromes" sections aim to make culturally sensitive psychiatric diagnoses. This concern for the articulation of cultural principles in the organization and content of the psychiatric diagnostic manual did not find much resonance in *DSM-III* (1980) or *DSM III-R* (1987) (Mezzich et al. 1996). In preparation for *DSM-III* (1987), the chair of the task force, Robert Spitzer, contacted Arthur Kleinman, a well-known medical anthropologist, and asked him for advice to caution mental health professionals about the potential misuse of the *DSM* when applied to minorities and non-Western societies. Kleinman answered this request with a five- or six-paragraph letter. To Kleinman's surprise, that letter was published but rewritten and condensed into two short paragraphs in the *DSM-III* Introduction. The inclusion of those two paragraphs symptomatically exposed the *DSM-III-R*'s limitations when applied across cultures.

Again, this time for *DSM-IV* (1994), very few of Kleinman's systematic recommendations were included. Kleinman (1996) argues that the way "cultural sensitivity" is understood by *DSM-IV* invites to "superficially stereotype entire groups—for example, 'This is the way Hispanics respond to depression!'—and to convey an erroneous sense that cultural orientations are conventions, mistaken beliefs that can be taken off and put back on again at will" (p. 16). Kleinman observes, "When applied in a narrow, mechanical fashion, *DSM-IV* is too easily turned into something it was never meant to be: an overly formalistic blueprint that pathologizes ordinary and extraordinary experience and that disaffirms the meaning-oriented subjectivity of suffering in favor of technical diagnoses that often lack personal and collective significance" (p. 20).

Unrelenting in his convictions, Kleinman recommends moving the section on cultural assessment from the Appendix to the Introduction as a first step toward a "culturally valid *DSM-V*." Since there is no direct correlation between specific *DSM* diagnosis and culture-bound syndromes, "key cultural idioms of distress such as *nervios* or *ataques* among Puerto Ricans should be introduced and it should be pointed out that these are common channels of communication and behavior that may express either normal or pathological states." Only including major culture-bound syndromes of American ethnic groups and major non-Western societies among the other *DSM* diagnoses would remedy the cultural inaccuracies of the manual noted by Kleinman: "90% of *DSM* categories are culture-bound to North America and Western Europe, the very idea of culture-bound as 'exotic' syndromes outside Euro-American culture itself is flawed; therefore, the use of this concept to label *only* non-Western or ethnic syndromes is biased and inappropriate" (p. 23).

AN IDEOLOGICAL LABEL

Existing only as the result of the intermeshing of various medical, supernatural, religious, and racist discourses, the Puerto Rican syndrome is determined by a particular historical context and a defined social location. Let us insist on the political element in the genealogy sketched so far. We have seen how U.S. military doctors invented a psychiatric postwar syndrome with a name tied exclusively to a national status, reserved for citizens of the misleadingly labeled Commonwealth *and* "freely associated state" (*Estado Libre Asociado*); the meanings diverge in English and in Spanish. Puerto Rico's American-born "foreign" citizens obtained self-government while establishing "permanent union" with the United States—the historical determinations seem to create a perfect double bind. The obvious reappearance of a spectacular mode of hysteria frozen in time testifies to the truth of Freud's motto that hysterics suffer from reminiscences. Their memory, symptomatically remembered in act, is both a gift and a relentless curse. The symptoms keep alive a *hystory*; then, the syndrome stands for a missing chapter in a national history that does not cease to be written.

The naming of the syndrome as "Puerto Rican" presupposes that nationalities are not just matters of geographical frontiers but of the geopolitics of the psyche. The medical construction of a Puerto Rican "illness" invents a syndrome that is exclusively Puerto Rican, thus creating a new representation, a new metaphor for the "imagined community" of the nation. The first published description of the Puerto Rican syndrome, explored in Chapter 4, includes an evocative "transient state of partial loss." Could it be that this label, a psychiatric syndrome with a name tied exclusively to one of the last surviving colonies, a label that involves a national status and includes a description of a *dissociative* condition of "transient state of loss," would inadvertently refer to an unresolved political status of the island? Puerto Rico is contradictorily both a Commonwealth and an *Estado libre asociado* (that is, a "freely associated state"), which suggests a "free association" that has very little of the psychoanalyst's technique since this state is caught up in a "permanent union." As we have seen, the same year that Puerto Rico changed its status, the word "hysteria" disappeared as a separate diagnosis from the official American psychiatric manuals. But it is precisely then that the diagnosis of the Puerto Rican syndrome, a psychiatric label attached to a national denomination for a nation that was not confirmed as an independent nation, was invented.

More than a century after the arrival of U.S. troops in Puerto Rico, the status of the island remains uncertain. The political debate is, however, heated and passionate. Nonetheless, in a postcolonial world that is being reshaped by globalization, Puerto Rican people remain ambiguous and undecided, unable to overcome their colonial conundrum.

The complex political status of Puerto Rico dates back to the times when it was a Spanish colony and it was not resolved when the United States granted citizenship in 1917, nor with the changed political status of 1952. Numerous plebiscites have not put an end to the debate on the island over the three main status options: statehood, independence, or a heightened commonwealth status.

The commonwealth has granted the United States a military outpost in the Caribbean and one of its biggest consumer markets while giving Puerto Ricans U.S. citizenship and one of the highest standards of living in Latin America. As U.S. citizens, Puerto Ricans have unequal rights and obligations: they are subject to federal law but do not pay most federal taxes, do not vote for presidents, and do not have full representation in Congress. Puerto Rico's own laws, taxes, and government are subject to United States law. Even with a federal aid of approximately $9 billion a year (equivalent to the total amount of U.S. aid to the rest of the world combined), the island faces substantial economic problems: an unemployment rate of 13 percent, 60 percent of the population living below the poverty line, crime rampant and worse than on the mainland, drug traffic from Puerto Rico to the United States escalating.

Repeated referendums have confirmed the commonwealth status quo but the Puerto Rican predicament has not been settled. The commonwealth status appears like a compromise formation full of contradictions: classes in school are taught in English and Spanish, both Puerto Rican and American flags are seen on public buildings and both national anthems are played at official events. Thus far, Congress has not made any effort to specify what "decolonization" approaches would be acceptable; issues of sovereignty have been hindered by discussions about the costs of incorporating a Spanish-speaking state if Puerto Ricans decided on statehood.

Since the Puerto Rican syndrome was first identified among Puerto Rican Korean War veterans, the nomenclature has forced us to take a closer look at the ideological determinations of that particular moment. Puerto Rican soldiers had joined U.S. armed forces to fight in a war aimed at stopping the Communist expansion in Korea. Military action took place on a territory that had been invaded and kept under the Japanese colonial power between 1905 and 1945. The war ended in an impasse—the peace negotiations drew a division line creating North and South Korea that was in fact not too far from the 38th parallel, the original boundary line of occupation. Fernando Pico (1988) observed that the Puerto Rican war veterans who served in the U.S. military in World War II and the Korean War returned home with two main attitudes: some veterans were left after military training and war experiences with a robust feeling of allegiance with U.S. institutions; others developed strong anti-militaristic feelings, acquired a powerful sense of Puerto Rican identity, and demanded social justice. On the whole, the issue of the military draft for Puerto Ricans continues to be very conflictive. As Frank Ramos (1970) puts it eloquently:

> Should a Puerto Rican who believes in independence be required to serve in the U.S. military, which he considers to be a "foreign" army? For that matter, should a resident of Puerto Rico, who considers himself loyal to the United States, be required to serve, if he cannot vote, either for the President, who is Commander-in-Chief of the Armed Forces, or for the members of Congress, which has power to declare war? The issue of the military draft is one of the several which remains unsolved, because of Puerto Rico's anomalous Commonwealth relationship with the United States.[4]

PR SYNDROME

The Puerto Rican syndrome was a new label for manifestations that were old, known, and culturally sanctioned. The illness was culture specific; it was transmitted not by a virus but by a particular culture, which made it no less contagious. What has to be underlined here is the global historical evolution: a local phenomenon transported to the U.S. armed forces in the context of the Cold War received the pompous name of "Puerto Rican syndrome." This unlikely name invented a diagnosis that has been actually used and is still present, although admittedly very few practitioners would use it today. Recently recognized as a "culture-bound" mental disorder, the *ataque* and *nervios*, as we have seen, appear in the most recent edition of the *DSM*. In the 1950s, the label was employed "strategically" in the Army for the disposition of U.S. Army veterans who had sudden outbursts of violence and partial loss of consciousness. Soon after, the burgeoning field

---

4. Ramos, F. *San Juan Star*, January 30, 1970, p. 33. (Wagenheim 1973, p. 292).

of social psychiatry adopted the denomination in the name of cultural awareness. As psychiatry receded in the 1960s under the pressure of antipsychiatry, the emerging field of mental health turned to the community to understand *ataques*.

In the 1970s and 1980s, Hispanic mental health workers did not question the denomination but rather adopted the name, sustaining an analysis that reversed that of the 1950s. They contested the alleged inadequacy of the syndrome, claiming that the *ataque* as social phenomenon was a response to stress, in fact a coping mechanism. During that same period, medical anthropologists pointed to the connections with Puerto Rican spiritual beliefs in *Espiritismo*. In the 1980s, feminists reevaluated the *ataque* as an acceptable form of expression of anger in women, in response to *machismo*. According to feminist critics, Puerto Rican women deal with higher levels of stress associated with a position of oppression and marginalization due to their gender, class, and color. Other critics interpreted the *ataque* as a culturally acceptable cry for help "expected from women when they do not get their own way or when they are faced with an act of aggression they cannot otherwise stop" (Harwood 1981, p. 419). Although not gender-specific, some studies indicate that sufferers are likely to be middle-aged women of a lower socioeconomical status (McCormick 1986).

The clinical significance of the diagnosis is limited. In a recent clinical study exploring the correlation between *ataque* and psychiatric disorders, Salmán (Salmán et al. 1998) notes that the concept *ataque* is overly broad. Varying subtypes of *ataque* would be required for determining the relationship between *ataques de nervios* and coexisting mental disorders. Salmán's research concludes that the *ataque* may be a useful clinical marker for detecting psychiatric disorders, but its relationship to psychiatric disorders as well as cultural, demographic, and environmental factors should be investigated more. Over several studies, Guarnaccia and colleagues have emphasized the inclusion of the social context in the understanding of *ataque de nervios*. Most recently, DeLaCancela and colleagues (1986) included other U.S. Hispanics in the *Puerto Rican* syndrome, arguing that one should not medicalize what are essentially social problems. For understanding individual cases of *ataques* one must take into account the impact of the "socioeconomic circumstances of colonialism experienced by *ataques* sufferers. *Ataques de nervios* provide Puerto Ricans and other Latinos opportunities for displacement of anger, secondary gains, and direct rebellion against repressive conditions" (p. 432). For these authors *ataques* are "cultural expressions of colonized classes" (p. 433). Since the manifestations gathered under the name *ataques* are found in other Latin American countries, further study is needed to examine the combined influence of the Catholic Church and Spanish colonial domination in the production of the popular label, as well as the relationship to cultural, demographic, and environmental factors.

It is by now obvious that the Puerto Rican syndrome is a racially charged construction still used today to identify symptom patterns related to the *ataque*. The multiple interpretations of the syndrome depend on the perspective of the observer, a perspective that is historically determined. What is also remarkable is that in the translations of the Puerto Rican syndrome one finds new levels of displacement or pathological dislocation as soon as we ask: Who is having the *ataques?* No longer is the *ataque* a manifestation reserved for a bourgeois Doña Concepción isolated in Puerto Rico as we shall see below, or a war-traumatized Private Ramirez lost somewhere in the U.S. Army. Today in the so-called Hispanic ghettos in New York, Chicago, Hartford, or Philadelphia, something called Puerto Rican syndrome, *ataque*, or "culture-bound" syndrome is being triggered as having an impact on others. The Puerto Rican syndrome is not limited to Puerto Ricans in their own territory, but has spread all over the continental United States. It promises to continue multiplying according to the demographic growth of the Hispanic populations; then perhaps one will call it the PR (public relations) syndrome.

CANDLE IN THE SUN

We have seen how by the time of the invention of the Puerto Rican syndrome, the *ataque* was a common occurrence within Puerto Rican culture. Typically, in *A Candle in the Sun*, a novel about the adventures of a young American woman in Puerto Rico that was published before World War II, Edith Robert (1937) begins her narrative with an evocative description of Doña Concepción's *ataque*:

> The four-poster rocked with it. The whole house vibrated to it. A purple and gilt image of Mary hanging against the blue wall at the head of the bed was particularly agitated. It seemed likely to fall and smash at any moment. [p. 9]

Doña Concepción's *ataque* had been triggered by the news that her son had married an American and was bringing her to the island. Although the situation of Puerto Rico in the late 1930s is part of the narratological structure of the novel that describes at length the cultural shock experienced by the newly wed American young woman, the reference to this political background is hazy and it is mostly used as a picturesque and exotic backdrop. Avery's gaze describes with astonishment the lives of the "others." Her distance and estrangement is only slightly mitigated by time and the birth of her Puerto Rican children. "Avery deliberately planned to live a lie. That was the paradoxical price placed upon happiness by convention" (Robert 1937, p. 388). Among the ingredients in the plot we find the expected oedipal rivalry between mother-in-law and daughter-in-law, the jealousy and petty misunderstandings in the newlyweds, a bookish brother-in-law who falls in love with Avery, an envious and vain sister-in-law who resents her while another sister is very shy but helped and "improved" by the young American woman (she loses weight and becomes a happier being, less subjected to the mother's influence), and the attendant clashes between the Puerto Rican and American cultural models. The novel mostly narrates how Avery resists the pressure of "the Puerto Rican Family" to make her convert to Catholicism and adopt a subservient role. Her husband turns out to be *machista* and a philanderer, and Avery ends up finding love outside her marriage, in the arms of another American. The self-effacing third person narrator makes tangential reference to the political background. Nonetheless, politics are a main character in the story: Avery's in-laws belong to the "Federals" whose "*cacique máximo*" is her husband's father. There is also repeated mention of anti-American feelings among the Family. Her being the *americanita* invites all kinds of political attacks from the opposing party to the Federals, the Progressives. Despite all this, it is only in brief and almost ironical tones that Avery thinks explicitly of the colonial status of the island. A few pages before the end, Avery is at another cocktail party and chats with an American expert in economics. The "Important Expert" appears more concerned with cocktails and picking up the local beauties than with discussing politics; Avery teases him with uncharacteristic impertinence until he is moved to ask her opinion:

> . . . . what would *you* suggest?
> "Independence," said Avery instantly and enigmatically. . . .
> Avery looked alarmed. "I didn't mean independence for the Island," she said quickly. "I just mean independence from busybody 'experts' like Dr. Manning." . . . For a few moments Avery considered the possibility of such a political upheaval, which would put in the shade every-

thing that happened up to now. But not for long. National problems, however great, faded into a dim perspective before the towering shadow of her personal trouble. [Robert 1937, p. 387]

With some interpretive effort, one may recognize references to the real events behind the imaginary characters and situations in this book. Let us take a look, for example, at the very ending of the novel:

> As she stopped before the country house, she saw that it was blazing with lights. A quite large cluster of peasants, numbers of whom were always passing along the busy highway, were staring across the hedge towards the dwelling from which poured the unmistakable sounds of Doña Concepción's hysteria.
>
> As these incoherent screams smote upon Avery's ear, something suddenly seemed to right itself in her throbbing head, as when in one of those aggravating glass-covered puzzles the little balls all at once click into place. Pushing by the gaping peasants who murmured "*La Americanita*," as she passed, she hastened to join the Family. [p. 391]

In Avery's decision "to join the Family," it is easy to see an allusion to *La gran familia puertorriqueña* (the great Puerto Rican Family), a slogan stressing unity that played a key role in the cultural discourse of the *autonomistas* movement of the turn of the nineteenth century. In this last scene, the *campesinos* (peasants) who stare across the hedge represent the impoverished working class witnessing the decline of the now disenfranchised upper-class matron Doña Concepción whose husband first loses the elections and then ends up in shameful poverty. Throughout the novel, Doña Concepción, a devoted Catholic, opposes the claim for women's rights upheld by Avery in open confrontations. According to Mariano Negrón-Portillo (1997), these two features—Catholicism and opposition to women's rights—defined the *unionistas*, a nationalist organization in the Puerto Rico of the 1930s. The Federals and Progressives of the novel call up the two main political parties that dominated Puerto Rican life. The "growing figure of the Laborite, Lorenzo Gomez . . . that gentleman, with his rolled-up shirt sleeves" (p. 384) evokes Pedro Albizu Campos, the leader of the newly founded pro-independence *Partido Nacionalista*. Since Albizu Campos entered politics as a member of the Unionist party and, later, of the Alianza, it is quite likely that Doña Concepción's defeated husband, Don Sancho, would have been displaced within his party by the emerging Albizu Campos; like Don Sancho and like most actors in the long elitist nationalist tradition, Albizu Campos defended the Catholic Church and invoked concepts like *La Raza*, claiming Hispanic ancestry based on Spanish soul, language, customs, and idiosyncrasy (Negrón-Portillo 1997). The main character is constanly reminding us of Puerto Rican animosity toward her as an American: she is perceived not just as a foreigner but as an antagonist.

On many occasions, however, Avery criticizes the arrogance, naiveté, and lack of good will of Washington-appointed bureaucrats, "just-at-the-moment-unoccupied Experts . . . aware that the hitherto obscure territory tucked away among the Indies had a PROBLEM" (Robert 1937, p. 385), which, by the way, was a position shared by officials of both the *Partido Unionista* and the *Partido Republicano*. Although if this novel gives voice to a political critique of the colonial situation the heroine observes, it is only obliquely. Just like Avery, who, as we have seen, glimpses momentous "National problems" but allows them to fade "into a dim perspective before the towering shadow of her personal trouble," author Edith Robert prefers to look elsewhere. She cautions us in the first page: "There has been no intention whatever to depict living persons or actual events either wholly or in part." This is true enough, for the political backdrop, a mere counterpoint for the story, has been blurred purposely by the author. If Avery blurts out "independence" as the only solution when she faces a U.S. expert, her statement is soon undercut by what appears as simple annoyance at American arrogance.

The context of this outburst should not be downplayed too much: the young American wife who is also a young mother is having an affair with a handsome American man who is soon to leave the island. The last chapter evokes the final nights of intimacy and her sadness at the end after he has left. Another male American friend tries to teach her to disguise her feelings in order to avoid a full-blown scandal. Still full of the memories of intense lovemaking, Avery returns to fetch the babies at her mother-in-law's and this is when she discovers that the latter is having an *ataque*. No clear reason for the outburst of hysteria is given; the reader is left to surmise its causes. Has the family heard of the affair? Has a new political event happened? Is it to be blamed on Doña Concepción's cycles of mood changes? More than any reason given to these ominous fits, what stands out as very revealing is that the book opens and closes with Doña Concepción having an *ataque*. This narrative twist reveals the *ataque*'s function: more than the exposition of a "native malady," it is a paradigm of how the colonizers see the "other" as other. The "incoherent screams" constitute a message addressed to the Other. The *ataque*—a precursor of the

Puerto Rican syndrome—epitomizes the view of the outsider who is surprised by such strange manifestations. Most importantly, this novel exemplifies the fact that the *ataque* always intertwines personal dilemmas and political upheavals. One could not fully understand the *ataque* just by focusing on the symptoms. In order to make sense of Doña Concepción's *ataques*, one must take into account the intense, explosive emotions triggered by a context determined by colonial politics, sexual betrayal, and divided allegiances.

7

The Puerto Rican Syndrome:
Anger and Justice

Early in the studies on the Puerto Rican syndrome, one common feature loomed large: anger. Still looking for a fundamental determination underlying all these various manifestations, one encounters on the way a basic passion, a passion that has clearly pathological overtones but that is also ethical and even political throughout. Among the teeming contradictions we have detected in current and past interpretations of the Puerto Rican syndrome, anger is the single key factor that has been continuously noticed by all observers; when it comes to this elementary passion, they speak as it were in one single voice. Let us quote some clinical vignettes; the following is a partial transcription of five sample case stories that come from actual hospital files.[1] All patients had been diagnosed with the "Puerto Rican syndrome."

> *Case 1*: The patient was a 23-year-old Army private who became acutely disturbed suddenly one day while sitting in his barracks. He got up, ran around the room, jumped on everybody's bed, screamed and yelled and had to be restrained. In the process of being subdued, the patient

---

1. Psychiatric Section of the Rodriguez U.S. Army Hospital.

became almost rigid, was breathing very heavily, rolled his eyes up so that only the whites were visible, foamed at the mouth and trembled all over. He was admitted to an Army hospital in the Continental United States where he remained for several weeks. During his hospitalization, there were several similar episodes somewhat milder but always marked by subsequent amnesia and mild confusion. . . .

Case 2: The patient was a 20-year-old Puerto Rican recruit who had gone AWOL for several days. He was brought to an Air Force base hospital on another part of the Island because he was running down the street with no clothes on and experiencing bizarre behavior and was screaming incoherently. . . .

Case 3: This patient has been AWOL from his unit for several days. Shortly after being apprehended by the military police, he was brought to this hospital, mute, uncooperative, violently twirling his arms around and hyperventilating. He refused to cooperate in examination procedures and intermittently cried profusely. He stated, in between periods of mutism, that he did not know who he was. He would pull his testicles and stated that he did this in order to see blood because he liked to see blood.

Case 4: The patient, a 19-year-old recruit, was admitted to the hospital confused, disoriented, moving his head back and forth, and hyperventilating. This episode subsided during the admission procedure, and when he was examined the patient stated that during his entire stay in the Army, he has been in continual trouble particularly for not carrying out orders. He stated that he had so many thoughts in his mind that, at times, he could not hear other people and was not aware that they were around. He stated that he hears people's voices but he is not sure what he hears. He later stated that for many years he had the feelings that there were people talking to him and they lived in his left ear.

Case 5: The last patient was an 18-year-old recruit who was found wandering around the post on the night of his admission to the hospital. When an effort was made to talk with him, he began to fight and struggle, hitting out at the persons who attempted to talk with him and struggling violently. He bit, kicked, and yelled and when finally apprehended became grossly tremulous, hyperventilated, foamed at the mouth and became mute. Following this, he appeared to make futile efforts to speak and would write incomprehensible symbols when offered a pencil and paper. [Mehlman 1961, pp. 328–330]

In the first clinical example, the so-called Case 1, we can see that the initial episode of what entered the records as "Puerto Rican syndrome" was triggered by anger at "his sergeant who, the patient said, was unfair." This patient, a 23-year-old Army private, mentioned that he would often experience intermittent headaches and giddiness when angry. During the diagnostic interviews, when he complained about the sergeant with an upsurge of anger, he "again began to experience giddiness, headache, and had trouble finding words." He also revealed that prior to his entry to the service, his anger centered around his father. Mehlman (1961) contends that the patient became overwhelmed with his own anger that "lit up unresolved feelings with respect to anger and feelings towards his parents" (pp. 328–329). Furthermore, Mehlman notices that the patient "had never worked out his feelings with respect to his father and his anger towards his sergeant was quite clearly a displacement of these unresolved feelings. Every time the patient came close to the awareness of his wish to kill his father, he had an acute 'ataque' or dissociative reaction" (p. 331). This connection with unresolved feelings of anger directed at the parents can also be also made about the second case of Puerto Rican syndrome quoted. Case 2 concerns a 20-year-old recruit who had gone AWOL, is a patient with violent and bizarre behavior who was hallucinating the voice of his mother, was concerned about his wife's impending delivery of their first child, and was resentful of his father from whom "he was inadequately seeking financial help." The third case, a patient who has been AWOL for several days, is about someone who, between periods of mutism "pulled his testicles and stated that he did this in order to see blood because he liked to see blood." If we pay attention to the literal meaning of the expression "to see blood," one can recognize the signifier of a Spanish idiom "*ensangrentar*" (literally, to stain with blood), which conveys the idea of becoming heated or fiery with the most intense rage. In this important study, Mehlman emphasizes the existence of a link between the symptoms of *ataques de nervios* and an "inability to manage anger" (p. 332).

IN THE NAME OF ANGER

The very first clinical example Mehlman gives, of a man enraged by an unjust sergeant, seems to perfectly illustrate the analysis of anger as a complex passion by one of the greatest philosophers of antiquity.[2] When Aristotle addresses the question of anger, he contends that

> acts proceeding from anger are rightly judged not to be done of malice aforethought; for it is not the man who acts in anger but he who enraged him that starts the mischief. Again, the matter in dispute is not whether the thing happened or not, but it is justice; for it is apparent injustice that occasions rage. [*Ethics*, 1980, 127]

Anger, in Aristotle's perspective, arises from a situation of injustice that needs to be corrected. "Let anger be [defined as] desire accompanied by [mental and physical] distress, for conspicuous retaliation because of a conspicuous slight that was directed, without justification, against oneself or those near to one" (*On Rhetoric* 1991, p. 124). Aristotle admits therefore that acts triggered by anger are not without virtue. "The man who is angry at the right things and with the right people, and, further, as he ought, when he ought, and as long as he ought, is praised" (*Ethics* 1980, p. 96). This naturally leads to a conception of anger as a handmaiden of justice. Moderate rage follows reason. Revenge would call for justice. Yet, this rage for justice is within measure—never excessive. For Aristotle the "good-tempered man" is not led by passion, tends to be unperturbed, and if he gets angry, he is angry "in the manner, at the things, and for the length of time, that the rule dictates." Nonetheless, let us note that Aristotle considers the lack of anger, or "unirascibility," undesirable:

> For those who are not angry at the things they should be angry at are thought to be fools, and so are those who are not angry in the right way, at the right time, with the right persons; for such a man is thought not to feel things nor to be pained by them, and, since he does not get angry, he is thought unlikely to defend himself; and to endure being insulted and put up with insult to one's friend is slavish. [*Ethics*, 1980, p. 97]

The use of the expression "they *should* be angry" betrays the policing aspect in anger. The ability to get angry at injustice would be a call to restore dignity and fair play, which may lead to correct the circumstances that elicited the anger in the first place. Anger, therefore, would be a political matter. Anger could be read as a message: *I don't like what you are doing.*

---

2. I thank Charlie Shepherdson for this useful insight.

You are not being fair. Do not enslave me. Give me justice. This message is addressed at the other who, one assumes, can influence the object of one's anger, that is, the other who is responsible, and who ought to behave differently. Anger expresses a sense that certain rules must be followed and therefore follows rules. It is elicited by a transgression of the rules and aims at ensuring that justice be respected, that the Law be honored. A similar perception of injustice was clearly illustrated by the main complaint of the patient in the clinical example mentioned above—he developed the Puerto Rican syndrome when angered by his sergeant's unfairness. Following Aristotle, we may say that these enraged patients diagnosed with Puerto Rican syndrome were defending themselves in the face of injustice. They were recognizing anger as the only passion capable of restoring justice. A detour through the "phenomenology of anger" (to quote the title of a poem by Adrienne Rich) will be henceforth inevitable.

POLICING ANGER

Mehlman (1961) emphasizes the existence of a link between the symptoms of *ataques de nervios* and an "inability to manage anger" (p. 332). We are living in times when anger-management seminars are becoming increasingly popular. In the last ten years, more than five hundred books on anger have been published in the United States. It is clear that anger has emerged as the dominant manifestation of an entire society's fear of its unconscious. Indeed, it looks as if the explosions of contemporary anger, like the epidemic of hysteria at the end of the nineteenth century, beg for nothing less than psychoanalysis. Today's anger and the attendant fear of anger look more and more symptomatic of the American fantasy of disciplining the unconscious through a total management, and call for some kind of intervention (not just from the police, one hopes) or at least for some kind of discourse.

Anger is an emotion neither new nor exclusive to the Puerto Rican syndrome.[3] Anger is as old as the world, at least as the ancient Greeks, but our society has a particularly difficult time dealing with it—defining it, coping with it, understanding it, not to say preventing the more and more common escalation of anger into murderous rage. Rage pops up just about

---

3. See Gherovici 2001.

anywhere; it surges with riots, flares with children taking guns to school, and erupts unexpectedly in the most familiar settings. Any post office, any high school, any broker's office, any university campus, any jammed highway can become the stage where this most American of symptoms will explode with a vengeance.

In order to elucidate the emergence of the phenomenon, one may go back to the ancient expression "*Ira brevis furor est*"—anger is a "brief fury," or better yet, a "momentary madness." Anger can alter one's mental condition, producing fits of madness. Such short-lived madness often had dire consequences for the Ancients. From Seneca's *Hercules Furens* to Ariosto's *Orlando Furioso*, one witnesses murder, slaughter of children or friends, all sorts of mayhem that will certainly remind us of recent events. Indeed, doesn't the standard American idiom equating "angry" with "mad" already imply that anger can make us lose our heads? We recognize the difference between being angry and acting out murderous fury, but what matters in the linguistic and psychological affinities between "mad" and "angry" is the stress on time: a "brief" madness—duration here is the key. The implication is that the intense emotional state induced by anger only takes place from time to time and for a *limited* time, as if an instant were enough to overcome a particular psychic threshold, after which we are expected to regain our senses.

"Daddy, are you mad at me?" Is this common expression the sign of a deeper fear of the uncontrollable upsurge of affects that anger elicits? Why do people sometimes go crazy for a while? Insane or not, nobody is a stranger to anger. If anger stubbornly insists throughout time, it is because anger somehow *works*. How does anger work and for whom in the context of the Puerto Rican syndrome? When stressing the links between anger and the perception of injustice brought to the fore by Aristotle, I have left aside, however, the second feature noted in Mehlman's (1961) observation of the Puerto Rican syndrome. Every time his patient reached an awareness of his wish to kill his father, he had an acute *ataque*. How to make sense of this unconscious murderous rage directed at the father? The incoherent manifestations provided by a phenomenology of anger require a more rigorous explanation; thus the key to the function of anger in the Puerto Rican syndrome can only be provided by a psychoanalytic rationale such as it has been brilliantly theorized by Gérard Pommier.

In a provocative and groundbreaking work, Pommier (2001) contends that anger originates in the field of love: in love and libido only can it be positively channeled. In anger one finds all the factors triggering complex forces that allow human sexuality to operate through the Oedipus complex. Just as all subjects experience the fate of castration and the oedipal complex, no one can escape falling once in a while under the spell of anger. For Pommier, anger forces us to engage actively with the trials and tribulations of the castration complex. "Castration" marks human beings and establishes a symbolic debt that everyone will have to pay back by becoming neurotic: here is the root of Freud's myth of the murder of the father. This myth helps us to understand how human "animals" become "subjects" by entering into the Law. In Lacanian theory, one has to look for the "name-of-the-father" to find the agency supporting the Law. Such agency is encountered in a father who is better dead than alive, or remembered by the ritual of the totemic feast. Thus, according to Freud, the father's law is effective only after his sons have killed him.

Lacan's ideas on aggression reach back to a narcissistic moment constructed in relation to the mirror stage. In *Ecrits* (1977b), when Lacan addresses the springs of aggressivity often motivating the technique of analysis, he emphasizes that an analyst can cure even the most serious cases of madness though dialogue. Aggressivity forms the negative transference that is the initial knot of the analytic drama. As aggression is fundamentally imaginary, it can be resolved in either murder or suicide, or pacified by an oedipal identification with the father—this is the common way leading to the possibility of engaging in social and cultural creativity. For Pommier, anger is both the consequence and the sign of the unrest created by the Oedipus complex. The oedipal moment is not just a too often rehearsed fable of love and hate; it is an operative structure that precedes the arrival of the subject. This structure "in waiting" will then introduce the subject into culture. We observe a double moment: on the one hand, prohibition gives rise to the taboo; on the other hand, it creates order—the organization of places and positions that allows the emergence of desire in culture.

Although anger is not a technical term in Freud's vocabulary, it is interesting to find the most detailed interpretation of anger in his classic analysis of an obsessional neurosis. There, too, anger will be seen working in connection with castration. In Freud's (1909b) Rat Man's case, anger intersects with eroticism via the father's fantasmatic assassination. Let us read more closely the "scene" of anger:

> When he was very small . . . he had done something naughty, for which his father had given him a beating. The little boy had flown into a terrible rage and had hurled abuse at his father even while he was under

> his blows. But as he knew no bad language, he had called him all the
> names of common objects that he could think of, and had screamed:
> "You lamp! You towel! You plate!" and so on. His father, shaken by such
> an outburst of elemental fury, had stopped beating him, and had de-
> clared: "The child will be either a great man or a great criminal!" The
> patient believed that the scene made a permanent impression upon
> himself as well as upon his father. . . . From that time forward he was a
> coward—out of fear of the violence of his own rage. [pp. 205–206]

This could be interpreted as a sort of inversion of the famous fantasy of "A
Child Is Being Beaten," for here the child assumes an active role and beats,
or at least defeats, the father rhetorically. In the course of being beaten,
the boy, later known as the Rat Man, somehow managed to express the
otherwise inexpressible excess of a terrifying and murderous rage. The
epithets hurled at his father stopped him cold and the boy was never beaten
again after this incident. However, the son will eventually internalize a
terrifying father whom he also adores. The Rat Man is stuck on the oedipal
path to Thebes. Freud discovers that the Rat Man's main symptom is the
fear of a horrible torture applied to the father, even though the father has
long since died by the time he enters analysis. He is obsessed with the idea
that if he were to declare his love to his revered Lady a rat would eat its
way up the father's anus.

We can understand this scene as the place where the etiology of the
subsequent neurosis must be sought. As Patrick Mahony (1986) notes, this
traumatic event was never anamnestically certified in the treatment; what
the Rat Man "remembered" was a tale reproduced by his mother (pp. 72–
75). The Rat Man mentions this infantile scene of rage, part of the family
romance, in the following way, immediately after an intervention of Freud.
Freud, who was obviously trying to help the Rat Man build his fundamental fantasy, presented a construction.

> I ventured to put forward a construction to the effect that when he was
> a child under six he had been guilty of some sexual misdemeanor con-
> nected with masturbation and had been soundly castigated by his fa-
> ther. This punishment had left behind an ineradicable grudge against
> his father and had established him for all time in his role of an inter-
> ferer with the patient's sexual enjoyment. [Freud 1909b, pp. 204–205]

The patient told Freud then that, indeed, his mother had repeatedly described to him an occurrence of this kind. But the patient himself had no

recollection of it. After this session, the Rat Man questioned his mother, who confirmed the story. The scene of rage has a structuring function, Freud tells us, because from that time forward the Rat Man was afraid of his own rage and all his life was terribly afraid of blows, and used to creep away and hide, filled with terror and indignation, when one of his brothers or sisters was beaten. The emergence of this childhood memory in his analysis shook the patient, who had thus far refused to believe Freud's contention that at some point in his childhood he had been seized by fury against the father whom he loved so much, a fury that had subsequently become latent. The incident surprised the Rat Man because it revealed some of his resentment against his father. Nevertheless, it had been described to him quite often, even by the father himself. Since the infantile memory was not a memory of the Rat Man but in fact a scene that his parents often narrated, here is a memory validated by the Other.

One remarkable element in this early scene of rage is that the Rat Man calls his father by the names of objects in the room: "You lamp! You towel! You plate!" rather than calling his father names. He is not calling him names but nouns, or more than nouns, inanimate objects. It was not as if he was calling his father an animated name, like a Schreber calling God a *Hure* (whore). The Rat Man could have called his father "you ass," "you pig." But in his choice of words the Rat Man dis-animates his father. This gesture institutes the father as not dead, not alive, but rather inanimate—this is the father of the Rat Man's subsequent neurosis: a father who cannot be killed because he is not mortal. He is showing to his father a pure signifier, as such, indestructible. By subverting the normal functioning of language, he creates an inverted metaphor whose arbitrariness forcefully struggles to undo the paternal metaphor. Being reminded of the arbitrariness of all signs, the father is left speechless and cannot tell the child that he has done something wrong and deserves to be punished. Falling under the contagion of this mute rage generated by the feeling of some terrible injustice, the father merely posits a universal law that functions as an oblique retaliation. This retaliation takes the abstract form of a maxim positing an alternative between opposing maxima, the maximum of greatness and the maximum of abjection. The father declared afterward: "The child will be either a great man or a great criminal!" He responds in the third person whereas the child had tried to address him directly—as a "You lamp!" But when the child says "You lamp," the father could have answered; "You spoiled little brat" or "I am not a lamp, I am your father." Instead of this exchange, what the child hears is not the inversion of his own speech but an address in the third person. The father's response introduces an obsessional trap in the pairing of superlatives: if both greatness or badness are equal options, they are reduced to the same. Whatever he does will be the best or the worst. Here is the dramatic alternative that posits the double model of obsessional neurosis.

Stuart Schneiderman (1986) has underlined the importance of this outburst of rage and contends that this scene destroys the father's desire when "the child accomplished as much in unnaming his father, in naming him as one of the objects of the household, to be more specific, of his mother's household." Schneiderman argues that the child's rage was not his, but rather the repressed rage of his mother. "In the scene that she repeated to him he was simply realizing her desire and in so doing sacrificing his own" (p. 83). Freud had also noted this identification with the mother, and was aware that the patient identified with his mother in his criticisms of his father, sustaining the disagreements between his parents within himself. However, even though some of the child's resentment toward the father was in fact his mother's, his anger's goal was to bring the father into the scene—the scene is in fact staged as a call for the father.

In the scene of rage, the father does not talk back to the child but speaks about the child to his wife. Avoiding a dialogical model, he sets the basis for the infantile neurosis by establishing the obsessional mechanism that recurs in the Rat Man's case. The father's response fixes the child's neurotic destiny: the father undoes the child's acting in the scene; he recognizes him and does not recognize him at the same time. The fact that the father addressed his wife instead of the child also reveals his position not as a subject but just as an object caught between the parents. The scene of anger elicits in the father the statement, which, as we have seen, is addressed to his wife: "The child will be either a great man or a great criminal!"[4] This either/or structure predicating a disjunction corresponds to what in logic is designated by the suggestive name of "the excluded third" or "excluded middle." The Rat Man's later dilemma will become: "I can marry this woman, but if I marry this woman I lose that other woman," thus always vacillating endlessly, unable to decide between opposing choices. Hence, the Rat Man's "solution" will be to suggest that the third is not really excluded: he will wait as if suspended in time for a sign that will come

---

4. Freud suggests in a footnote that these options do not exhaust the possibilities; the most common symptomatic resolution for the repression of anger is neurosis.

and make him choose one way or another. By not choosing, he can have both, and of course neither. In other words, his either/or becomes a neither/nor.

We see here links between obsessional neurosis and the self-prohibition against a kind of rage that exceeds linguistic categories, a rage triggered by an excess of injustice or justice (for they cannot be distinguished anymore, since the father's voice fails at the moment when it could articulate this crucial difference), a rage quite close to what in French is called *rage mue* or mute fury. The Rat Man's father was in fact a good person with a passionate temper and a violence that he found hard to control. Above all, he was unable to use or transmit his own anger "well." This misuse of anger became an obstacle and prevented the resolution that would have been essential for the consummation of the Rat Man's sexuality. Therefore, the Rat Man's father complex manifested itself as a ferocious struggle between the persistent influence of his father and his own amorous predilections. This reveals the double nature of an interdiction that both restricts sexual enjoyment and makes it possible. Because the Rat Man's father was actually a good man, and father and son lived together like best friends, nevertheless this harmony stood between father and son and returned later as a symptom evinced in the Rat Man's sexuality. As a friend, his father was also not father enough. Could it be that the Rat Man's obsessional and recurrent fear that his father might die, which persisted even years after his actual passing away, confirms that his neurosis encountered an obstacle: the dreadful feeling that his father could never be killed? In other words, in order for his sexuality to be realized, the dead father needed to be killed again in the son's fantasy. Even though his father was long dead, the Rat Man was still trying to reach him by way of his self-imposed prohibitions; he was seeking a father beyond death in order to kill him and inherit his phallic power.

This is confirmed by a revealing incident in the Rat Man's life. "Several years after his father's death, the first time he experienced the pleasurable sensations of copulation, an idea sprang to his mind: 'This is glorious! One might murder one's father for this!'" (Freud 1909b, p. 201). This looks like a classic oedipal plot; yet, the rivalry with the father for a loved object (the mother) is a battle that the boy has lost (the father has kept the mother), forcing him to occupy a passive position (the boy renounces the mother and has to look for another woman outside the endogamic circle). The boy fantasizes that he did not lose the battle (he kept the mother), thus identifying with the victor (his own father), and inheriting his phallic power that is essential in his access to sexual enjoyment. We could conclude that this thought is evidence for the necessity of the murder of the father in fantasy, a transgression that is required for a sexual act to occur. The father needs to be killed over and over again for him to operate as the symbolic father that guarantees the function of castration.

By articulating death, castration, and anger, are we opening the curtain on the Freudian theater of war that produces the fantasmatic assassination of the father? In the 1975 Seminar *Le Sinthome*, Lacan presents the oedipal complex as a symptom. However, its status as symptom does not make it less necessary. The prevalence of anger is a visible trace of human sexuality as "symptom." Freud's originality was to discover that there is no "normal" sexuality. Furthermore, there is a common foundation in "normal" and "abnormal" sexuality. If a sexual object appears, it is contingent; the relationship to this object is enigmatic at least, for the drive's aim is variable and its object uncertain. As Lacan (1977b) notes, Freud called attention to the "skewed" relation of subjects to their sexuality (p. 297).

In obsessional neurosis, anger is closely related to the function of the father. The obsessional subject needs someone who would recognize him as a desiring subject, an other who is the father. Lacan has pointed out that the problem here is not initially the castrating father, the father who interferes with the sexual enjoyment of the child, in spite the fact that that seems to be what Freud is trying to make the patient accept. According to the family romance of the Rat Man's lineage, the father had married for money and not for love; he had sold on his desire and was unworthy of her love. Because of the mother's deprecation of his father's desire (as a man who married her for her money, not for love), the Rat Man found that this father had nothing worth appropriating. The Rat Man's anger repositioned the father in a desiring place where he could function as a father. Anger and transgression thus intersect along the lines of particular economies.

In order to make sense of the anger lurking in the Puerto Rican syndrome and of the oedipal logic that might underpin it, it is crucial to establish whether the Rat Man's anger is specific to the complex structure of obsessional neurosis or depends upon the simpler structure of hysteria. The relation of obsessional neurosis to hysteria was established by Freud (1915) when he claimed, "The language of an obsessional neurosis . . . is, as it were, only a dialect of the language of hysteria" (p. 258). Lacan insists upon this point when he too states that obsessional neurosis is "a jargon of hysteria" (quoted in Ragland-Sullivan 1988, p. 69). Although hysteria appears as a more basic structure, Freud (1926) notes that obsessional neurosis and hysteria originate in the same situation—the oedipal complex. He adds that "every obsessional neurosis seems to have a substratum of hysterical symptoms that had been formed at a very early stage" (p. 113). Hysterical and obsessional anger thus essentially share the castration complex. Humanity overcomes mortality through sexual reproduction. Conversely, the death drive stamps sexuality with a touch of lethal anxiety.

When the opposites of sex and death meet, it is not so much because the sexual act signifies eventually death but because access to sexuality implies a power fundamentally based on a fantasmatic murder. Castration does not curtail potency—it makes it possible. The boy inherits the insignias of a virile power equal to his father's—the phallic gift—when the father castrates him. However, in order to earn these marks of honor, the boy has to do away with the father. Does the aggression presented by destructive anger facing the paternal complex operate similarly in hysteria and obsessional neurosis? This problem will have important consequences on our understanding of the Puerto Rican predicament; we will thus need to explore the differences between Freud's Rat Man's anger and the anger of the *Ur*-patient of psychoanalysis, its most famous hysteric, Anna O.

8

From Obsessional Rage
to Hysterical Fury

We doubt that many clinicians at the present time see patients like
Anna O. For this reason *DSM-III-R* does not have a single category
that would encompass the variety of symptoms and the often chronic
course that correspond to the traditional concept of Hysteria. Anna
O. is therefore a diagnostic enigma for today's clinician.

Robert Spitzer (Spitzer et al. 1989, p. 465)

In the literature on psychopathology among Puerto Ricans, it is
widely reported that hysterical behavior is more common and
generally accepted in Puerto Rican culture than in the United States.

Christine Torres-Matrullo (1976, p. 712)

We have seen how classical hysteria overlaps with the Puerto Rican syndrome, and how both are underpinned by the common phenomenon of
anger. Obessional rage can nevertheless lead us to a hidden core of classical hysteria. The vantage point provided by our new understanding of the
centrality of anger in the Puerto Rican syndrome will help us reopen the

famous history of Anna O. I will use a fictionalized treatment of this famous hysteric that lays the stress on the issue of anger. Anger, as an affect, underpins both Anna O.'s symptomatology and the Puerto Rican syndrome, and has to be reinscribed in Freud and Breuer's (1895) *Studies on Hysteria* via a Lacanian approach to hysteria. Hopefully, revisiting the case of Anna O. through the problematics of anger will in the end confirm the fecundity of a Lacanian theory of hysteria. With these methodological issues in mind, let us quote excerpts from Lucy Freeman's (1972) fictionalized account of Breuer's treatment of Anna O.

> "You *are* helping my daughter, Dr. Breuer," she said. "Today she talked to me. In anger, but she talked." [p. 13]
>
> "I couldn't think very clearly today, Dr. Breuer. My mind seemed all mixed up. And I felt as if the walls of the room would topple over on me."
>
> After he had placed her in the trance, he asked, "What were you thinking today?"
>
> "I was very angry." [p. 17]
>
> "Dr. Breuer—please hurry. We can't control her."
>
> He saw his young patient on the bed, angrily trying to thrust herself out if it, her mother holding her back. [p. 21]
>
> At times he [Breuer] would find her in such rage that even under hypnosis she remained mute no matter how persistently he pleaded with her to speak. [p. 30]
>
> "What torments you?" he asked.
>
> The words exploded from her parched lips. . . . Her eyes simmered with rage. "I wanted to tell her what I thought. . . . But I held my tongue because I have been brought up to be polite to people, whatever their station in life. . . . And, with these words, she seized an embroidered pillow with her left hand and hurled it venomously across the room as though it were a stick of dynamite she threw at an enemy. [p. 32]

This dramatized rendering is not pure invention, as Freeman has studied Breuer's notes and the whole clinical history of Anna O. Even though the style is fictional, these excerpts are based on documented facts. Breuer (Freud and Breuer 1895) himself mentions in his case story:

> Two entirely distinct states of consciousness. . . . [In one state] she was melancholy and anxious, but relatively normal. In the other state she hallucinated and was "naughty"—that is to say, she was abusive, used to throw cushions at people, so far as the contractures at various times

allowed, tore buttons off her bedclothes and linen with those fingers which she could move and so on. [p. 24]

Anna had frequent fits of anger, and Breuer experienced difficulties in calming her down. When long lapses of time would stretch between each of her "talking-cure" sessions, Breuer would find Anna "increasingly moody, contrary and unpleasant" (p. 30). She would enter "a wretched moral state, inert, unamenable, ill-tempered, even malicious" (p. 31). This state of mind not only made her unpleasant: Breuer notes that it would even dry up her florid poetic vein.[1] Her anger was clearly related to the amount of time elapsed between her verbal utterances: "On the day after giving verbal utterance to her fantasies she was amiable and cheerful, on the second day she was more irritable and less agreeable and on the third positively 'nasty'" (p. 32). When Anna's mind was clear she would complain "of the profound darkness in her head, of not being able to think, of becoming blind and deaf, of having two selves, a real one and an evil one which forced her to behave badly, and so on" (p. 24). Even when she was in a very bad condition her "good self" prevailed as witness, "a clear-sighted and calm observer sat, as she put it, in a corner of her brain and looked at all the mad business" (p. 46). Anna was aware that when she got mad, she was unable to think, becoming blind and deaf in rage. Her split condition calls up once more "*Ira brevis furor est*"—anger is a "momentary madness."

Breuer was greatly surprised when he noticed that the hysterical phenomena brought to a verbal utterance made the symptoms disappear; the demons were exorcised in speech. Underscoring its prevalence, Breuer chose a symptom caused by repressed anger to illustrate the therapeutic efficacy of what he called "abreaction": during a period of extreme heat in the summer, Anna developed a phobia to water. She suffered very badly from thirst and found it impossible to drink, living only on fruits as the source of fluids. This lasted for some six weeks. Finally, "After giving further energetic expression to the *anger* she had held back, she asked for something to drink, drank a large quantity of water without any difficulty and woke from her hypnosis with the glass at her lips; and thereupon the disturbance vanished, never to return" (pp. 34–35, italics mine).

---

1. Under this disposition, Anna's narratives "were merely formulated in stereotyped images rather than elaborated into poetic productions" (p. 31).

In order to broach both the meaning of the recurrent appearance of anger throughout this case of hysteria and to understand the promising effect of her verbal utterances, let us take a look at the function of fantasy. Since the very beginning, hysteria and fantasy appear closely linked in Freud's theoretical map. In his search of an origin for hysteria, clinical difficulties led Freud from the seduction theory (the supposition of a real sexual trauma) to the idea of fantasy. Freud's change in his understanding of the etiology of hysteria was strategic. Trauma, nevertheless, remained at the origin of the Freudian elaboration: it was no longer reality that mattered but trauma. For Lacan, trauma is always Real since it marks the encounter of the subject with the desire of the Other. We shall return to this crucial clinical issue in Chapter 15 by way of a case history.

As Verhaeghe (1999) notes, fantasies are not merely attempts at escaping a frustrating world but rather they organize the way we perceive, or better said, construct, reality. Anna O.'s life history "is an excellent demonstration of the thesis that the development of a basic fantasy determines the way one lives one's life" (p. 167). Breuer (Freud and Breuer 1895) has mentioned that his patient would complain that "something was tormenting her—or rather, she would keep the impersonal form 'tormenting, tormenting'" (p. 25). In Freeman's fictionalized biographical account of Anna O., who, as we know, Ernest Jones disclosed in 1953 was Bertha Pappenheim, we see a life evolving as if some fundamental fantasy had remained untouched. Even before she consulted Breuer, Bertha used to spend hours daydreaming, living fairy tales in her "private theater," caught in a "systematic daydreaming." Her fantasies changed during her life. Freeman (1972), however, claims these were "tormenting phantoms, phantoms she spoke of in the treatment with Breuer that she later managed to keep under control but that never really let her be. The same phantoms haunting her at her father's bedside haunted her as a child and were to haunt her the rest of her life" (p. 212). We shall explore what Freeman alludes to when she mentions lifetime haunting phantoms or fantasies that possessed Anna and "never really let her be." The most intriguing elements about Breuer's pioneer work with Anna may look idiosyncratic; yet they allow us to speculate on some of hysteria's general features. Anger will bring the illumination that will shed light on the conceptualization of the castration fantasy underlying hysteria.

Breuer (Freud and Breuer 1895) observed that the stories Bertha told him were "always sad and some of them very charming, in the style of Hans

Andersen's *Picture Book without Pictures*, and, indeed they were probably constructed in that model" (p. 29). We can see how she "uses enchantment" by focusing on one of her early "private theater" fantasies that she narrated to Breuer. The following fairy tale was told immediately after a violent fit of anger during which she threw a pillow at her mother. The plot summary goes like this: a poor orphan girl wanders into a house in search of somebody to love. There, she finds a father suffering from an incurable disease, soon to die. His wife has given him up. The little orphan, refusing to believe that he is doomed, sits by his bed day and night, takes care of all his needs. Slowly, he comes back to life and is so grateful that he adopts the child who indeed had found somebody to love (Freeman 1972). As Verhaeghe has noted, Bertha's uncertainty about the father figure increased her uncertainty about her female identity. As in the classical scenarios for hysteria, Bertha is looking toward a father so as to signify her female sexual identity. Thus, following her fit of anger (addressed at a mother in whose discourse she finds only a failing father), she invents for herself her own potent father figure and comes to occupy this place herself. This is what Lacan (1998b) describes as *"Elle fait l'homme."* The phrase has a double meaning in French, "playing the man's part" and "making the man," in the sense of making a man of him (p. 85). The little orphan was in quest not so much of someone to love but of a father to love and to be loved by. The mother had given him up; yet the girl could not believe that he was doomed because, if he was, she would be doomed as well. Bertha's resentment was directed at her mother for not explicitly finding the phallus in the father and her anger was vividly expressed in several instances throughout the case. In Bertha's fairy tale, when the father is helped until he comes back to life, a happy ending leads to the girl's being "adopted," that is, inscribed in a symbolic structure on top of having found an object of love. This is a fundamental, almost basic hysterical fantasy that can remind us of other hysterics like Dora. This basic fantasy persists with slight variations throughout Bertha Pappenheim's life. Not only did Bertha take care of her dying father by nursing him night and day, but after her treatment with Breuer she "played the man": she became the father she never had by becoming the benefactor of an orphanage. To fully understand the impact of the oedipal and castration complexes, it is crucial to keep in mind that the father here is not just a third term introduced between mother and child; he is in fact placed as a fourth term due to the presence of an inexistent phallus.

What can we learn from Anna O.'s case that could help us elucidate the hysterical structure that underpins the Puerto Rican syndrome? We may note that the curious label contains the name of the Puerto Rican people's *patria*, their *father*land. In hysteria this reference to the father is of great significance; hysteria always constructs a scene with a father and a trauma, and then some knowledge is generated by their interaction. The Puerto Rican syndrome's hysteria might be telling us something that has to do with the father's memory, the lost ideals of independence and nationalism. We shall return in some detail to this political aspect in the next chapter. Let us now focus on the figure of the father who is always so present in hysteria.

THE FATHER'S SEDUCTION

Applying what he had learned from his patients' most intimate associations, Freud's early architecture of hysteria considers heredity as the transmitter of hysteria by way of the seduction of the father. At the origin of the hysteria, one always finds a trauma produced by the father's "seduction." Catherine Millot (1988) argues that Freud conceived of hysteria not as a rejection of sexuality but as a rejection of the seducer himself, the father (p. 14). Freud (1954) found in the recounted infantile memories of his hysterics not just a sexual source, but a source of sexual perversion at the origin of hysteria. In his letter No. 52 to Fliess, he states that

> the essential point of hysteria is that it is the result of perversion on the part of the seducer; and that heredity is seduction by the father. Thus a change occurs between generations: 1st generation: Perversion. 2nd generation: Hysteria. . . . Thus hysteria is repudiated *perversion*. [p. 180]

One can hear in hysteria's repudiation of perversion Lacan's play on *perversion* as *père-version* (father's version) and thus think of hysteria as repudiated *père*-version, a contention to which we shall return soon.

Freud's striking statement exposes the peculiar, yet structural, role of the father in hysterization. Millot notes that in hysteria we have a double figure of the paternal lack: an impotent or dead father on the one hand, and a perverted father who is a seducer, on the other hand.[2] In Bertha

---

2. We can already find in the first psychoanalytical texts this double feature of the father. If we follow the cases in the *Studies*, Millot (1988) adds, we find fathers who are

Pappenheim's life, however, one can clearly see a progression whose pace is marked by her relationship to her mother. This is because if Anna O. could find a less dissatisfying "father," it would be found in her mother's castration, since the maternal castration precedes what the paternal castration simply substitutes for. Castration for Lacan refers to the alienating impact of language on the subject that can be traced back to the primordial experiences of the infant and the Other (mother).

ANGRY FIGHTER

Examining her early years as a leading feminist, Marion Kaplan (1984) states: "Pappenheim's outrage at the injustice faced by women made her an indomitable fighter for equality. . . . Her anger against male dominance increased over the course of her career" (p. 101). Although her anger finds socially productive outlets, one can detect the overdeterminations in the evolution of her anger by following the variations in her fundamental fantasy. Her first publication, in 1890, was *In der Trodelbude* (*In the Thrift-Store*), a collection of fairy tales similar to those she would extemporize during her treatment with Breuer. Marion Kaplan and Max Rosenbaum (1984) agree that it was only after the publication of this book that Bertha Pappenheim could become an active worker in the feminist movement. It is noteworthy that when she chose a pseudonym, she called the book's author Paul Berthold, masculinizing Bertha in her patronymic since Berthold is the masculine version of her first name. Thus, she seemed to refuse her last name, the one she received from her father, and chose instead to turn the first name she received from her parents into a patronymic element. That name is neither a name she shares with the family nor a name she would have received from a husband. Her *nom-de-plume* "Berthold" is a relatively common name suggesting in German beautiful (*bert*) and pure (*hold*), thus condensing mystical and romantic ideas.

Bertha may refuse her father's actual name but since the *Nom-du-Père* articulates the *no* to questions of naming, by disguising her first name as a

---

severely sick, even dying. Anna O. and Elizabeth von R. fell ill when the fathers they had been nursing for a long time died. Emmy von N. developed her symptoms after the death of a much older husband, while Katharina and Rosalia H. become ill as the result of a traumatic sexual scene during which their fathers tried to seduce them.

man's name, she reinstitutes the father, playing herself the man's part and thus "making the man."[3] Like any "good hysteric," Bertha Pappenheim challenges and sustains at once the father/man, supporting him while "making a man of him," teaching him the right way to be a father/man, even if the pedagogic enterprise may happen to entail some transgendered impersonation. As Lacan contends, the hysteric "constitutes the man." The hysteric "puts the man at the center," a feature that will become clear in the evolution of Bertha Pappenheim's feminism.

As noted before, the hysteric has the unique power of playing a constituent role in producing a man who could conceive of woman as equal yet different. As Diane Hunter (1983) argues, "feminism is transformed hysteria, or more precisely, that hysteria is feminism lacking a social network in the outer world" (p. 485). Politically, hysteria tends toward a self-defeating conclusion—no sooner is the Master dethroned than another Master has to appear on a new pedestal.

These contradictions, which are at the kernel of the hysteric's fundamental fantasy, can be illustrated by the literary and political career of Anna O. Her stories of In der Trodelbude describe family tragedies following an oedipal structure: the basic plot of the stories concerns a man who has been abandoned by his wife and who regains his happiness when the lost daughter moves back with him (see Verhaeghe 1999, pp. 167–168). In 1899 she financed the publication of her translation into German of A Vindication of the Right of Women, written in 1792 by one of the founders of feminism, Mary Wollstonecraft (who was the mother of Mary Shelley), and published a three-act play, Women's Right.

The play marks the beginning of a new stage. The classic oedipal plot is abandoned and the play focuses on the failure of the father, and more

---

3. Let us recall that Lacan describes the function and duplicitous role of the father by playing with the French phrase Nom du père, in which one can both hear the "name" and the "no" of the father (non du père). The double dimension—the nom-du-père and the NO du père—articulate this NO to questions of naming; the name appears there where the father prohibits something from happening. This nom/non castrates. On the one hand, it enforces the prohibition of incest (paternal metaphor), breaking the illusion of an imaginary complementarity of the child and the mother. On the other hand, it guarantees the incorporation into the realm of language, of culture, of law; it inscribes the child in a genealogy, it gives the child a symbolic place in the social world. This is a no that is introduced by the mother's discourse, a discourse determined by her desire, that is, by her own oedipal drama as mother, daughter, lover. Therefore, the father's double role as husband and lover will remain at the origin of the symptom for both women and men.

precisely on how his failure yields to the unscrupulous sexual exploitation of women. Succinctly, the play tells the story of a single mother, sick and poor, and a wealthy woman married to a lawyer who wishes to help her. The husband does not want to help the sick woman. His wife insists until the couple visits the poor ailing mother. In that encounter, it is revealed that the man had been the lover of the destitute woman and that he had abandoned her while she was pregnant. The wife is shocked about her findings but chooses to stay with her husband for the sake of her children while refusing future sexual contacts—thus exercising Lysistrata's "women's right." In short, the male characters (one a rake, the other an irresponsible seducer) appear as hostile victimizers and women are depicted as helpless preys of male exploitation.

The central position of the woman/mother in the plot marked an original turn in Bertha Pappenheim's fantasy that generated a third position. This new mode of fantasy appeared after a period during which Bertha had been very aggressive toward her mother. In the early 1890s, she started reclaiming her Jewish identity (which is completely erased in Breuer's account of her case) and engaged in active community work: from soup kitchens for eastern-European Jewish immigrants to classes teaching basic practical jobs to young women. By 1895 (coincidentally, the year the Anna O. case was published) she became the directress ("housemother") of a Jewish orphanage for girls. Although the post was temporary, she held that position for twelve years while becoming a pioneering social worker.

THE WOMAN THE FATHER OUGHT TO HAVE

In her role as housemother, her model of femininity seemed the exact opposite of her mother's—she set up a sewing school, insisted that young women should learn practical skills, and above all be provided with more cultural and educational opportunities (women should be "educated like men"). As Kaplan (1984) contends, Bertha Pappenheim's illness was a cultural construct that one could trace back to conflicts in the position of women of her day. Possibly, some of her hostility toward her mother was aimed at the reduced social role allowed to women, which was entirely condoned by her mother's beliefs. Her animosity, however, was also motivated by a classic complaint of the hysteric: she reproaches her mother "for not being the woman the father ought to have," as described by Lucien Israël (1979). In her new stage, she overcame this grudge and seemed to be reconciled with her mother. Thus, Bertha became very interested in her mother's family background and found out that through her, she was related to Gluckel von Hameln, a widow of Jewish background who lived in Germany between the turn of the seventeenth and eighteenth centuries. This discovery about her maternal lineage to an admirable foremother was powerful enough to let her reclaim her proper name. The new appraisal of her mother made her rise in Bertha's esteem. Only then could she find in the mother's discourse the Name-of-the-Father. And through her writings and publications, she finally reclaimed a name of her own. The first step was taken in 1900 when the name "Bertha Pappenheim" appeared in a parenthesis next to "P. Berthold" in a publication. Let us note here that the name Paul is reduced to the initial letter, leaving the name and hence the gender of the author more uncertain. This publication was *The Jewish Problem in Galicia*, a short pamphlet denouncing the connection between poor education and poverty in Jewish girls.

Her distant relative Gluckel von Hameln was a remarkable woman, someone whom Mary Wollstonecraft deeply venerated. In 1910 Bertha Pappenheim translated into German and published Gluckel von Hameln's memoirs, using for the first time her given name. In 1913 and 1916 she published another play and several short stories. New themes cropping up are anti-Semitism, white slavery, and the unfulfilled needs of young mothers. Bertha Pappenheim is by then concerned with the Other (sex). Of her many writings, her most well known one is *Sisyphus Work*, published in 1924, a report on prostitution and white slavery in eastern Europe and the Middle East, which, unhappily, was used by the Nazis in the aim of anti-Semitic propaganda. Bertha Pappenheim was aware that when she denounced how young Jewish women were sold into brothels by an organized white-slave traffic of which some Jews were part, this was a predicament likely to be turned against the Jewish community by anti-Semites. She did not withdraw from her plight; her decision to not flinch from telling the truth at any cost illustrates the proverbial love for truth of the hysteric (and the price to pay). As she was terminally ill, she was questioned by the Gestapo. Mercifully, Bertha Pappenheim died in 1936 before the Nazis destroyed the homes she had created (one home was burned, another was turned into a brothel). Many of the women were sent to concentration camps; some committed suicide to avoid being sent to brothels organized for the German military.

Bertha Pappenheim, or Anna O., is known in the annals of psychoanalysis as a "successful" hysteric (Forrester and Appignanesi 2000, p. 80). Her many achievements were widely acknowledged in 1954 when the German government issued a Bertha Pappenheim stamp, honoring her as a pioneer German social worker. In a review of her life history, Max Rosenbaum (1984) mentions that although later in life she showed almost no trace of her earlier emotional difficulties, "her associates described her as being overly sensitive or subject to outbursts of anger" (p. 19). Her unrelenting anger was a Prime Mover affecting her whole life, inciting her defense of the weak and oppressed, inspiring her to accomplish difficult, heroic humanitarian deeds. This anger was elicited by horrible social injustices she fought to change. Her plea for equality and her admirable deeds found resonance, however, in the structural peculiarities of hysteria concerning the paternal complex. This complex in hysteria is structured around the construction of a certain father, the missing signifier for The Woman, and the nonexistence of sexual rapport. The hysteric constructs a particular type of father, a Master who will know the answer to the question "What is a Woman?" and thus render a female identity possible (there would be a signifier for femininity and thus a promise of complementarity between the sexes). This fantasy fails because the Other happens to be castrated. There is no total Other; the lack in the Other is irremediable. Let us note that Bertha's real father, like all fathers, was a "castrated" father—hers was weak and ill, and died early.

In what can evoke the obsessional's strategy, the hysteric wishes to sustain a failing father by idealizing the father figure. This Ideal father is not just a father, he is much more: he is complete, he is in the position of a Master, and he is freed from all desire. No longer subjected to a primary loss, this Ideal father can produce in his own name a particular knowledge about *jouissance*. This tendency toward creating an ideal, impossible father is illustrated by Bertha Pappenheim, who in 1922 wrote, "If there is justice in the world to come, women will be lawgivers, and men have to have babies" (Freeman 1972, p. 59). Are we returning to Aristotle's theory of a "just" anger when confronting injustice? Is Anna O. angry because without a father, there is no justice? According to her fantasy, however, "justice in the world to come" is not far from the infantile sexual theories concerning the timeless question of origin—"Where do babies come from?" As one can often see in clinical work with children, questions about pregnancy and birth query the role of the father since "*Mater certa est, pater semper incertus est*" (the mother is certain; the father is always uncertain).

How can there be any justice when the "law" is marked by sexual difference? We now see the root of the difference between the Rat Man's perception of injustice and the hysteric structure. Both face the unspeakable excess of a subjective destitution facing injustice, but their strategies and aims diverge in their efforts to restore speech, therefore the possibility of justice. Both address a law that seems compounded of impossible alternatives and tricky disjunctions.

In both structures, it is the father's part in the process of procreation that creates the first riddle.[4] Anna O.'s difficulties in understanding "what is to be a father" in the sense of procreation relate hysteria's refusal to accept the phallic attribution of the father. However, despite her concern for justice and the anger generated in the process, Bertha Pappenheim's construction does not reverse the patriarchal model: for her, mothers should also be lawgivers, which means that they can occupy the place of the Other as locus of the signifier, or agents of a law they represent and are subjected to. The fantasy confirms the Lacanian theory that when mothers acknowledge the father as the one "who lays down the law," it is a mere function, since "father" refers to that position, a name/no that appears in the mother's discourse. The mother is a central figure in this drama since she has to acknowledge the father as a third party between her and her child; this is a father who, as Lacan says, "lays down the law" with the mother's complicity. The father of the law, the father who underpins symbolic justice, is an agency leading each child to the recognition of castration. Can Bertha differentiate between the Law (the primal patriarch) and the representative of the Law (a father)? Her fantasy reinstates a Master-father-man who can "make" Woman and give her what she is lacking to become The Woman. Anna O. ended her treatment with Breuer with a hysterical pregnancy—could motherhood have been the attempted answer to the mystery of what is a woman? Another element to consider in understanding her phantom pregnancy is the phonetic similarity in English of her own name *Bertha* with the signifier "birth." English became the only language she could or would speak at the time of her illness, one of whose signs was that she seemed to have forgotten her mother tongue. Thus a long segment of her "talk-therapy"

---

4. The difficulties in understanding "What is to be a father" in the sense of procreation, led Lacan (1994) to state that "the question *'What is the father?'* is placed at the center of the analytic experience, left eternally unsettled, at least for us, psychoanalysts" (p. 372).

treatment with Breuer was conducted in English. Another language allows her to posit another access to the law.

Anna O. ended her "talking cure" dramatically with a scene of hysterical childbirth and saying, "Now Dr. B.'s baby is coming!"—an exclamation that declares Breuer as the phantom father-to-be. This outcry and her 1922 statement "If there is justice in the world to come, women will be lawgivers, and men have to have babies" (Pappenheim quoted in Freeman 1972, p. 59) reveal her insistence on the question of a procreative process in which fathers would have to occupy a central position. A father who can have babies suggests a complete father: he can get pregnant, carry a child, and successfully sexualize his child as female. This Ideal Father is whole and fares much better than the mythic father of the horde: he not only enjoys all the women as The Woman but becomes Woman and can have a child. The only problem is that a father who is a complete Other, thus an Ideal father able to provide a specific signifier for a specific sexual feminine identity, remains an impossible father. The law the Ideal father embodies is as impossible as the law of either grandeur or ignominy laid down by the Rat Man's father. For both obsessionals and hysterics, then, it looks as if there was little justice to expect from the world to come.

A VOLCANO LIVED IN THIS WOMAN

Bertha Pappenheim's obituaries in 1936 are filled with allusions to her angry disposition and explosive character. This is one of them: "A volcano lived in this woman; it erupted if someone angered her" (Cora Berliner, quoted in Freeman 1972, pp. 174–175). From the volcano emerged not lava, but a bubbling crucible with generous passions inside. Bertha Pappenheim lived an exemplary life rescuing the frail, assisting the poor, aiding the helpless.

Where was her anger put to "good" use unconsciously stemming from? Anna's anger is produced by an injustice and her anger is an attempt to recuperate what she believes to be in the possession of the Other; it is what arouses the Other's desire while showing that the Other desires that which the Other lacks. This sends us back to the early seduction theory: whether the account of sexual abuse during an infantile seduction scene is genuine or not, it is an accusation of the Other. As Lacan notes, the Other is of extreme importance in hysteria (as we have seen, often this Other is a woman, the Other woman), for the hysteric's desire is the Other's desire. Wajeman (1986) notes that the hysteric is a speaking riddle who commands the Other to answer the question, "What am I?" This demand compels speech and expects an answer. This answer is marked by an essential flaw. When the Other responds to the question with a "You are this," it reduces the subject's search to a finite object. But no answer can settle the hysteric's question. The object of the hysteric riddle, contained in the statement "You are . . . ," is inevitably dropped as a lost object, as *object petit a*. Paradoxically, the only true answer to the question is no answer at all—silence.

When the hysteric exposes the insufficiency of the answer offered by the Other (whatever the answer may be), the hysteric is making visible the place where the Other is lacking, a lack that the hysteric is in fact occupying as the insurmountable enigma. Identified with the Other's lack, the hysteric can fantasize becoming the Other's desire. This is a double gesture: on the one hand, it uncovers the Other's lack, yet on the other hand, the hysteric offers herself completely as a plug to cover up the void in the Other. The hysteric's reproach shows the Other's failure, but if there is any room at all for reproach it is because the Other was expected to be complete, to have all answers, and so on. This position of being the "artificial appendix" for the Other's lack is often observed in the devoted sacrifice of the hysteric. Hysterics are often willing to put themselves at the service of another, renouncing their desire in favor of the Other.[5]

Nestor Braunstein (1990) observes that the hysteric places herself as the object that supports the partner; it does not in fact deny the castration in the Other but rather the hysteric's (the hysteric does not have the phallus but may well *be* it). The hysteric aims at occupying a fundamental role for the Other: that of being the object in the Other's fantasy. As we can imagine, the Other is never worth such tremendous sacrifice. Braunstein contends that behind the "sacrificial offering of hysteria" of "all for the other" there is a hope of finding an absolute Other to whom one may offer it All. This "all for the other" reveals that the absolute Other pursued is none other than the Ideal Father, the mythical father proposed by Freud in *Totem and Taboo*. This is a primal father, complete but al-

---

5. Lacan (1991c, p. 289), in Seminar 8, describes this operation with the following formula: $\dfrac{a}{-\varphi} \diamond A$

ways dead, whom the hysteric passionately "sustains beyond all contradictions" (Braunstein 1990, p. 156). Obviously, compared with this Ideal father, anyone will be deficient. What the hysteric is searching for is not her father, but an improved and revised version of him—the complete mythical father. In this sense, we can understand that the hysteric is in fact looking for a Master.

In order to be more precise, let us say that hysteria entails a defensive strategy to avoid all issues raised by castration: hysterics delude the Master, making him believe he is complete, all powerful, and thus they avoid confronting their own castration; they do not deny the Other's castration but rather strategically conceal their own castration. Here castration should be understood as the impossibility of achieving a harmonious rapport between the sexes, because the realization of such utopia of complementarity would require the denial of sexual difference. Even though hysterics try to fill the Other's lack, they never fully succeed in doing so (this is an important difference with perversion).

Millot (1988) has identified this search for a noncastrated primal Ideal father/Master as one of the main features of hysteria. Bertha is looking for a father that would confirm her in her feminine identity. She institutes a father, in fact an Ideal father, the impossible father of the mythical primal horde. Her anger results from the entrapments of the doomed enterprise of finding this primitive father, a noncastrated Other, an Ideal, impossible, dead *Urvater*. She is irritated by the failure of the father but at the same time her ire itself reinstates the father to the position of primal father/Master with all answers/absolute Other.

One may wonder why the hysteric is always hoping to find an absolute Other. This image of paternal omnipotence would correspond to a father that is above desire and would offer the missing guarantee against *jouissance*—an ideal that only a dead or impotent father can fully satisfy (which may explain why the hysteric often encounters that kind of father). The hopeless search for an omnipotent father is structurally comparable to the prospect of being the phallus for the mother, and thus sustains the fantasy of an Other who lacks nothing and desires nothing.[6]

---

6. In the Oedipus complex, initially desire is the desire to become the maternal phallus, the Other's phallus. Nonetheless, the subject always desires from the point of view of another, not just any other but the prehistoric, unforgettable other: the Other.

In order to conceal the anxiety raised by the lack in the Other, the hysteric reduces herself or himself to that which fills the Other's lack. Thus, anger in hysteria is both the result of the unbearable lack of the Other, and of the refusal to be reduced to the object a that fills the other's lack. This specific form of anger can be located in Lacan's formula of hysterical fantasy:

$$\frac{a}{-\varphi} <> A$$

This is how Lacan (1991c) explains this formula: "a [is] the substitutive or metaphorical object, under which something is hiding, this is, the *minus phi*, its own imaginary castration in rapport with the Other" (p. 289). Lacan suggests that we may read this formula as a formula of *desire*. This is to say that through her identification to the objects sustained in the imaginary castration, the hysteric relates to the Other's desire. Let us then read again the formula in this way: the hysteric looks at the castrated Other (A). Confronted with this castration, the hysteric places herself as the object (a) that covers up the Other's castration by identifying with the imaginary object the Other lacks (phallus as an image of loss, $-\varphi$). The (a) concealing the phallus as an image of loss ($-\varphi$) is where the hysteric is placed in relation to/as desire of ($<>$) the Other (A). This "fake" object (a) is the bait the hysteric offers to the Other as a demand that urges the Other to do something, to desire. In order to hide and expose at the same time the Other's castration, the hysteric will rush to become whatever will maintain the fragile illusion of a complete Other. And, as we have seen earlier, the hysteric will be converted into an object tailored to the Other's desire—she will be a witch for the witch hunter, a saint for the believer, someone with the Puerto Rican syndrome for the astounded Army doctor. Robert Levy (1996) argues that Lacan's formula of hysterical fantasy explains why hysteria can be seen as the "structure of all dangers" because it implies the traumatic recognition of the Other (p. 172).

Lacan's formula of hysterical fantasy shows how the hysteric relates to the Other identified to the lack as an object that causes the Other's desire but without a desire of her own. As seen earlier, this Other is the seductive, traumatizing father. The hysteric's love for the father maintains active this fantasy of a dominating Other. Is hysterical anger an expression of a desire to castrate the father? Is this desire to castrate the father equivalent to the desire to kill him? In her anger, the hysteric kills the father but only under the condition that the father will not die.

ELLE FAIT L'HOMME

In Bertha Pappenheim's particular architecture of hysteria, the basic fantasy evolves from impersonating a man—*elle fait l'homme*—and temporarily becoming Paul Berthold, to identifying with her mother and other women and searching for a father. Siding with women, she engages in a quest for the vindication of women versus men. According to the portrait she renders in her early plays, it all suggests that men remain, however, still a little too close to the model of the gluttony of the "always-enjoying" totemic father to whom nothing is forbidden. Her "Women's Right," founded on the refusal to have sexual intercourse, may aim at preserving the belief in "the" woman for whom there would be a sexual rapport. Her concern about prostitutes, as Verhaeghe (1999) contends, tends to preserve the belief in the existence of a sexual rapport: the sexual relationship is a fraud, a make-believe. Only prostitutes (taken advantage of by men) would consent to this deception; "the" woman can only refuse such a fraud and the hysteric will be there to denounce it.

One can see that Bertha Pappenheim's evolution takes a new turn when she starts to follow the discourse of the mother. Her renewed interest in Judaism and her plight against the assimilation of Jews and the decline of religion (Judaism, as we know, is inherited through the mother) came at the same time as she discovered that through her mother she was related to an illustrious feminist heroine. This change in allegiances accompanied her transformation of her oedipal desires. Her antagonism toward her mother became anger at her father as identification with her mother's resentment toward him, which later became a political statement: full-fledged feminism in the name of all women.

By then, she recovered her given name, was recognized for her writings, and achieved wide social recognition for her accomplishments as a social worker. As a response in compensation for the castration of the Other, the former Anna O. longed all her life for a social rapport—her hysterical fantasy, however, produced a life of generous humanitarian deeds and social achievements. The inscription on the German Bertha Pappenheim stamp reads, "*Helfer der Menschheit*" (helper of humanity) (Verhaeghe 1999, p. 142).

In Bertha Pappenheim's case we see anger delineating a *colère*-version as a way of inscribing a particular version of the father. Here one can find an equivalence between Lacan's idea of *père*-version, perversion as a version of the father, and the dynamic role of anger we have sketched both for obsessional neurosis and hysteria. In the first session of his 1975 seminar *Le Sinthome*,[7] Lacan introduced the notion of the father at the core of perversion. "*Perversion*" was understood as "version" toward (*vers*) the father (*père*). Lacan shows that "perversion does not mean anything other than version towards (*vers*) the father (*père*)." His contention underlines the close connection existing in perversion with the law, as well as highlighting the fact that being a father is a doomed enterprise. In this new view on perversion he remarks on the fact that perversion "tends to"; it is not a static construct but rather a movement whose destination is the father. In the case of anger, we also see a movement of investiture and elimination that seems to be toward (*vers*) the father; it even institutes it. Anger is in the name of the father and is directed toward the father supporting the name.

ANNA IN THE TROPICS

The obvious prevalence of anger in Anna O.'s case and in the Puerto Rican syndrome can send us once more to Anna O.'s case. One could even re-baptize this Jewish upper-middle-class hysteric "Ana," and imagine her as a young woman suffering from the Puerto Rican syndrome. The reader should not object too strongly to this forced Hispanization of the most famous hysteric: her symptoms were motor and sensory disturbances (scattered anesthesias, loss of hearing, contractures of extremities, bizarre visual distortion), conditions of "absence," confusion, delirium, alterations of her personality, finally, paroxysms of anxiety and rage. Her hysteric manifestations are exactly the same as those that were identified in descriptions of *ataque de nervios*, the traditional Puerto Rican idiom of distress. Let us not be misled by the commonality of mere symptoms, no matter how striking it appears. All these patients are in fact determined by a common structure, a structure that Anna relentlessly subverts in a paradoxical and paroxysmic (if not always self-defeating) manner: Anna O.'s hysteria did invent many things (psychoanalysis, among others) but it also launched the strategy of defensive attack. Doing this, she ushered in not just a set of pathological symptoms but a whole historical situation; this will be the object of my next chapter.

---

7. Unpublished seminar, class of November 18, 1975.

9

Ataques: *Defensive Violence?*

> Equating hysteria with disadvantage misses half the problem.
> This half is the issue of hysterical violence.
>
> *Juliet Mitchell* (2000, p. x)

The attack has been mentioned in connection to hysteria for centuries—from the Hippocratic corpus, in descriptions of the convulsions caused by the *globus hystericus*, to Charcot's groundbreaking systematization of the *attaque* in four stages uniform in all his patients. Is the hysterical attack so permeable to the prevailing medical paradigms that its rise and changes follow those of medical theories and practice? What are the political implications of its showing primarily among working-class Parisian women in one century and resurfacing among minority members from a marginal social location like New York's *barrio* seven decades later? Let us note that the word *attack* has roots in the Old Italian *attaccare* (to attack, to alter), akin also to the Old Italian *estaccare* (to attach) and to the Old English *staka* (stake). Do the attack's alterations attach, this is, create a link, make a discourse? What is at stake in this mode of attachment?

To answer these questions, let us momentarily put aside its etymology and browse instead through current uses of the word *attack*. As a verb, it is paired with others like assail, assault, bombard, storm, rape, ravish, seize upon. All actions imply forced or violent use of brute strength, bitter words, or weapons. The noun is used to convey an access of disease—a fit of sickness, the duration of a destructive process, an aggression, an offense, an assault, destruction, and warlike moves. There is, however, one interesting definition: in phonetics, by analogy with the bow's touch on the strings in a musical instrument, the attack is the start of articulation of a speech sound. Between the ability to create a discourse and the initiation or articulation of speech, let us hear what the *ataque* might have to say, taking up Lacan's longing remark in Chapter 3, "Where have they gone, the hysterics of olden times . . . ?" (Lacan, 1977a) that reminds us of Freud's main lesson on hysteria: there are illnesses that can speak and convey a truth in what they are saying.

DEFENSIVE VIOLENCE

What truth is the attack conveying? Is the attack a life-preserving strategy or is it self-destructive? Behavioral science has placed a lot of emphasis on the alleged survival value of aggression for the preservation of the species. For Darwin, it was always good for the future of a species if the stronger male rival takes possession of the territory or of the desired female. Obviously, this "Man Meets Dog" model has limits. When animal behavior is applied to humans, one forgets the qualitative jump brought about by language. "Dog barks, Man talks" would be a more adequate slogan. More importantly, the Darwinian model of the survival of the fittest has an ideological function since it easily justifies the colonialist desire to conquer; colonization becomes then something natural to the species and even genetically desirable. This view could be used in the nineteenth century to naturalize imperialism while concealing economic and political dialectics inherent to the colonial encounter, but is hardly tenable today as we are aware of the process by which "primitiveness" was manipulated by ethnocentricism and political domination. The limits of social Darwinism are also clear from a Freudian perspective because homo sapiens acquire not only language but also the death drive. This has to be taken into account whenever we attempt to describe the strategy of the attack.

The death drive and the attack are closely linked. Such connection became clear after four commercial airplanes were hijacked and used as missiles to destroy the World Trade Center and hit the Pentagon. After September 11, 2001, that is, after the *New York Times*'s front page titled "U.S. Attacked" and dense television coverage endlessly repeating the phrase "Attack On America," *attack* now calls up terror, terrorism and threats of war. In all accounts of the tragedy, the term "attack" reappeared over and over again. In the aftershock of the atrocious destruction, a consuming sense of vulnerability settled—the United States and the whole world were shaken by very tangible acts and further threats of destruction. The monumentality of the events and the strong symbolism of the attacks were painful reminders of the proximity of death and devastation. As the country struggled to make sense of the catastrophe, death drive and attacks tended to merge. What was new in this strategy was the fact that suicide bombers were ready to die when perpetrating their actions. They had actually turned the hijacked victims into other suicide killers, thus making their own death drive strategic, which entailed totally new sets of preventive measures. What had often been described as the weapon of weak and dispossessed minorities, like blowing oneself up with lots of explosives in a crowd, had become an engine of mass destruction. Terrorism opens an era of new warfare, where the strategy "You die and I survive" is replaced by a new strategy: "We will all die and use our deaths to kill even more people."

Yet, was the attack mere terrorism or really already war? In response to the attack, the idea of war crept in, from Pearl Harbor to cries of military revenge. The enemy behind all this was not a government but an elusive multinational organization that knew how to exploit the death drive with political vengeance. A schoolboy interviewed on TV in the aftermath asked the naïve but obvious question: "What have we done to them to make them so mad at us?" While the terrorists who organized and carried out mass slaughter did not issue any demand or proposition, the attacks spelled out anti-American feelings fueled by fundamentalist discourse. It was more than hatred of modernity or technology-envy that incensed them. The U.S. involvement in the complex global reality beyond its frontiers, including its whole foreign policy, past interventions, economic sanctions, military occupations, having financed and supported rebel groups in various countries, demanded serious discussion. The fundamentalist discourse that elicited such heinous acts provoked cries for revenge, feelings of rage, and a sense of righteousness that seemed disquietingly similar to the arguments put forward by the terrorists. They suggested a dichotomy, an "us" and "them" mentality. Did this all stem from the same aggression, the same death drive? Or is it that radically suicidal mass destruction is the only discourse of resistance possible? Why is this discourse that speaks through acts and not words the only way out when facing a superpower perceived as controlling all the strings at work behind a globalization—a process that is seen as ensnaring the entire world in an ineluctable logic of imperialistic domination?

To explain this, we need to have recourse to the notion of *jouissance*. Both at a political and individual level, imaginary thresholds separate people from each other, justify labels, underpin bellicose cries and creeds, prevent us from sharing our destinies. As we have seen, the way reality becomes real is through fantasy since fantasy is the window through which we frame and construct reality. It is also fantasy that underlines national discourses or ideological positions—fantasy regulates the relationships of individuals to the collective and to each other.[1] When one may fear that the other threatens "our way of life" or turns into "a godless devil," what is at play is a logic according to which the Other has an excess enjoyment, a surplus *jouissance* that excludes me and threatens my integrity. Since fantasy is primary to politics, one can see how acting out fantasies of survival and destruction perpetuate the fear of the other—this fear increases once the other is attacked or even destroyed. From the social horror of terrorism to our everyday dislikes of neighbors, we are made aware of the primacy of deadly impulses. While the aim of all life is death, civilization imposes the renunciation of powerful drives, not always successfully serving the purpose of protecting human beings from themselves. The practice of listening to the unconscious teaches us that the horror of this *jouissance* is not only to be found in others, but also is in fact lurking in us.

MAL DE PELEA[2]

In a similar manner, war, death, and mass destruction were also at the core of the Puerto Rican syndrome. Why is the term *ataque*'s polysemy so prevalent and charged by military overtones? Let us reexamine the situation of

---

1. A community is held together by a shared rapport to the Thing and this rapport is sustained by fantasy.
2. Disease of fighting.

those Puerto Rican soldiers initially diagnosed with Puerto Rican syndrome in the 1950s, during the military training process leading to the Korean War battlefield, suffering strange symptoms that defied anatomy and resembled those of classic hysteria. Those men seemed to have been made sick by the perspective of a war situation. Given their colonial situation, they not only had been the victims of previous aggressions but they were being trained to become aggressors themselves. They were armed, they were dangerous, they were given power. The taboo of killing was temporarily going to be suspended for them—they were not only victims of war who killed and feared retaliation but they could be allowed to enjoy killing enemies. They were to be permitted the exercise of a forbidden pleasure. They were going to be authorized by the state of war to act out unconscious deadly impulses. Were they prepared to process the psychic implications of acting out something destined to remain just a fantasy? War was forcing them to confront the actuality of the hatred of the neighbor, the subjectivation of one's own death, the horror of something in front of which words stop. Their symptoms attempted to answer the heavy load of questions brought about by murderous or suicidal aggressiveness. Required to confront the impossible, they found in their very dead-end the life force of action. The *ataque de nervios*, also known as *mal de pelea* (fighting disease), calls up the ancient dictum "The best defense is attack." For human beings, as Lacan (1977b) contends, "constitute [their] world by [their] suicide" (p. 28). According to this death drive-laden logic, in a dead-end situation, the attack, or *ataque*, appears as the best defense.

We have noted how from the early texts on the Puerto Rican syndrome to the recent literature on *ataque de nervios* most interpretations take divergent points of view with one notable exception: reiterated issues of control, aggression, and anger emerge as the main common feature. As we have seen, very early on Rothenberg (1964) identifies aggressiveness as a predominant aspect of what he names "Puerto Rican hysterical attacks." Rothenberg also notes that his patients commonly used the term "nervousness" to mean anger. This suggests that *nervios* (nerves) contains "anger." An *ataque de nervios*, then, becomes an anger attack, or even better, a substitute for an angry attack. The clinical examples he quotes confirm this claim: "A 40-year-old Puerto Rican Army specialist requested psychiatric treatment. . . . When asked what he meant by 'nervousness,' he replied, 'When I'm working and can't get something done, I get frustrated and then I get nervous. Also, when I'm home sitting in front of the television set I get, like you say, angry about something and I'm nervous.'"[3] He quotes another example of a 29-year-old Puerto Rican Army cook who requested treatment for "nervousness" (p. 965). Further exploration showed that after one violent episode in the kitchen he was afraid that he was going to lose his temper. Yet, he described his emotions as "nervousness." Rothenberg further elaborates that the use of the word "nervousness" instead of rage or anger betrays a distinctively Puerto Rican cultural phenomenon. He notes that Puerto Ricans emphasize personal qualities of *dignidad* (dignity) and *hospitalidad* (hospitality), suppressing assertiveness and aggressiveness. This repression tends to create sudden outbursts of anger. Let us not forget the troubling proximity in their Latin roots between *hostis* (host, enemy) and *hospes* (refuge). Hospitality is never far from hostility. Rothenberg argues, "In Puerto Rican hysterical attacks, one important kind of fantasy frequently represented in the direct violence, the hyperkinesis and the self-mutilation, is an *aggressive* one" (p. 963). Is *aggression* (that has nothing to do with reality and that is mostly an imaginary relation), or rather *aggressivity*, the "strangulated affect" that cannot find a way out through speech? Rothenberg contends that "[a]ctually, the superficially warm, friendly Puerto Rican is a slighty passive, unassertive person, who at times can be moved to extreme outbursts of anger" (p. 965). Rothenberg's analyses are revealing:

> Puerto Ricans are not particularly militaristic. They are generally not attracted to the military service, the organization which provides social sanction for violence (at least in time of war). Among many of the Puerto Rican pre-inductees evaluated psychiatrically by the present author and his associates over a period of two years, in fact, anxiety appears significantly increased simply because of being called for induction. A prominent factor in their anxiety seemed to be that the military was seen as a symbol of violence. This was true for those of this group who were ultimately rejected because of severe symptomatology. Such a finding is probably common in pre-inductees everywhere. For the Puerto Rican, however, it is in sharp contrast to the high level of actual violence on the island. Moreover, exceptional fear of violence is often indicative of repressed hostility. [p. 965]

---

3. Note that Rothenberg clarifies that "like you say" in this example does not refer to anything anyone actually said to the patient.

ATAQUES: DOMINATION, SLAVERY, COLONIALISM

The *ataque* appears more and more clearly as a strategy of defense. Therefore, one may wonder about the real source of the violence the *ataque* is still defending against today. Unhappily, the oppressive conditions that may exercise violence have not changed since Rothenberg identified them in 1964. Besides a long history of colonization, he notes the oppressive role of the military in Puerto Rican history, the rupture of the family unit brought about by industrialization, migration, and high unemployment. How could Puerto Ricans be attracted to the military service when the U.S. Army embodies a colonial power that denies their status as other, positioning colonized subjects as an inferior counterpart, as a subaltern? Like more recent analyses by DeLaCancela and colleagues (1986), Iris Zavala-Martínez (1981) interprets *ataques* by taking into account the disempowering effect of the colonial experience. She argues that *ataques* communicate anger at and resistance to oppression, whether generated by the family or social institutions. Guarnaccia and colleagues (1989) include this sociocultural perspective when referring to the "micro-politics of Puerto Rican gender and social relations" and to "the macro-political impacts of changing gender roles and social relationships resulting from the industrialization of the Island as part of the on-going colonial status of Puerto Rico" (p. 361).

If we look at the wider political dimension of the *ataque*, we need to understand the semantic and political logic behind the translation of *ataque de nervios* into the pejorative dubbing of "Puerto Rican syndrome" in the 1950s. The new label suppressed an important word that functioned as a fundamental signifier—"attack." The history of Puerto Rico offers a potent armory of events for opening up what appears as a long history of recurrent attacks, as if the word *ataque* could provide a key concept in colonial strategies. Hence the relation of hysteria to history cannot be disregarded. The historical context of such *ataques* spans over five centuries. In pre-Columbian times, the Caribes attacked several times the indigenous Taínos who populated Borinquen (land of the Haughty Lord), as the island of Puerto Rico was then named. The Taínos were an agricultural, peaceful, cooperative tribal community, a subculture of the Arawaks from South America estimated in numbers from 50,000 to 70,000. On November 19, 1493, guided by Taíno Indians who had formerly been prisoners of the Caribes, Christopher Columbus identified Borinquen and "discovered" it. By renaming it San Juan Bautista, he claimed the island for the Spanish crown.

The first years of Spanish domination were peaceful. René Marqués (1972) attributes the controversial Puerto Rican people's "docility and hospitality" to the Taínos' nonviolent nature. "Docility" is a national feature that has been the focus of analysis in numerous essays on Puerto Rican identity; it has been interpreted as a sign of insularity, as an irrepressible propensity to laziness, even as a feminine trait. Nonetheless, following Freud's (1930) argument in *Civilization and Its Discontents*, one might be tempted to see in this feature less an indication of weakness than a sign of a higher level of civilization. If, as Freud explains, society is always threatened with disintegration under the force of aggressive drives, civilization "obtains mastery over the individual's dangerous desire for aggression by disarming it and by setting up an agency within to watch over it, like a garrison in a conquered city" (p. 84). We shall return to this point soon. Let us also take into consideration that the Taínos' deferential attitude toward the Spaniards was in conformity with their religious credo—they believed the Spaniards were immortal gods claiming a wealth belonging to them. Thus, during the first thirty years of Spanish settlement, the mineral reserves of the island—rich in gold— were almost depleted. By 1570 the production of gold had ceased altogether. The initial financial success and mineral wealth of the colony may be partly responsible for the new name "Puerto Rico" or "rich port." Paradoxically, once the gold mines were depleted, this "rich port" became one of the poorest islands in the Caribbean. As the natural resources diminished, so did the tales of riches, and the struggling colony became more clearly a military outpost.

A CYCLE OF AGGRESSION

Initially, the European colonizers profited hugely from the power conferred by the sacred position they had been endowed with by the religious beliefs of the Taínos. In addition, the Spanish crown created the *encomienda* system that assigned to each Spanish colonizer from thirty-three to 300 Indians who were to serve them in exchange for being taught Catholic religion and being assimilated into Spanish culture. In face of the violence of the exploitation, such peaceful cohabitation could not last.

Before planning any attack, the local Taínos conducted an experiment that dramatically challenged their belief in the Spaniards' immortality. Led by Gurayoian, an elder cacique, they immersed a young Spanish officer for several hours in a river. When he clearly did not awake, the caciques declared war and attacked the new settlers. The Spaniards, who were better armed, subdued the uprising. Ponce de León ordered 6,000 to be killed. The survivors escaped to the mountains or left the island altogether. In 1514, the Spanish crown granted Spaniards permission to marry Taíno Indians. That same year the Caribe Indians attacked and destroyed several Spanish settlements. In 1529, once again there was an attack—Caribes assailed the new settlers. And thus a history of endless attacks to the island began. Now, new attacks also came from European floats. Arturo Morales Carrión[4] identifies "a cycle of aggression," a pattern of repeated foreign attacks that wore out the colony and retarded its growth.

> [T]he social history of Puerto Rico is inseparably linked with the international chaos that reigned in the Caribbean as Spain's enemies swarmed into the vital area to plunder, sack or destroy the offshoots of the empire. The attacks upon the island hindered the colonization process and, hardly profitable to the aggressor, were partially responsible for bringing about a schism in the social life of the colony throughout the first three centuries of Spanish rule. [quoted in Caro Costas 1977, pp. 216–217]

For centuries, the Caribbean was a battlefield for Europe. Between 1527 and 1576 alone, we can list English, French, and Dutch raids on San Juan Bautista. Buccaneers, filibusters, corsairs, and pirates joined the attacks. To respond and resist the repeated sallies, *El morro*, the famous stone-sentry of San Juan de Puerto Rico, was reinforced. Even a rebuilt fort was not strong enough to protect the city from further offensives. Therefore, in 1634 a "major defensive structure," a wall 21 feet high and 18 feet wide circumvallating the city, started construction (Morales Carrión 1983, pp. 22–23). Centuries of overseas armed assaults from European powers followed until 1898, when an American nation attacked Puerto Rico—on May 12, U.S. Navy bombs exploded against this very wall in San Juan during the Spanish-American war. This attack proved successful and on July 25, 1898, U.S. troops came ashore in the south-

---

4. Morales Carrión, A. *Puerto Rico and the Non Hispanic Caribbean: A Study in the Decline of Spanish Exclusivism.* Rio Piedras: University of Puerto Rico Press, in Caro Costas 1977.

ern town of Guánica, landed unopposed, and started the invasion of the Puerto Rican territory.

PUERTO RICO: THE UNIVERSITY OF WAR

Since the history of Puerto Rico is a history of attacks (the island suffered the natural assaults of hurricanes and disease as well as the attacks of soldiers and pirates), the role played by the military in Puerto Rico reveals the island's major strategic position in colonial policy, be it Spanish or American. Ever since the beginning of Spanish rule the island was built as a garrison state with troops massed in the capital's fortress. This strong armed forces presence created what Gordon Lewis (1963) calls a military society. From the very first days of the conquest of the New World, the island's privileged geographical location as a key position in the defense of the Spanish Empire was evident. Puerto Rico was the stopping and storing port for Spanish ships full of cargo with treasures and supplies. The island is situated between the Caribbean and Atlantic, becoming a strategic link between the two continents. All European navies wanted to invade the island and gain control of this crucial place, guaranteeing military hegemony and control in the Caribbean.[5] The politics of such a geographically advantageous location have not changed. In hearings in 1980 before the Committee on Armed Services, Rear Admiral Arthur Knoizen pondered the advantages of the strategic position of U.S. military facilities in Puerto Rico, now at the center of the U.S. military training—"our university of the sea."

> Only in the Roosevelt Roads complex we train simultaneously in all varieties of missile firings, air to ground ordinance, surface gunfire support, underwater, surface, and air launched torpedo firing, submarine calibrations, amphibious operations, and electronic warfare. All this . . . makes the complex our university of the sea for training our Atlantic Fleet and allied navies.[6]

---

5. Cuba is a similar case—let us recall that the Spanish-American War was waged initially to liberate Cuba from Spanish rule.

6. Naval training activities on the island of Vieques, Puerto Rico. Hearings before the Committee on Armed Services, House, 96th Congress, second session, Washington, DC, 1980, p. 100, quoted in Fernández 1994, p. 101.

Admiral William O'Connor made the following declaration in 1985. When praising the advantages of Puerto Rico, he again uses the rhetorics of a "university of war." We do not need further commentary:

> Puerto Rico is the best training field in the world for the U.S. Army. Here we can combine all elements and practice each stage of naval war, as we would do it in combat. The Navy truly desires this 'piece of real estate' and enjoys being down here with the Puerto Rican people. We can realize shooting practices with missile ships; we can bring airplanes from the United States to attack our fighting groups and be intercepted by war airplanes that take off from our ships. . . . Therefore in the zone of operations of Puerto Rico we can practice all the aspects of Naval war. . . . [Puerto Rico] is like a university of naval war. [Estades Font 1988, back cover]

From the beginning of American rule, the United Sates established a military occupation of the island. Two years after the invasion, Puerto Rico was granted its first civilian government (a United States-appointed governor). Puerto Rico was then called an "unincorporated territory"[7] and the population was called "the People of Puerto Rico." Not only was the new civilian government under the jurisdiction of the U.S. Department of War, but the first civilian governor appointed, Charles Allen, arrived in Puerto Rico after leaving his post as Sub-Secretary of the Navy. In 1917, during World War I, the government of the island was reorganized. The U.S. Congress granted citizenship to Puerto Ricans and drafted them as soldiers immediately. By 1918, of the 236,853 Puerto Ricans who had been registered only 17,855 were actually drafted, mostly due to obstacles created by the prevailing system of racial segregation in the Army at the time (Estades Font 1988). There was no training camp on the island that could accommodate the new recruits, and the alleged reason for not sending them to the U. S. South was that they did not speak English and would not like the colder weather. Finally, a training camp and a military hospital were built in Puerto Rico in 1918, consolidating the presence of a stronger U.S. military structure that included the "natives." Altogether, the participation of Puerto Rican soldiers in twentieth-century wars, from

---

7. The wording of the Foraker Act may remind us of the 1903 U.S. treaty with France for Louisiana and the 1819 U.S treaty with Spain acquiring Florida. In both the unincorporated territories, natives were not granted citizenship.

World War I and World War II to Korea and Vietnam, has been proportionally much higher than that of any U.S. state (Garcia Passalacqua 1984). Of the more than 90,000 Puerto Ricans who served in the armed forces during the Korean War, 90 percent were volunteers.[8] Not surprisingly Gordon Lewis (1963) notes that in Puerto Rico "it would be difficult . . . to find any small town on the island that does not possess its quota of younger people with stateside experience, or of veterans of American Armed Services" (p. 7).

ATTACKS AND ASSAULTS

In order to interpret the political meaning of the translation of the *ataque* as the Puerto Rican syndrome, let us explore the Puerto Rican context of what should now be called a "defensive attack." I will focus specifically on the 1950s, time of the invention of the Puerto Rican syndrome, but also a period of intense unrest that turned out to be the real breeding ground for this hysteria.

During that time Puerto Rico passed through troubled waters. Political turmoil was marked by numerous violent attacks. This was a decade of nationalist uprisings and bloody demonstrations. Among the preceding events we may underline that 1948 was a stormy year—the first election of a governor was celebrated and the FBI recovered 10,000 rounds of stolen ammunition that were rumored to be seized by Nationalists. Also early in 1948, President Truman visited the island and declared that "Puerto Rican people should have the right to determine for themselves Puerto Rico's political relationship to the continental United States" (Johnson 1980, p. 33). Truman's message raised expectations. Tumultuous Nationalist-linked demonstrations at the university unfolded and they were broken up by the police with tear gas. The newly elected governor, Luis Munoz Marin, formerly pro-independence, began pushing the commonwealth idea. Roberta Ann Johnson (1980) notes that while Muñoz Marín and his party tried to legitimize a commonwealth as a viable and dignified status alternative, the Nationalists responded with a terrorist campaign. On October 30, 1950, just days before the registration

---

8. Commonwealth of Puerto Rico, *Facts and Figures, 1964, 1965*, p. 8, quoted in Johnson 1980.

for the first referendum that would give Puerto Rico the option of remaining a colony or changing status, Nationalists launched armed attacks in several Puerto Rican towns. The Nationalists represented a minority and the revolt started more as a gesture of protest aiming at attracting the world's attention to the cause of independence than an effective plan to overthrow the government. The old Nationalist leader from the 1930s, Dr. Pedro Albizu Campos, was surrounded on the island after a two-day siege of his house by the police and led into captivity on November 2, 1950. In the meanwhile there had been another attack, this time on the U.S. mainland. On November 1, 1950, two New York Nationalists, Oscar Collazo and Griselo Torresola, attacked the residence of President Harry S Truman. One Secret Service man was killed, another wounded, while Torresola was shot and killed and Collazo wounded in the chest (Ribes Tovar 1973). Again, the death of President Truman was not their aim. According to Fernández, who interviewed one surviving perpetrator, Collazo and Torresola had taken an oath to defend their *patria*—they assaulted Blair House "to focus the attention of the world on the colonial status of Puerto Rico and its people" (Fernández 1994, p. 80).

Four years later, on March 1, 1954, Lolita Lebrón, Andrés Figueroa, Rafael Cancel Miranda, and Irving Flores, all from New York, unfurled a Puerto Rican flag at the visitors' gallery of the House of Representatives in Washington, DC, shouting, "Long live free Puerto Rico!" Then they started shooting at the members of Congress; five of them were wounded. A note in English was found in Lolita Lebrón's handbag. It read: "I give my life for the liberty of my country. I take full responsibility for everything" (Ribes Tovar 1973, p. 526). Seventeen Puerto Ricans were implicated and charged with conspiracy; of them, thirteen were found guilty (Hunter 1966, p. 125). In the trials that followed these two last Puerto Rican attacks, Oscar Collazo rejected any suggestion that his defense would be based on a plea of insanity. He was condemned to the electric chair (Fernández 1994). Albizu Campos, who was charged on six counts that included subversive activities, attack with intent to kill, and four violations of a law requiring registration of firearms (Johnson 1980), was considered by the U.S. authorities "a psychopathic case, perhaps actually insane."[9] In a congressman's report, Albizu Campos's powerful rhetoric appeared described as "acid tongue," mainly

9. Acosta, I. (1987). *La Mordaza*. Río Piedras: Edit, p. 48, quoted by Fernández, 1994, p. 76.

understood in terms of personal pathology.[10] During the trial of Lolita Lebrón and her three co-defendants, she interrupted the proceedings, crying "No!" three times when lawyer Ehrich tried to claim that the defendants were insane (Ribes Tovar 1973, p. 528). During Lebrón's trial, Rafael Cancel Miranda declared that "as self respecting Puerto Ricans they could no longer live without protesting the aggression against Puerto Rico" (p. 529). While it would be rash or misleading to collapse the hysterical symptoms manifested by Puerto Rican soldiers during the Korean War and the violent political actions led by various groups of nationalists because they somehow took place at the same time, I wish to stress the similar pathologization of these disruptive manifestations. While violent demonstrations, shootings, and rioting in the name of nationalist resistance cannot be called hysteria but political struggle, when this is perceived from the point of view of the Other—that is, in this case, from the American doxa of law and order—then the subversion of order can only be made sense of by being reduced to a madness seen as stubbornly opposing civilization.

THE ATTACK COUNTERATTACKS

Reviewing the most recent bibliography on *ataque*, we confirm that *ataque* continues to represent the challenges and symptomatic formations produced by the "inability to manage anger" (Mehlman 1961, p. 332) in what is repeatedly described as a peaceful and hospitable community. However, we should emphasize that the *ataque* can also be interpreted as an inventive way around the restrictions imposed by prohibitions of any direct expression of anger. Lillian Comas-Díaz (1982) argues that in a culture in which the expression of anger is repressed, the *ataque* serves to release aggression in a relatively acceptable way. In a similar manner, Nydia Garcia-Prieto (1982) claims that Puerto Ricans handle anger by having *ataques de nervios.*

> Anger, which is usually precipitated by discord in social relationships, is discharged, and secondary gains, such as being able to exercise control over one's family or to receive protective care and attention from others, may result. Whatever guilt may be associated with the aggressive behavior is alleviated by claiming amnesia. [p. 174]

---

10. See "The Nationalist Party," a report prepared at the request of Hon. Fred Crawford, member of the Committee of Interior and Insular Affairs, Washington DC, 1951, quoted by Fernández 1994, p. 76.

According to García-Prieto and Comas-Díaz, when Puerto Ricans are in distress and can no longer contain their exasperation, the *ataque* is the best way of losing control, discharging pent-up anger, and obtaining gains like the activation of the social support system. Thus an interesting and revelatory new feature of the *ataque* emerges: the multiple dimension of an experience of "loss of control" that reflects an unsettling social and personal context yet paradoxically serves the purpose of regaining control.

A very detailed and rigorous study conducted recently by Guarnaccia and colleagues (1996) based on numerous individual descriptions of *ataques de nervios* has concluded that in all accounts the dominant theme was "an over-riding sense of loss of control; a threat to the person's social order; emotions of sadness and anger; and expressions of distress in the form of physical symptoms, aggressive outbursts and loss of consciousness" (p. 350). In another landmark study, Roberto Lewis-Fernández (1998) expands the scope of the experience of "loss of control" and identifies it as the core feature in both *ataques* (the paroxysm) and "nerves" (the condition). But what is this "nervous" need to exercise "control" over anger that reaches an outbreak in the *ataque*? And how can loss of control contribute to exercise of control? To answer these questions, let us return to what many literary classics as well as canonical social studies on the Caribbean have defined as a main cultural feature: the "docility" or "passivity" of Caribbean people (see Marqués 1972, Pedreira 1934). As we have seen, these characteristics have been associated with lack of virility, resistance to progress, laziness, a fragile national project, or even the inability to build a nation-state. Lewis-Fernández (1998) contends that the "tranquility" of Puerto Ricans stems from a prevalent cultural system of "control." "Tranquility" here is neither a sign of weakness nor a negative feature. For Lewis-Fernandez follows Antonio Benitez-Rojo's contention that people from Caribbean cultures have a model of "performance" according to which dance substitutes for war (the *Capoeira* of slaves in Brazil seems to confirm this claim—a martial art disguised as dance). According to Benitez-Rojo, Caribbeans confront situations not directly but in a "sinuous," "acuatic," or "rhythmic" manner. Thus, Lewis-Fernández interprets the "performative" not as a passive response but rather as an active defense (in the Freudian sense) against violence. For him, "control" opposes aggressiveness; remaining calm or "in control," one can disarm violence.

Negrón-Muntaner, Grosfoguel, and Georas (Negrón-Muntaner and Grosfoguel 1997) have postulated a similar form of performance as a strategy that makes survival and subversion possible, despite its contradictions.

These authors call it *jaiba* politics (p. 30). They take this metaphor from *jaiba*, a mountain crab that advances by moving sideways. In Puerto Rican usage, the word *jaiberia* refers to collective practices of nonconfrontation and evasion. We may note an interesting homology of structure between *jaiberia* and *ataque*: both are forms of rebellion, "of complicitous critique or subversive complicity [that] point to an acknowledgment of being in a disadvantageous position within a particular field of power. A non-heroic position, *jaiberia* favors endurance over physical strength, and privileges ambiguity over clarity." *Ataque* and *jaiberia* both follow "an active, low-intensity strategy to obtain the maximum benefits of a situation with the minimum blood spilled" (p. 31). Negrón-Muntaner, Grosfoguel, and Georas put *jaiberia* in line with Diana Fuss's (1994) "mimicry without identification" (pp. 28–29) and Linda Hutcheon's (1989) "postmodernist parody" (p. 26).

A WAY OUT WHEN THERE IS NONE

Joseph Heller's (1971) famous novel that popularized the expression "Catch-22" both exemplifies the ancient dictum that says "the best defense is attack" and offers us a good illustration of how the *ataque's* strategy of what we may call *jaiba* nonheroism, nonconfrontation, and evasion could become liberating in an otherwise impossible situation. If Yossarian, the main character of the novel, would not be a paranoiac, as it is commonly said, but a hysteric, he would have found a compromise solution—getting sick and tired of war, he would have developed bizarre inexplicable symptoms that no Army psychiatrist could decode. Rather than producing unpalatable paranoid delusions, if Yossarian would have fallen to the floor, foamed at the mouth, and fainted, or would have had nonepileptic seizures and sudden outbursts of anger, he would have fulfilled the requirements of the label of Puerto Rican syndrome. Confronted with an otherwise impossible situation, the *ataque* would have crippled Yossarian although offering a way out when there is none.

If one wants to avoid the trap of treating the Puerto Rican syndrome as a conscious strategy of manipulation, one should approach the *ataque* or Puerto Rican syndrome by interrogating the unconscious desire contained in this symptomatic formation. Let us go back to the five clinical examples quoted in Chapter 7. Those scared and disoriented soldiers running around the rooms screaming, twirling their arms, and having seizures were creating a spectacle that shook those in a position of authority and forced them to see something different. It is as if those extravagant manifestations that entered medical records under the label "Puerto Rican syndrome" were in fact messages, at times opaque, neither comprehended nor controlled by the subject, offered to the field of the Other—messages staged as a provocation, a call for attention, still awaiting the right decoding, the just interpretation.

In those examples, the *ataque* "makes a scene," stages a desire not fully integrated in the Symbolic, which remains mostly enacted in the field of the Imaginary. This form of hysterical attack, as acting out, includes a deferred verbalization that is addressed to an Other that fails to recognize the other as its *semblable* or resembling other (we shall return to this point in the next chapter). Within this logic, the *ataque* is both a reconstruction and a manifestation; it is a defense: "Here I am, without my understanding of what it means" or "My dramatic, at times explosive, symptoms will force you to recognize me."

MULTIPLE PURPOSES OF THE ATTACK

Freud mentions the fact that the hysterical attack is made to serve multiple purposes, at times contradictory. To illustrate it, he gives the example of the case of an hysteric patient who tore off her dress with one hand while she struggled to keep the dress in place with the other hand. This contradiction that appears as a general feature of the attack reveals its enabling and disabling aspect, in which opposite tendencies are acted out and coexist.

Since the Puerto Rican syndrome was initially a label created in a military setting in the aftermath of an inconclusive war and in order to give an account of mysterious symptoms in Puerto Rican soldiers, it is interesting to note how the dynamics and politics of the syndrome evolve according to the logics of a hysterical mode of discourse. The syndrome serves a double purpose: on the one hand, the "mirror stage" dread of fragmentation may be resolved in violence. Yet on the other hand, these soldiers do not completely identify with the Master. Their violence, which presupposes a symbolic destitution, is sent back to the Master. Thus, the Puerto Rican syndrome could express a return to the Other of its message in an inverted form. The message would be: "I will turn you into an efficient soldier in the best army in the world on behalf of your belonging to a greater nation, the U.S." In return, the message traverses a "conversion" and becomes: "I'm incapable of being efficient, soldierly, 'aggressive' in my violence. The only violence you can release in me is uncontrollable. It 'attacks' others or myself without discrimination. Therefore I cannot be useful for your imperialist program. I'm disabled." This explains why this violence is not directed toward one particular figure as would be the case in a paranoia geared at the hated mimetic double. This is a mode of violence that is discriminatory but has no definite object. Unlike paranoiac violence, it is a pantomimic violence that represents the Other's violence. The *ataque* mimics so as to render the Other inconsistent, absurd, senseless.

The Puerto Rican syndrome contains a violence that "explodes" by rebelling against a situation of subjection, and that disqualifies the subject of violence. The histrionic paroxysm of the Puerto Rican syndrome shows that it is not simply violence; it is a defense, but at the same time a dramatization (a *mise en scène*) of the vacillations of Puerto Rican nationalism. They no longer restore the union, they explode. Their explosion destroys also their own homes and damages their own people; it seems to be violence in search of a limit. The *ataque* is a message sent to the Other in want of a response, in the hope of a better sublimation of aggressiveness.

As with any hysteria, the Puerto Rican syndrome presents itself as a riddle. This riddle supposes an other (an Army doctor, an *espiritista*, a social worker, a psychoanalyst) capable of solving it. This enigmatic set of symptoms compels this other to respond: as if asking the question "What am I?" or better said, "Tell me who am I so that I can know what you want me to be." These questions ask, in fact: "What am I for the Other?" This is a question that asks for an answer that is doomed to fail, because no answer can make things whole. The Puerto Rican syndrome, as it were, responds, "I am not a soldier to exercise your violence with, but someone who resists your violence and challenges it, making it explode." In previous chapters we have seen veterans expecting some compensation for the state of permanent disability, the "deficiency" produced by the training. Their subjectivity is asserted when it is "pathologically" expressed in the attack. The attack comprises pathological manifestations that resist a position of service, but once they have been discharged from service, soldiers expect to be awarded compensation or pension benefits. Here is a refusal that is enabling, a rebellious aspect that challenges the Master's discourse. It is true that it is doubled by a disabling aspect: it seems that in many cases a compensation is expected as the only outcome of war, a permanent status as a disabled veteran. One may question the enjoyment represented by the disability compensation that appears as a surplus production of enjoyment in the transaction with the Master.

From a social perspective one could say that the patients diagnosed with Puerto Rican syndrome identify with the object *petit a*, the object cause of desire, sacrificing themselves to cause the desire of the Master while sustaining the illusion of a complete Master. Identified with the object *a*, their fate is that of any object located as *a*—soon to be discarded, "disabled." Here, the fascination with the demand of the Master becomes a trap that prevents the possibility of the subject to assume his or her own speech and act. However, the hysterical structure prevails: the Master will eventually be shown lacking and be dismissed. Looking for an ideal father, the hysteric will find a new Master to appoint, and the cycle is renewed.

The ataque is prevalently described in the bibliography as an experience of being *fuera de control* (out/outside control) (Lewis-Fernandez 1998). Attention to these specific signifiers reveals a double meaning: being *out* of control may entail a lack of control over a situation. However, being *out of* or *outside* control may also convey liberation from an oppressive situation or state. Guarnaccia and colleagues (1996) contend that the *ataque de nervios* is a metaphor that encapsulates social bodily experiences that can be heard as an enraged voice of resistance: "One can also read *ataques de nervios* as a voice of protest against the neo-colonial transformations of Puerto Rico which in many ways have undone the lives of working class poor women *and* men in Puerto Rico" (p. 362).

Since no definition can fully encompass the Puerto Rican syndrome, it always leaves something to be desired. The Puerto Rican syndrome stages a failed encounter, and could be read as a hysterical seduction of the Master, a seduction that challenges the imaginary wholeness of the Master. The return of the violence seems the only possible defense: the *ataque* is the way a hysteric can send back to the Master his message in an inverted form. Thus, all the expressions used in colonial discourse tend to reappear (with a significant difference) in the discourse of the colonized. For instance, the vernacular use of the expression *dar coraje* (literally, give courage—a quality after all, essential if one wants to produce good soldiers) is used typically in Puerto Rico to mean "anger." It is as if the word rage could be heard in "courage." This sounds like a pun, almost like the English idiom "rage in courage," but obeys the same logic of semantic reversibility.

A similar logic of reversible appropriations underpins the way American culture prepared for the incorporation of the new Puerto Rican state. One of the first actions in U.S. colonial policy was to change the name of the island from *Puerto* Rico to *Porto* Rico. This modification was preceded by a notorious hesitation in the spelling of the name of the island before the island was invaded by U.S. troops. In the news coverage and documentation of the period immediately preceding the U.S. invasion, the island appeared already alternatively "Americanized" as "Porto Rico" or in its original Spanish name. Immediately following the invasion, on July 30, 1898, the *Times* was faithful to the Spanish when reporting that "the American troops were received by the entire population, . . . the piers, balconies, roofs and streets being alive with *Puertoricans* representing every class" (OED 1989, italics mine). This indecision about what language to use for the island's name can be read as revealing the "unsayable" within the contradictions of a country that is not prepared yet to think of itself as "colonial."

The official new name was a straightforward derivation from a common designation for the island in nineteenth-century English. Yet, while the island was called Porto Rico also in French and Dutch, in English the islanders were called both Porto Ricans and Porto Riqueneans.[11]

Evidently, the change in appellation constitutes a first colonial act of appropriation. Nonetheless, as Nancy Morris (1995) notes, the change in name was produced by an official misspelling, one may say, by an official parapraxis. "A curious oversight in the drafting of the Foraker Act caused the name of the island to be officially misspelled. The law established a civil government for the island of 'Porto Rico.' In writing the bill, Congress followed the spelling in the English text of the Treaty of Paris, the document through which Spain had ceded the island to the United States" (p. 27). This transcription error had momentous political implications. As Hugo Rodríguez-Vecchini notes, "By virtue of the Foraker Act, the previous Spanish citizens of Puerto Rico became the citizens of *Porto Rico* (sic), i.e. citizens legally and orthographically without a country or citizenship" (Torre et al. 1994, p. 69). Thus, in an "imperialist" parapraxis, Puerto Rico became Porto Rico. This renaming carried along important consequences

---

11. The *Oxford English Dictionary* quotes in the entry "*Puerto Rican*" the 1858 J.T. O'Neil, *Mem. Island Porto Rico* in R.S. Fisher *Spanish West Indies,* p. 152: "The Porto Riqueneans . . . are generally indolent." 1891 R.T. Hill, *Cuba and Porto Rico* xv, p. 146: "The Cubans are fired with the spirit of progress and infected with American notions, while the Porto Ricans are plodding along in contentment."

regarding the legitimization of imperialist expansion and a practice of linguistic colonial domination (see Hill 1899).

The officially misspelled new name was easier to pronounce for English speakers and corresponded to the standard English designation at the time. Yet the new name did not conform to the actual name found in the original treaty of annexation but to that of its translation. "Porto Rico," as it were, was a new place with a new name. Regarding the transliteration from Puerto Rico to Porto Rico, it is interesting to note that "Porto" does not mean *port*. "Porto" constitutes a new signifier, a neologism in English and in Spanish that retains in its exotism a middle position between *puerto* and *port*, ironically illustrating the ambiguous and intermediate situation, the "in-between" of the Puerto Rican population. Even though the official designation Porto Rico was changed back to Puerto Rico in 1932, the issue of Puerto Rican identity, what has been called "Puertoricanness," remains a problematic one.[12]

Puerto Rican referential ambiguity is symptomatic of a long history of colonialism—500 years of elusive identity. The first Spanish colonizers called the island San Juan Bautista for St. John the Baptist, and the main town was named Puerto Rico for its rich potential. In 1521 the city and the island exchanged names: the city of San Juan Bautista de Puerto Rico became the official city of the island of Puerto Rico. Still today the first Taíno name, Boriken or Borinquén, is also used to designate the people and island of Puerto Rico.

"For years, I was called a *Boricua*, never knowing what it meant," writes Roberto Santiago (1995). "*Boricua* was the word that turned strangers into friends when used as a greeting" (p. xiii).

> I imagined that *Boricua* was just affectionate slang for *Puerto Rican*. I guessed that *Boricua* was just a word that proclaimed that you were down with your people and your culture—no different from *brother* and *sister*, the terms of endearment used by African Americans. [p. xiii] . . . Then in a tiny book tucked away on a dusty shelf in the Aguilar library, I discovered what "*Boricua*" actually stood for. It meant "Brave Lord," which is what the Puerto Rican natives—the Arawak indians—called their island before Christopher Columbus confiscated it for the Spanish crown in 1493. [pp. xvii–xviii]

---

12. The official designation "Porto Rico" was modified in 1932 by the War Department (U.S. Geographic Board 1933:622; U.S. War Department 1932:14). See Morris 1995.

For Santiago, *Boricua* is an assertive moniker, a performative naming that transcends class and gender by sending everyone to the origins of the Puerto Rican people. In fact, as in all colonial histories, any account is partial and flawed with contradictions; in the endless rewriting of origins most "facts" appear expunged from memory. According to Santiago, even the name "Taíno," given to the island's natives, results from a colonial oversight. Columbus called the Arawak Indians "Taíno," a word that means peace and that was used by the natives to greet the Europeans when they first stepped ashore on the island (p. xix).

WHAT IS A PROPER NAME?

From an analytical point of view, any parapraxis is always extremely revealing. Naming is a symbolic act that often forces us to acknowlege our alienation in the Other, since most of the time we just inherit our first and last names, we do not choose them—one can rarely name oneself. Our name forces us to accept the radical alterity of the dimension of the Other while establishing a symbolic kinship that offers a place within a symbolic network. A name offers the subject a place in the Other anterior to the subject's very appearance. Finally, the process of naming entails always a lack, that is, the subject's castration or the subject's division by the signifier. Between the name and what is named, there is always a gap. Thus, for Lacan, naming ultimately sends us to the metaphor of the Name-of-the-Father, while embodying the irreversible division of the speaking subject as an effect of the signifier.

Lacan argues that the name's site is the edge of the hole of the Symbolic: "I am called Jacques Lacan, but as something that can be missing, for which the name will tend to cover over another lack. The proper name, therefore, is a moveable function to fill the hole, to put a stopper, to give a false appearance of suture" (Lacan 1965). Identity, as alienating and precarious as it can be, is established by naming. Names, however, do not necessarily have meaning—they are not descriptions of properties.[13] In the unpublished (1961–1962) *Seminar 9: Identification*, Lacan states that the

---

13. This is the thesis of Saul Kripke (1982), who contradicts the dominant belief of analytic philosophers (the "Frege-Russell thesis") for whom the reference of a proper name is determinable only through definite descriptions: If someone mentions the name "Jacques Lacan," the answer to the question "Which Jacques Lacan?" would call for a description like "the French psychoanalyst" or "the author of *Ecrits*" (pp. 27–28).

proper name designates the subject's rootedness in the Symbolic as such. The proper name bears a mark; it is tied to the trace in a form that is not translated from one language to another since it is simply transposed or transferred:

> My name is Lacan in all languages, and this is true also for you, each one of you, as you are called by your own names. This is neither a contingent fact nor an element of limitation . . . since on the contrary . . . herein resides the very particular ownership . . . of the proper name . . . this does not mean that each of us is forced to ask ourselves what there is in this radical and archaic point, which we must absolutely suppose lies at the origin of the unconscious . . . this is to say, the name which names the subject as the subject of an utterance.

Having opened that session of his seminar with the general question "What is a proper name?," Lacan concludes that "there can be no definition of proper names except insofar as we perceive the relation of the naming utterance to something that is, in its radical nature, of the order of the letter." It is precisely when an impropriety appears in the letter itself of a so-called "proper" name that this function appears most clearly. This detour through the Lacanian theory of the name is necessary in order to underline the importance of a bureaucratic parapraxis that ended up divesting Puerto Rico of its proper name between 1900 and 1932. Not only were Puerto Ricans transformed into citizens without a country (until 1917, when they became U.S. citizens) but they were robbed of a name that had represented them symbolically for more than 400 years. The transformation of the island's proper name was a colonial act that involved a destitution, an effacement of singularity, a form of erasing their history.

Clara Rodriguez (1995) notes that "when asked that divisive question 'What are you?,' Puerto Ricans of all colors and ancestry answer, 'Puerto Rican,' while most New Yorkers answer, black, Jewish or perhaps, 'of Italian descent'" (p. 82). Just as the American imposition of a new name on the conquered territory appeared as a cruel subjugation, the psychiatric labeling of male hysterics in the U.S. Army revealed a similar absurdity. The *ataque*'s defensive violence reveals the struggle of people caught up in an absurd, impossible situation. The "Puerto Rican" syndrome has shown us how the Symbolic precedes the imaginary aspect of representation; the aggressiveness of the image has been subordinated to the Symbolic in the process by which the Puerto Rican proper name emerged, and signed itself, as it were, through its syndrome.

10

Awake from the Ataque

Despierta, Borinqueña,
Que han dado la señal.
Despierta de ese sueño,
Que es hora de luchar
(Awake Borinqueña,
They have given the sign.
Awake from this dream.
It is the moment to fight)
First stanza of the National Anthem of Puerto Rico
(*Words and music by Lola Rodríguez de Tió*[1])

In a footnote added in 1909 to *The Interpretation of Dreams*, Freud (1900) states that with hysterical patients dreams frequently substitute for attacks. In an article of the same year (1909b) specifically devoted to the topic of hysterical attacks, Freud goes further and explains that besides replacing an attack, a dream "still more frequently helps to explain one, since the

---

1. As specified above, all translations from Spanish are mine.

same fantasy finds different forms of expression both in dreams and in attacks" (pp. 227–228). Furthermore, he argues that the same analytic procedure of dream interpretation can render intelligible the phenomenon of hysterical attack. We may remember that with the quintessential hysteric Freud called "Dora," it was not her suicidal gesture but one attack accompanied by convulsions and a delirious state that finally convinced her father to bring his reluctant daughter to be treated by Freud. Freud (1905) adds in a footnote (p. 17) that the attack, which had been preceded by a trivial argument between father and daughter, was subsequently covered by amnesia: it was never reached by analysis or by trustworthy recollections. The illuminating case study of Dora, however, was at first an expansion of *The Interpretation of Dreams.* Its original title, "Dream and Hysteria," fittingly summarizes Freud's purpose. Dora's clinical report, a "fragment" of a psychoanalytic treatment "grouped around two dreams," is less an analysis of the hysterical structure than a probing of how dreams provide a key to the links between hysteria, seduction, oedipal quandaries, and gender trouble.

Without questioning the obvious relevance of dream interpretation to clinical practice (and to the general understanding of psychic life), we may wonder—given the disparity in the actual production of dreams and of hysterical attacks—how we may make sense of Freud's insistence on equating the two. Whereas dreams are generated through condensation and displacement, in a dynamism resulting from the combination of metaphor and metonymy that parallels the movement that produces poetic creations, hysterical manifestations crystallize language. To give an example, let us revisit the case of hysteria treated by Freud and written up in the *Studies on Hysteria* (Freud and Breuer 1895).

Elisabeth von R. was a 24-year-old who suffered astasia-abasia: she experienced pains in her legs and had difficulties walking. Freud's clinical description captures something poignant about his patient—she endured her pains with *belle indifférence.* To determine that this was a case of true hysteria, Freud paid attention to the way the patient *talked* about her symptoms. He noted that Elisabeth, an otherwise extremely intelligent woman, was unable to render a definite description of her pains. Freud knew that usually patients suffering organic pains describe them clearly and calmly. For neurotic pains, however, language seems too poor to convey something unique and inexhaustible. Neurotics, Freud noted, never tire of adding new details, feeling that they can never make themselves fully understood. The pains attract their whole attention, as if the pain were merely an excuse to talk endlessly. Like dreams, they can be excuses to tell a story.

Indeed, neurotic symptoms are very subjective; they carry the imprint of the patient's subjectivity being the point of departure for endless stories with an inescapable vortex. Like dreams, they are a formation of the unconscious. Here we see Freud already, in 1892, making a diagnosis based on the way a patient talks about her symptoms! Already then, Freud was diagnosing, treating, and curing with and within language.

We can also see that Freud productively "used" the symptom: he did not simply consider it an annoying disturbance one should get rid of rapidly, but instead he let the symptom be a point of departure, a guide in the cure, because contained in the symptom were both the secrets of its origin and the pathway to its resolution. In order to effect the cure, he concentrated on the particular words chosen by the patient to describe her ailments. They contained some knowledge about the symptom, knowledge that the patient possessed without knowing it, and which was revealed unwittingly whenever she spoke of her ailments. Elisabeth's painful legs began to "join in the conversation" (p. 148).

At very precise moments, Elisabeth's pain "spoke," indicating that something had been left unsaid. The physical sensation of pain behaved like a message sent to Freud, thus calling for an interpretation. The symptomatic pain diagnosed as "neurotic" within speech then "joined in the conversation" in order to be "talked away" in the analysis.

With Elisabeth's case one can see that Freud was a careful listener, attentive to the syntax and semantics of symptoms as well as to the signifiers that were used by her significant others in their relations to her. This is exactly how he progressed, paying close attention to linguistic elaboration. Her pains, which prevented her from walking, represented her impotence, her feeling unable to "take a step forward." This is the exact, even literal meaning that Freud discovered. She felt unable to "take a single step forward" (*nicht von der Stelle kommen*) because of "not having anything to lean on" (*keinen Anhalt haben*), and complained that "standing alone" (*Alleinstehen*) was too painful for her. She literalized her inability to "take a step forward," her not being able to "stand alone" on her own, or having something "to lean on." Her symptoms moved across the lines of polysemy—the signifiers remained untouched while the signified would change. For Freud, Elisabeth's abasia was a symbolic expression of mental pain that became a physical sensation of pain. "I feel that I cannot move forward; therefore, I actually cannot move forward."

Thus, the hysterical symptom took the place of an utterance. This perspective was revolutionary insofar as it broke with the medical tradition that remained fascinated with simply staring at the hysterical spectacle. The analyst no longer took into account only what he was seeing; rather he focused exactly on what he was hearing. This new style of "analytic listening" to hysterical symptoms involved detecting signifying plays on words that affected *both* body and soul. Freud worked directly on the pain, decoding the function of the word *pain* (*Schmerz*) itself. He used this privileged signifier "like a compass" guiding to the articulation of soul and body, returning, by way of the word, from the physical pain to the psychic pain that caused it. Its meaning was changed once narrated, even if the pain persisted.

Indeed, after ending her treatment with Freud, Elisabeth suffered occasionally from slight pains. Nonetheless, in the spring of 1894, Freud got himself invited to a private ball that he knew his former patient might attend. He did not want to miss the opportunity to see how she was doing after the cure. His efforts were rewarded: from a distance he could see Elisabeth, the first patient ever treated with his new method, whirling about in lively dance steps.

Freud's major innovation in his treatment of hysteria was to assume that the body *speaks* in symptoms: he remained silent in order to let the body speak its distorted discourse of gagged utterances "converted" into anesthesia and paralysis. Freud is in fact asking: "What does this paralysis, this attack, or this dream have to say?" In his meticulous analyses, such a strategy makes him turn his interest away from the symptoms themselves to the fantasies out of which they proceed (see Freud 1908, p. 229).

Freud's radical originality resided in his *listening* to motor symptoms rather than looking at them. Here is what he discovered: "When one psychoanalyses a patient subject to hysterical attacks, one soon gains the conviction that these attacks are nothing but fantasies translated into motor activities and represented in pantomime" (1909a, p. 227). Thus, "when someone psychoanalyses" (that is, when someone listens attentively to the nuances in verbal expression), one may undo the path of the "conversion" (retracing the process by which a psychic affect passes into a bodily innervation), thus grasping the psychic content that during the crises is "translated" (transported) and represented in "pantomimes" (dramatic performances in which a story is told).

Why does he conclude with a homology between the images and forms of a dream, and the hysterical symptoms that are "translated" in a pantomime? While attacks or paralysis are symptoms, dreams are universal to all psychic structures and are not a sign of pathology. Despite the obvious difference, one can no longer be deceived by the slippery terrain of hysterical symptoms, or lose access to the unconscious desire revealed by dreams, if one looks at their common kernel. Freud can put forward a reciprocal equivalence because he does something we may sum up as "fantasmatizing" the dream and the attacks. That is why one can replace the other: Freud observes that both express unconscious fantasies that undergo equivalent distortions.

HYSTERICAL POETRY

The new common dimension introduced by fantasy helps us understand Freud's observation that poetic creations and hysterical fantasies obey the same mechanism. A few years after he had successfully treated Elisabeth von R., and just a few months before he would completely transform his interpretation of hysteria, abandoning the "seduction theory," Freud (1985) wrote to Fliess: "The mechanism of poetic creation [*Dichtung*] is the same as that of hysterical fantasies" (p. 251, translation slightly modified). Like the poets, the hysterics use language for its associations, for its images, in ways that are creative, and at times, can even subvert commonsensical expressions, producing a new grammar of metaphor. Freud is probably all the more aware of the poetic condensation at work in the discourse and bodily symptoms of the hysterics, as his own literary preferences go to the principles at work, devices and motifs, form and structure, of the novel (in his youth, he filled empty hours meticulously rereading one of the greatest novels ever written, *Don Quixote*, in its original language). Let us recall that Freud's style, as he himself admits, is the short story. And he was a very gifted writer: In 1930, Freud was awarded the coveted Goethe Prize for his talents as a writer and scholar. He appealed to the rhetorical strategies of poets and hysterics—using language in innovative ways, both challenging and enlightening.

We shall insist on the importance of fantasy, because fantasy lurks at the heart of dreams, attacks, paralyses, poetic creation, and even ideologies and political claims. They all share the fact that fantasy is a possible answer that allows one to imagine a relationship to the Thing. Our relationship to this traumatic real kernel is negotiated by way of fantasies that create a relationship to the Other. Fundamentally, fantasy is produced to answer the impossible question: What is the desire of the Other?

Following Freud's lead, we may say that the hysterical attacks we have dealt with so far are pantomimic representations of a fantasy. The distortions fantasy undergoes in an *ataque* are quite similar to those that crop up in dreams. The *ataque*, despite its theatrical features, is still not wholly trans-parent, but it can be rendered intelligible if we apply Freud's method of dream analysis while keeping in mind Lacan's postulates about fantasy. This technique allows us to work with the *ataque* as structured along linguistic lines, attending closely to the wordplay of the specific signifiers chosen by the analysands when they talk about the *ataque*. Thus, employing the Freudian technique of dream interpretation that emphasizes the linguistic dimension of the dream, we will approach the *ataque* as a rebus to be deciphered. Lacan's conception of fantasy also emphasizes its linguistic aspect, for fantasy is an enigmatic scenario condensed in a phrase that allows the analyst to catch something crucial in the subject's fundamental desire.

That the *ataque* represents a fantasy is crucial since, as noted earlier, for Lacan reality as such is lost; for fantasy not only organizes "reality," it also keeps the Real at a safe distance. To understand more precisely this function of fantasy, I will rapidly allude to Lacan's interpretation of the famous "burning child" dream analyzed by Freud (1900; see especially Chapter 7). This puz-zling and pathetic dream can be summed up as follows: The father of a re-cently deceased child had spent the previous days and nights nursing his terminally ill son. After the child's death, he went to the next room to lie down, leaving the door half open so that he could still see his son's body surrounded by tall candles. There, he had a dream in which his son, stand-ing beside him, caught him by the arm and asked reproachfully: "Father, don't you see I'm burning?" He immediately woke up and hurried to the room, only to discover that one of the arms of his cherished child had been burned by a fallen candle (Freud 1900, p. 652). Lacan's peculiar interpretation of the logic behind the father's painful awakening modifies Freud's interpreta-tion. Freud contended that dreams are the guardian of sleep, assuming that we dream in order to continue sleeping. For that purpose, we include in a dream disruptive stimuli such as the smells of something burning or the sound of an alarm clock or radio. When the disturbing external stimulation becomes too strong, the dreamer wakes up. Lacan explains the moment of awaken-ing differently: for him, the dreamer awakes to escape from the Real of his desire by returning to reality.

BURNING DESIRE

What kind of desire is realized in this tormenting dream? The moment of the awakening can give us a clue. The father woke up from his dream of anxiety when it reached an unbearable point. This moment is unbearable because it has to do with an encounter, the stage in the dream when the father gets too close to the Real of his guilt for his son's death. The phrase "Father, don't you see I'm burning?" marks an encounter with the Real of his son's death. Freud states that the dream allows the realization of a desire—the desire to see the son come alive beside the father, thus allowing the father "not to see" his death. This dream became a nightmare because it went too far in the realization of its desire; ultimately, it failed to conceal its *jouissance* any longer. In this case, the father woke up from a bad dream in order to escape to a reality that is excessively Real. He woke up to see the excruciating sight of his son's dead body, whose flesh had been caught in flames while he was sleeping.

Paradoxically, one dreams not to wake up. Usually, when one wakes up from a bad dream (we may say, from too Real a dream), one feels relieved to escape into so-called reality. Thus, one feels alleviated, able to keep dreaming awake, avoiding the truth of one's unconscious desire. As we saw, the Lacanian concept of reality is a fantasy that masks the Real: fantasy simply protects us from the Real. In view of this logic, we should not be tempted to conclude too quickly, "Everything is simple, life is but a dream." If "Life is but a dream," then "Life is all too Real." In the dream one can grasp something of the Real, an encounter that is accompanied by anxiety; when the dream does not stop at the *encounter* with the Real and goes too far, it becomes a nightmare. According to Freud, a nightmare is a failed dream—the *jouissance* that the dream was to conceal is exposed and the dreamer awakes. The point of awakening is the dream's umbilicus, the place where the *jouissance* of the Other would be revealed. Hence in the dream we have a *via regia* leading to the core of truth of our being, to the fantasy that determines the way we construct our waking reality and with it, to the beyond that supports it. Following Freud's insight into the interchangeability of dreams and attacks, the *ataque* should lead us to the same hard kernel of the Real that concerns the truth of our desire.

Fantasy leads to new insights because of the Lacanian barred subject that is partly made whole by fantasy. It is therefore constitutive for the subject while remaining enigmatic, almost inaccessible. This separation of the subject from its most intimate reality illustrates Lacan's idea of the constitutive decentering of the speaking being. This is even more unsettling than a "loss of control" since it expresses the subject's exclusion from the very truth of his or her being—no one can consciously know what guarantees the kernel of one's being. From this perspective, the *ataque* reveals the division of the subject; this is a division that, as the formula of the fantasy ($<>a) tells us, can be plugged with an object. While for Freud the fantasy is an imaginary scenario of fulfillment of an unconscious wish/ desire (*Wunsch*), for Lacan a fantasy gives to reality its consistency. Fantasy is central in psychoanalysis because it aims to uncover the object *petit a*, a remainder of the operation called by Lacan the "causation" of the subject. This operates in a twofold logic: *alienation*—the subject is a signifier for another signifier—and *separation* from the other by whom the subject was constituted.

A vignette from a case story demonstrates how the combined insights of Freud and Lacan can illuminate the understanding of the *ataque*. This is what I was told during the preliminary interview of someone I will call Consuelo, a 43-year-old woman from a small Puerto Rican town in the southern part of the island, who has been living in Philadelphia's "Hispanic" ghetto for the past twelve years. Initially, she moved here to take care of a sister who *perdió la mente* (lost her mind), but then her own failing health and the access to better health services motivated her to stay. In her first visit she explained why she had come to see me:

> I have this inside me. *Me agito* (I'm hurried/stressed) and something goes up to my head. I feel in despair. My head trembles—my head becomes strange as if something would be walking in my head. All my life I've suffered from my nerves . . . I take pills for my *nervios* (Xanax) and still get easily irritated.

It is always revealing to learn the reason that decides someone to pursue therapy or analysis at a given juncture. Consuelo's mother had died in the past year and she had come to see me exactly four days before the first anniversary of this death. Her father had also died around the same time of the year, four years earlier, but she could not recall the exact date. He was a sugar cane worker who "drank his salary" and stopped this habit only when he developed *delirium tremens*. He died of a stroke, just weeks after a failed suicide attempt; it was not his first attempt. She was one of eleven siblings—two died in childhood of a disease she did not recall but she remembered her mother saying that they could not breathe well and had weak lungs. She, like her mother, was the fourth girl in a large family and felt rejected by a mother who was particularly "severe" with her. Consuelo mentioned having experienced *ataques*:

My nerves have always been *altered*. Once I lost my mind. We were in Puerto Rico and my daughter was very young. I needed a gallbladder operation. But the doctor scared me, telling me that I could die if I did not take better care of myself. I felt such big despair but told nobody and went into the operating room feeling under intense tension. The surgery went well but my mind was taken over by despair. I worried about me, my baby daughter, my then husband. When I returned home I could not be by myself, and I would cry whenever my husband left for work, begging him to stay. During my convalescence worse things happened. I started feeling a strange itch on my skin and took a cold shower to calm it. Rather than feeling refreshed, I felt even hotter. I ran into the streets feeling sick all over. I reached my mother's house crying, unable to control myself, as if I was not myself. My whole body shook and I felt that my head was about to explode. I went to the window, I wanted to jump. They took me to the hospital. There, a psychiatrist saw me and gave me some medication. I slept for days.

Let us note that this very *ataque* that this woman described so vividly took place twenty years before. However, she chose to describe it in the first interview for a reason. She assumed that the *ataque* had a meaning relevant to my understanding of her *nervios*. By telling me about it, she hoped that I would explain a meaning from which she herself is excluded. Thus, Consuelo lays down the basic element of psychoanalytic transference: a supposition of knowledge (I am the subject supposed to possess knowledge about her symptoms). In fact, I do not actually know what her *ataque* means. Consuelo attributes to the Other what she lacks. In transference, the analyst is placed initially as Other: it is supposed to possess knowledge about that object that in Lacanian algebra represents the object of desire, that is, the object that *causes* desire, the object Lacan calls *petit a* (small a); this is an object that insofar as it is absent, can cause desire. If I would try to find an actual reassurance of my knowledge by applying general rules at this early stage—like predicting that *ataques de nervios* represent psychological distress or are a modulation of anger—I would pretend that I possess the answers (I would appear as noncastrated Other—and soon become another Master destined to be deposed). Besides, I would foreclose any possibility of actually deciphering its content and miss the particular meaning the *ataque* may have for Consuelo, thus suppressing her individuality, erasing any trace of her subjectivity, preventing her from questioning her own desire.

She offers her *ataque* as an enigma to read, to decipher, to learn about. I will wait and let her pose the question and find the answer herself. Several months of associations will be needed to identify the fantasy that the *ataque* expresses. At the very beginning of a treatment, the analysand is alienated in this attribution of knowledge. In a second moment, a separation takes place and the object *a* is thus produced as the leftover of the operation of separation. If there is any restitution of knowledge possible, it will happen by allowing the knowledge already there to emerge in dreams, slips of the tongue, or even new instances of *ataques*.

Thus as a first step, the emerging question posed to the *ataque* will be twofold: the Freudian interrogation ("What does it want to say?") should become a more radical "What does it want?," meaning "What does it desire?" The *ataque* expresses a fantasy, a fantasy that offers an *object a* occupying an empty place in the Other, the place of the Other's cause of desire. This displacement already presupposes that empty place in the Other; it implies a castrated/barred Other, as we will later see with Consuelo. Here it is instructive to note, once more, how the *ataque* functions as an appeal to the Other. As we have seen, Freud observed that hysterical attacks are aimed at *another person*, the primeval and "unforgettable" other person whom no one coming after can equal. This "other person" is the primordial Other that was instrumental in structuring the subject's desire (since the object of desire, as we have seen, is the Other's desire). The *ataque* can let us glimpse onto the object that the subject was for the Other, and the separation that was operated when the subject fell from that position of *object a*. Being addressed to the Other, the *ataque* functions as a possible answer to the question of the Other's desire, thus combining the fundamental elements at stake in a psychoanalytic cure that is key in the process of subjective destitution. Let us stop here for now, only underlining that in the *ataque* we have already a whole network of symbolic overdeterminations that can tell a lot about the psychic singularity of Consuelo (we shall return to her case story in greater detail in Chapter 15).

Following the reciprocity between dreams and hysterical attacks already discussed, we will turn to one revelatory dream as a means of access to the so-called Puerto Rican syndrome. As we have seen, both the hysterical attack and the dream are formations of the unconscious that undergo similar distortions when expressing fantasy. In our search for a better understanding of the *ataque* we will try to grasp the unconscious fantasies underpinning the *ataque* by way of one of Freud's dreams. We will then return to a dream poignantly traversed by colonial history, a dream analyzed in detail in *The Interpretation of Dreams* (1900, pp. 463–464). This is a dream of a castle by the sea, and a dream of naval war too, a complex dream that happens to deal with the Hispanic-American War. This was the very war that ended with the annexation of Puerto Rico to the United States; it meant the end of 400 years of Spanish domination of the island and it inaugurated a new form of colonialism for the United States.

FREUD AND THE SPANISH-AMERICAN WAR

Let us not hide our surprise and excitement at the discovery that this crucial historical incident in the history of the Puerto Rican syndrome had left unmistakable traces in Freud's own dreams.

We tend to forget the echoes of colonial struggles that found their way into *The Interpretation of Dreams*, above all because we rarely associate the Austrian context of the turn of the century with overseas imperialism. By a curious historical coincidence, Freud's discovery of the meaning of dreams, one of the most influential findings of the twentieth century, took place at the same time that Puerto Rico was passing to U.S. control.

In the name of liberty, justice, and humanity, American forces took control of Puerto Rico, beginning a new chapter in the Caribbean island's colonial history. Upon occupation of the island on July 25, 1898, Major General Nelson A. Miles, as commander in chief, issued a historical proclamation:

> We have not come to make war upon the people of a country that for centuries has been oppressed, but, on the contrary, to bring you protection, not only to yourselves but to your property, to promote your prosperity, and to bestow upon you the immunities and blessings of the liberal institutions of our government. It is not our purpose to interfere with any existing laws and customs that are wholesome and beneficial to your people as long as they conform to the rules of military administration, of order, and justice. This is not a war of devastation, but one to give to all the control of its military and naval forces the advantages of enlightened civilization.[2]

---

2. This proclamation can be found in the *Annual Reports of the War Department*, Washington DC, 1902, Vol. 1, pp. 13–15. Reprinted in *Documents on the Constitutional History of Puerto Rico*, 2nd ed., Washington, 1964, p. 55.

In his invasion speech, General Miles announced the "advantages and benefits of civilization" while expressing his desire "to put the conscience of the American people into the island" (Hancock 1960, p. 69). If the conscience of the American people was going to be put into the island, one may wonder, however, about the fate of the Freudian repressed, and most importantly, of the unconscious, now "under the control of military and naval forces." To start answering, let me quote Freud (1900); here is his dream.

> A castle by the sea; later it was no longer immediately on the sea, but on a narrow canal leading to the sea. The governor was a Herr P. I am standing with him in a big three-windowed salon, in front of which rise projections of walls like fortress battlements. I belong to the garrison, perhaps as a volunteer naval officer. We fear the arrival of enemy warships, because we are in a state of war. Herr P. has the intention of going away; he is giving me instructions what to do in case of what we fear. His sick wife is with his children in the besieged castle. When the bombardment begins, the big hall is to be vacated. He breathes heavily and tries to get away; I hold him back and ask him in what manner I should let news reach him in case of need. Then he says something else, but at once his head sinks down dead. I may have overstrained him unnecessarily with questions. After his death, which makes no further impression on me, I wonder whether the widow should remain in the castle, whether I ought to announce the death to the Higher Command, and whether I should take over the control of the castle as next in command. Now I stand at the window and inspect the ships, which are passing by; they are merchant vessels, which rush rapidly past on the dark water, some with several stacks, others with bulging decks. Then my brother is standing beside me, and we both look out the window upon the canal. At one ship we are frightened and cry: "There comes the warship." But it turns out that only the same ships are coming back which we have already seen. Now comes a little ship, comically cut off so that it ends in the middle at its broadest; on a deck there are peculiar cup or box-like things. We cry out in one voice: "That is the breakfast ship." [pp. 463–464; translation slightly modified]

In his analysis of this dream, Freud acknowledges that the dream contains allusions to the maritime war between America and Spain and to anxieties it had created about the fate of his relatives who have recently moved to New York. Freud explains that the deceased Herr P. appears as a substitute for himself, from which we may infer that he was one of the first casualties of the Spanish-American War. Freud's personal connection with the Spanish-American War could be seen as having wider implications. Perhaps the creator of psychoanalysis was already aware of the ominous consequences of American colonialist aspirations at a time when the United States looked to the Caribbean islands as a territory to conquer. What is even more ominous is that the dream describes an Etruscan urn looking like a boat, quite similar to the Greek urn in which Freud's ashes were to be deposited in 1939.

In order to understand better the political implications of the day-residues that have elicited this dream, it is indispensable to recapitulate certain events that Freud does not develop in his analysis of the dream but that quite strikingly reappear in his recollection of the dream. They arouse our suspicion since they emerge in Freud's dream not just as distorted remnants but almost word-for-word transcriptions of what he had read in Austrian newspapers about the Spanish-American War. Although Freud's interpretation of the dream alludes to them in passing, since he seems more interested in idiosyncratic or private associations leading to a distant past (an enjoyable Easter trip to the Adriatic, a trip to Venice, some Etruscan pottery, mourning customs, funeral boats, gloomy thoughts of an unknown future), the material of the dream is brought by the curious historical events that took place in the month preceding it. In order to enhance scientific neutrality, in his narrative Freud chooses to downplay the obvious political content of the dream.

After a careful examination of all the issues of the daily paper, Leslie Adams (1953) asserts that this dream must have taken place on the night of May 10–11, 1898. This thesis is confirmed by all the curious details that crop up in the dream. At this time there were fears that New York might be attacked by the Spanish fleet. Freud's dream recombines elements of the battle of Manila, which was fought on May 1st and news of which reached the media by cable only a week after, on May 7. It is clear that Freud had read the relatively bewildering account of the battle that was spread over the first three pages of the *Neue Freie Presse* on the morning of May 10, 1898.

Here are the events that preceded the dream. After mounting tension between the Americans and the Spaniards, the U.S.S. *Maine*, which had come to the harbor of La Havana on a friendly visit, was shattered by an explosion and sank on February 15, 1898. President McKinley was notified in his bedchamber that 266 Americans had been killed. The Hearst press began throwing the people into fury with a saga involving an endangered, virginal, beautiful young woman who was kept unjustly imprisoned by the Spaniards. The actual war was declared two months later, on April 22. By

May 2, the world press reported that a strong Spanish squadron under Admiral Cervera had left the Azores and taken to the high seas in a westward direction. Would it attack America or the West Indies? The fear extended across the coast reaching as far as New York. Lighthouses were dimmed and buoys were set from Maine to Florida. The whole Atlantic coast was on the lookout for enemy ships. Worried watchfulness was the mood in every newspaper during the following days (Adams 1953). On May 11 only the *Neue Freie Presse* made it clear that the Spanish fleet had been sighted off Puerto Rico, which implied that it was headed for the Antilles and not New York.

While this international drama developed, a dreamlike series of events had unfolded elsewhere. Admiral Dewey, in charge of part of the American fleet, had been in Hong Kong when the war began; he then sailed into the Pacific and had been lost to view. On the night of April 30, Dewey, on his flagship *Olympia*, led his fleet into the harbor of Manila.[3] This action should have led to certain destruction according to the principles of warfare, for the Spanish fleet was entrenched and supplied in a land-locked harbor, and well protected by the guns of fortresses. At 5 o'clock on Sunday morning, May 1, Dewey's fleet swept in single file as in a parade in front of the enemy squadron. The Spanish fleet began to fire, but the American ships swept on, not answering the fire in exasperating contempt of the poor marksmanship of the enemy—it looks indeed as if the historical event had already the structure of a dream.

"CALL OFF FOR BREAKFAST!"

The most astounding element was the behavior of Admiral Dewey. According to contemporary press reports, including the Viennese papers that covered the battle in great detail, he stood on his bridge quietly, remarking on the weather and the distant hills, saying that they reminded him of his native Vermont. Half an hour went by while his fleet swept back and forth, coming into ever-close range. He finally uttered: "You may fire when you are ready, Gridley." Sailing in closer ellipses, the American ships all

---

3. Dream leftovers make their way into daytime reality. In an outstanding coincidence, we can find one crucial element of Freud's dream reemerge in present-day reality: The flagship Olympia itself is permanently anchored in Philadelphia's Penn's Landing Seaport Museum not too far away from the *barrio*.

opened fire. At half past seven, after two terrible hours of steady firing, Dewey ordered: "Call off for breakfast!"—this was a command that became world famous. Admiral Dewey interrupted the battle at breakfast time, just when the execution was excellent and there was no resistance on the enemy's side. Some men cried out, "For God's sake, Captain, to hell with breakfast; give it to them now," while the Spaniards raised a great shout as they thought that the Americans were fleeing. After breakfast, the firing resumed and lasted several hours. Finally, when the smoke was gone, the Americans could see that all the Spanish ships were sinking or on fire. Captain Cadarso, commander of the *Reina María Cristina*, had fallen dead on the bridge, having been replaced by his second in command, who was immediately killed. The rear half of the ship had been blown up, and Admiral Montojo, commander of the fleet, would not quit the other half. The marksmanship of the Spaniards was obviously terrible: during the battle not one shot of theirs hit any target. Half an hour past noon, in time for lunch, the Spanish fortress hoisted the white flag. Even if the scene of destruction was awful with flaming hulks, shattered fragments of ships, and the water-battery devastated on the Spanish side, this was a "clean war" for the Americans since not one single person on their side was killed.

During the breakfast truce the Spanish who controlled the city of Manila had sent a message of victory to Madrid. Later on, they sent a second message of defeat concealed in comforting euphemisms. Although victorious, Dewey was prevented by the Spaniards from using the cable. Exasperated, he fished it from the sea and cut it. As a result, the outcome of the battle was learned much later, when a ship reached Hong Kong. Thus, for a whole week, the Americans knew confusedly that there had been a battle but were not sure whether Dewey had won or whether the Spanish fleet was heading to New York. Finally, the full story was published in Vienna on the morning of May 10. Only a week after the battle did the public realize that the Spaniards had been defeated and that New York was out of danger.

We see many elements of the dream appearing as repetitions of the battle events. Let us review just a few: Freud talks about "the arrival of enemy warships, because we are in a state of war," "I hold him [Herr P.] back and ask him in what manner I should let news reach him in case of need. Then he says something else, but at once his head sinks down dead. I may have overstrained him unnecessarily with questions." It is easy to assume how "overstrained" the international public may have been then, submerged in a tense expectation, hearing contradictory accounts, fearing an attack to New York, worried by the uncertain results of the battle. "I wonder whether I ought to announce the death to the Higher Command, and whether I should take over the control of the castle as next in command." During the battle, Captain Cadarso, commander of the *Reina María Cristina*, was killed and like Herr P., he was replaced by his second in command. Since the cable had been cut after the battle, not only the general public but even the Higher Command was not properly informed—who was in control "of the castle" remained unknown between May 1 and May 10.

"At one ship we are frightened and cry: 'There comes the warship.' . . . Now comes a little ship, comically cut off so that it ends in the middle at its broadest; on a deck there are peculiar cup- or box-like things. We cry out in one voice: 'That is the breakfast ship.'" As for the "little ship, comically cut off so that it ends in the middle at its broadest," let us recall that the rear half of Captain Cardarso's ship had been blown up, and Admiral Montojo, commander of the fleet, would not quit the other half. The appearance of the seemingly nonsensical "breakfast ship" is self-explanatory after Dewey's striking dreamlike breakfast truce and his famous command.

This dream of Freud's (1900) provides us with an excellent example of the function of overdetermination—"two interpretations are not mutually contradictory, but both cover the same ground; they are a good instance of the fact that dreams, like all other psychopathological structures, regularly have more than one meaning" (p. 149). Let us note that in this dream the day-residues do not seem to undergo many distortions—they are not mere allusions but reappear almost intact in the dream material. Since, as Freud says, "our dream thoughts are dominated by the same material that has occupied us during the day and we only bother to dream of things which have given us cause for reflection in the daytime" (p. 174), the political implications of the dream are even more relevant.

I will now concentrate on the striking political and historical relevance of this dream, taking advantage of the positive character of overdetermination. Freud does not see the dream as having only one unique and exhaustive meaning, but he rather sees it as a point of emergence of a series of meanings. Louis Althusser's concept of overdetermination (for something to occur there must be several conflicts at work) can help in this case, since the Freudian heritage in Althusser's "symptomatic reading" of Marx's *Das Capital* confirms that we need to cross the gap between the social and the individual. Each of Freud's dream elements is overdetermined; even when motivated by very personal and idiosyncratic circumstances, they are still traversed by the effects of a wider context, betraying a connection with the social structure. Following Lacan's topological model, one can read the dream as a knot tying different meanings corresponding to various levels. From this perspective, the Freudian idea of overdetermination demonstrates that the dream has several causes working together, bringing about a new concept of causality. However, if the manifest content of the dream seems to be motivated by very identifiable daytime ideas, I do not want to stress only one meaning. Thus, I would also like to speculate on the psychic factors instigating this dream in order to trace back its latent content. In that regard, Freud himself offers a lucid interpretation of the dream. Freud alludes to a line of Schiller, "*Still, auf gerettetem Boot, triebt in den hafen der Greis*" (Safe on his ship, the old man quietly sails into port), allegorizing life and death. He analyzes this dream as expressing fears about his own death. Interestingly, Freud notes that the Governor's death left him quite indifferent despite the fact that his analysis showed that Herr P. was a substitute for himself. Freud's fears concern the future of his family after his premature death. The profound impression awoken by the arrival of the warship led him to recall an event that occurred a year earlier while he was in a "magically beautiful day at the room on the Riva degli Schiavoni" in Venice. At the sight of a ship, his wife had cried out "gaily as a child: *Here comes the English warship*." When those words reappear in the dream, they are cause for deep fright.

The "tense and sinister impression" at the end of the dream is produced by the return of the shipwreck (*Shiffbruch*, literally "ship-break")— the cut-off, broken-off ship. Freud analyzes the appearance of the "breakfast ship" by referring to the world *English*, which is the leftover of his wife's phrase *Here comes the English warship* that in the dream becomes *Here comes the warship*. We can locate this missing signifier when it reappears in the English word "breakfast." "Break" relates to ship-*break* and "fast" becomes "fasting," then connected to a mourning dress. Freud notes that the breakfast ship was comically cut off and on the deck had peculiar cup- or box-like things that had great resemblance to some objects that had attracted his attention when he had seen them in Etruscan museums. They were rectangular trays of black pottery similar to modern-day breakfast sets. These were in fact the *toilette* objects of an Etruscan lady. The idea of black "toilette" related also to a mourning dress, thus is making a direct reference to death. Then, Freud attributes the origin of the "breakfast ship" to the English word breakfast (literally, breaking fast), linked to both ship-breaking and the black mourning dress.

[B]ut it was only the *name* of the breakfast ship that was newly constructed by the dream. The *thing* had existed and reminded me of one of the most enjoyable parts of my last trip. Mistrusting that food would be provided at Aquileia we had brought provisions with us. . . . And while the little mail steamer made its way slowly through the *"Canale delle Mee"* across the empty lagoon to Grado we, who were the only passengers, ate our breakfast on deck in the highest spirits, and we had rarely tasted a better one. This then, was the "breakfast-ship," and it was precisely behind this memory of the most cheerful *joie de vivre* that the dream concealed the gloomiest thoughts of an unknown and uncanny future. [p. 466]

Life and death converge in a pagan wake, in which intense joy and deep fear get all played out in this rich dream. Behind a memory of the happiest *joie de vivre*, the *jouissance de vivre* emerges. Freud's analysis about what lies behind the coining of the "breakfast ship" includes the phrase "The *thing* had existed." It is almost impossible not to hear echoes of both Freud's and Lacan's elaborations on *das Ding*, the "unforgettable thing" that exists beyond our attempts at symbolization. The dream stops when the domain of the Real is encountered.

Freud, still and all, chose not to explore the evident parallel between his inner thoughts and the sociopolitical realm. However, the impact of the historical events that may have brought up "the gloomiest thoughts of an unknown and uncanny future" were clearly there.

SO THE DREAM WILL BE

In a letter to Fliess written exactly one year after the dream (May 28, 1899), Freud (1985) calls the *Traumdentung* simply *der Traum* (the dream) and writes: "So the dream will be. That this Austria is supposed to perish in the next two weeks made my decision easier. Why should the dream perish with it?" (p. 353). As William McGrath (1986) observes, even though Freud's

ironic estimate of Austria's durability was not borne out, Freud's sense of impending political disintegration was well founded. The bitter divisions over language, nationality, and class that beset the Hapsburg Empire seemed to threaten its existence repeatedly during the closing years of the nineteenth century, when Freud was engaged in what proved to be his most important scientific project. [p. 15]

As McGrath notes, Freud's comment sets the writing of *The Interpretation of Dreams* against its political background, demonstrating Freud's awareness of how profoundly influenced his "dream" had been by the political conditions of his day.

During his analysis of what is called "The castle by the sea dream," Freud mentions that the dream-work brings about a *suppression of affects*. Thus, it reduces intense emotions to a level of indifference. Since political issues often raise intense emotions, can we say that the suppression of the political implications of a dream is due to their highly emotional tone? I will contend that political elements not only make their way into the dream, but that the collective is a formation of the unconscious comparable to a dream.

Manila's almost surrealist battle had baffled the principle of noncontradiction since both sides were uncertain about the issue for a while. If there were political allegiances for Freud, they were mixed. On the one hand, he was worried about his relatives living in New York. Four years earlier, in 1892, the brother of Freud's wife, Eli Bernays, who was married to Freud's sister, Anna, immigrated to the United States and in 1898 his relatives were living at 1883 Madison Avenue (between 121 and 122 Streets). However, Freud's position in the dream fearing the arrival and attack of the breakfast ship may remind us that he was not very fond of America, that he considered it a "gigantic mistake," being the "anti-Paradise" and "useful to nothing else but to supply money" (Gay 1986, p. 563). We may assume that Freud regretted the defeat of the Spanish, perhaps in the name of a long-standing Spanish-Austrian allegiance, and sided with the former Empire, now weakened and victimized.

An earlier event in Freud's life will shed more light on the content of this dream. Freud had a particular transferential relationship to the Spanish language, which he fondly called "the beautiful Castillian tongue" and that he had learned on his own at a young age. As an adolescent, Freud founded an exclusive secret society with his intimate friend Eduard Silberstein. This he called the "Spanish Academy."[4] As a secret language, not to allow the others to understand, they used Spanish. Freud had taught himself Spanish in order to read *Don Quixote* in the original language. Per-

---

4. Freud wrote that with Eduard Silberstein, a young Rumanian, "We founded a peculiar learned association, the Academia Española Castellana" (quoted in Clark 1980, p. 23).

haps, in the same way, he had set aside, in fact he had abandoned, hypnosis to teach himself a new language, psychoanalysis, in order to listen to the unconscious in the original dialect of hysteria.

Let us be reminded that Freud had this dream in 1898, three years after the publication of *Studies on Hysteria*, at a time when he was establishing the foundations of psychoanalysis. When Freud abandoned hypnosis and created psychoanalysis, he abandoned a therapy that was structured like a crowd according to the demonstration of *Massenpsychologie* (Freud states that in hypnosis as in the crowd, the psychic mechanism at work is basically the same).

Freud's main thesis describes hypnosis as a crowd of two, an idea that is taken not in a metaphorical sense, but quite literally. What is at stake for both hypnosis and for the crowd is group identity. Crowds erase difference because they crave conformity—they need a Master to love and to be loved by without any concern for truth. Whenever we find mass phenomena, we encounter segregation. Segregation is not a secondary consequence but a crowd's formation. Segregation is what constitutes the crowd.

Segregation is the disavowal of difference. All group formations erase difference since their constitution is based on a principle of identity. Any attempt at stressing differences, no matter how minimal, can be experienced by the crowd as an attack that threatens its very existence. Against the grain of the logic of group formations, psychoanalysis opens up a space of tolerance for difference if analysts are prudent (remaining on their guard against the temptation of playing the prophet or the Master), if they stubbornly refrain from the practice of suggestion, that is, if they abstain from exercising a form of hypnosis (and from producing a therapy that could be called "a crowd of two").

THE CROWD, THE DREAM OF DREAMS

Freud rendered the meaning of dreams intelligible; he made the royal path to the unconscious interpretable. Nonetheless, as we have seen, he chose to disregard in his analysis of this dream any of the obvious political implications of its content. Is this because psychoanalysis is a clinical practice built upon singularity, difference, and particularity? Then how can it stand up to the challenge of history that entails an engagement with collective formations? How is the psychoanalytic practice affected by the political conditions of its day? How far do the affairs of the city extend? Could it be that psychoanalysis, in spite of its love for knowledge, passionately ignores, in fact actively "resists," the social?

At the very end of the dream, Freud and his brother cried in one voice, "Here comes the breakfast ship." Freud tells us about this last scene of his dream: "the rapid movements of the ships, the deep dark blue water and the brown smoke of the funnels—all this combined to create a tense and sinister impression." What we see rising at the end of this dream seems clearly to be anxiety. As Freud and Lacan formulate it, anxiety would be the radical way in which the subject sustains, even in an unsustainable way, a relationship with his or her own desire. Freud's dream ends with breakfast, marking the end of the night, satisfying the desire for hunger, waking up from history to concrete needs of everyday rituals: it is time for breakfast; the war, even the dream, can wait. Admiral Dewey repeated this gesture, going from the collective of the war to the individual need for food, punctually interrupting the battle to have breakfast.

The dream ends with the brothers Freud crying in one voice; "as of one mouth" is the literal translation of the German. Precisely, I want to refer to "one mouth," the one and only mouth, the open mouth at the back of which Freud found out the secret of dreams. When Lacan (1991b) discusses in *Seminar II* the dream of dreams, the dream princeps, the dream of Irma's injection, he mentions in passing this very dream of Freud about the Hispanic-American war. There, in fact, Lacan establishes a peculiar connection between language, segregation, and psychoanalysis when he proposes a correlation between the crowd and the dream. His specific topic of discussion is the *ego* under the light of his mirror-stage logic. He notes that the narcissism we see in dreams is not there from the start but rather is a "new psychic act," as Freud calls it. It comes into being in the mirror stage; the *ego* does not exist before a relationship with a semblable is started. The borrowed image of one's own body is appropriated in anticipation and it becomes the principle of every unity the subject may perceive in objects. Lacan at the time was still telling the ego psychologists that the subject of the unconscious is decentered in respect to the *ego*. Thus, this subject is alienated and in a constant state of tension, perpetually in a state of fictitious unity in a world structured around the wandering shadow of the ego. Lacan even says an "egomorphic" world.

In the dream, because of an easing of imaginary relations, this constitutive alienation is even more poignant. The very truth of the subject appears exposed in its decomposition, in the Real brought by the night that usually culminates in anxiety. Lacan adds, referring to Irma's dream, that there is a moment when something of the Real, something at its most un-fathomable, is attained. Lacan therefore explains how the quest for signi-fication contains a moment at which the meaning of the dream of Irma's injection is revealed to Freud. Strikingly, Lacan names this moment *the crowd*, stating that this crowd is not just any crowd, but a crowd that is structured "like the Freudian crowd" (1991b, p. 160).

What is Lacan doing when he establishes an equivalence between the dream and the crowd? Lacan puts the dream side by side with the Freud-ian crowd (the type of crowd that Freud analyzes in *Massenpsychologie und Ich-Analyse*) because he locates an analogy in their structures; the dream and the crowd are formations of the unconscious that result from a failed *jouissance* and as such are equivalent to other formations of the unconscious-like parapraxes, slips of the tongue, and symptoms.

It is well known that Irma's dream allowed Freud to discover the royal path to unconscious desire. If dreams and the Freudian crowd share a common structure, a dream or a crowd can be read as an "inmixing of subjects" (1991b, p. 160). This corresponds to the dialectics of intersub-jectivity taking place when a subject interacts, "mixes" with things or with other subjects as counterparts. Using these sets of equivalencies, one could better understand how the ahistoricity of the unconscious is traversed by history, how the political is articulated with the subjective, how the sexual and the group life are intertwined.

The crowd illustrates the relationship of each member with its own image. If Lacan compares the dream to the Freudian crowd it is precisely because this crowd, according to Lacan's reading of Freud, is structured as the image of the body of the subject: indeed, a polycephalic subject or even an *acephalic* (headless)[5] subject, which speaks the discourse of the uncon-scious (1991b, p. 167). The acephalic subject speaks beyond the ego the nonsense of the dream revealing a knowledge, for instance, of the arrival of the uncanny breakfast ship of the Spanish-American War—a war that was called by the American Secretary of State, John Hay, a "splendid little

---

5. After a short-lived journal called *Contre-Attaque* (Counterattack), George Bataille launched the review *Acéphale*. Bataille proposed "headlessness"—abandoning the enlight-enment of the civilized world for the ecstatic power of worlds that had disappeared. This proposal can be read as an uncanny response to Major General Miles' invasion proclama-tion. Let us note as well that Bataille was a great reader of Freud ever since he came across *Group Psychology and the Analysis of the Ego*. For more on Bataille and *Acéphale* see Roudinesco 1997, pp. 131–137.

war," that included both the famous battle of Manila, which was punctually called off for a breakfast break, and an invasion of Puerto Rico often described in military records as a "picnic."

FREUD'S DREAM OF AMERIKA

According to Freud's logic in *Group Psychology and the Analysis of the Ego* (1921), even though Freud's "Spanish Academy" had but two members, it was already a collective formation, a crowd of two, and conceivably a repetition of the mythical primal horde. This myth, often contested because of its weak anthropological foundations, is in fact an ahistorical myth used by Freud because the Darwinian fantasy allows him to explain the function of the father that guarantees the place of a speaker who may believe that *jouissance* is possible. However, it is at the level of the brothers who feel guilty afterward that things start to move for civilization. Let us note that in Freud's dream, Herr P. is dead, left are his wife and children. Freud and his brother stay alone in charge of the garrison, taking care of the castle and of the wife and children (recall that the brother of Freud's wife who was married to Freud's sister was at the time living in the United States). Is Freud's dream a replay of the old Totemic myth or the family romance revisited?

The immediate historical context traverses his dream, creating a continuum between his private psychic life and the political world. The collective is not opposed to the unconscious. As Freud's dream illustrates, the collective becomes itself a formation of the unconscious. Why is Freud dreaming about this war fought in foreign lands far away? His interest in the war was probably influenced by the political situation of Vienna at the time and by the prevailing sense of looming disintegration. The 1897 government of Count Badeni obtained the anti-Semitic Christian Socials' support, which had a profound emotional significance for both Jews and German nationalists.[6] Freud may have been identified with both groups. We also know of the growing antisemitism in Vienna at the time, and of the

---

6. As William McGrath (1986) notes, the language conflict between Czechs and Germans was resolved by the government of Badeni who had the support of Karl Lueger's anti-Semitic Christian Socials. They assured him their support or abstention in parliament in return for the confirmation of Lueger as mayor of Vienna. This development offered cause for profound anxiety to all Jews living in Vienna.

direct impact it had on Freud's career. His dream of his uncle with the yellow beard (February 1897) shows his concern about his university appointment being blocked by antisemitic pressure. Freud was obviously in the position of segregated other. On the other hand, Peter Gay (1986) notes that Freud honestly admits in *The Interpretation of Dreams* that in his life he needed an enemy as much as a friend. Therefore, Gay understands Freud's lifelong staunch anti-Americanism as a construction of a gigantic collective manifestation of the enemy he said he couldn't do without.

The Viennese Jew, Freud, may have seen America as "Amerika," that is, as a mystic writing pad on which to project his experience of otherness as it may have been the case for the Czech Jew, Kafka. Neither Kafka when he wrote *Amerika*, nor Freud at the time of the dream, had visited the United States. America was the most familiar and strange at the same time, fascinating in its otherness.

IDENTITY IS STRUCTURED LIKE A CROWD

Lacan notes that Freud says about his dream something he paraphrases as *"I'm not in the dream where one might think. The character who just died, this commandant who is with me, it is he who is I."*[7] The fact that Freud was not situated in the dream where one might suppose him uncovers the unfathomable fundamental component of the narcissistic relation upon which identity is based. This is the same type of relation revealed by the crowd as by hypnosis—an identity always constructed in alienation, that is, as other. This dialectic entails a passionate rapture and overjoy: I am the other, the other is me.

In the dream context, the Spanish-American War to which Freud is alluding resulted in a new form of colonialism for the U.S. and has had lasting consequences that still impact America's identity today. The rise of the Hispanic "crowd" brings up questions about race, identity, and culture, since it can be seen as the repudiated other of the construction of American identity.

If the Hispanic as other is segregated, we could say that this separation occurs precisely because of its role as the leftover other upon which

---

7. This passage that Lacan (1991b, p. 167) mentions is found in *Standard Edition* 5: 467/448/464.

identification has been built. The mirror stage is replayed through racial disarray. The anticipated specular image of the body, being the paradigm of all forms of resemblance, functions as an alienating image working through a fictional figure. This fascination with the image of the other will bring over onto the world of objects a tinge of hostility or transgression, by projecting on them the manifestation of the narcissistic image. When facing a fellow being, the pleasure that can be derived from meeting one-self in the mirror transforms into an outlet for the most intimate aggres-siveness. This aggressiveness emerges full force in racism and runs the risk of being resolved through murderous or suicidal aggressiveness (Lacan 1977b). The logic of identification entails that one cannot see oneself, yet one can find one's image in the neighbor of the crowd, provided that there is a leader that occupies the place of the ideal.

Freud's dream collapses the individual with the collective because they are in fact inseparable: identity is structured like a crowd. The fundamen-tal transference, without which groups do not cohere, is part of a move-ment triggered by love that always includes some narcissistic element, and can at times crystallize into a "crowd of two" when the object is placed in the position of ego ideal (*Ichideal*), as happens in the process of hypnosis.

How could the crowd be the model for subjective identity? What is often asserted is just the contrary: a crowd abolishes the subjects that give up their individuality in order to "belong." But the logical order is reversed: first we have the crowd, then the individual; first the dream, then the sub-ject (Pommier 1990). Something quite extreme takes place both in the crowd and in the dream. Besides, something has been lost in translation: Why is Freud's *Massenpsychologie* mistranslated into English as "Group Psychology"? Why does the signifier "group" replace the crowd? Interest-ingly, the Spanish version of Freud's complete works has a number of il-lustrations accompanying the text of *Massenpsychologie*, among which are two pictures taken in the United States circa 1920: the captions claim that crowds became part of American life years before crowds appeared in European countries. William MacDougall, whose classic *The Group Mind* (1920) is quoted at length by Freud, makes clear that a group is not a crowd. MacDougall draws a sharp distinction between "the mental and moral de-fects of the crowd and its degrading effects upon all those who are caught up in it and carried away by the contagion of its reckless spirit" and the higher degree of organization of the group. Conversely, group life is "the great ennobling influence by aid of which alone man rises a little above the animals and may even aspire to fellowship with the angels" (p. 28).

If there is a translation discrepancy, the reasons are both geopolitical and chronological. It seems that the first part of this century has been rightly called the age of the masses, from Le Bon to Canetti (1962), and that the end of this century has been variously described as the age of nationalities or the age of minorities. Could it be that we need to shift our conceptual paradigms to address a different situation, described by Michel de Certeau (1999) as one of "culture in the plural"? Can we overhaul the model of identification, mass hysterization, and mass delusion of which we have made great use formerly? Is the mass phenomenon extinguished and replaced by the mass-media phenomenon? Or is the idle crowd of *Massenpsychologie*, mistranslated as "group," returning with a vengeance in the new "mass" of the Hispanic minority?

11

La Raza

> . . . in old San Juan
> a black Puerto Rican talks
> about "the race"
> he talks of Boricuas
> who are in New York on welfare
> and on lines waiting for food stamps,
> "yes, it's true, they have been taken out
> and sent abroad and those that
> went over tell me that they're
> doing better over there than here
> they tell me they get money
> and medical aid
> that their rent is paid
> that their clothes get bought
> that their teeth get fixed
> is that true?" . . . don't believe the deadly game
> of Northern cities paved with gold and plenty . . .
>
> From *A Mongo Affair* by Miguel Algarin
> (cited in Santiago 1995, pp. 108–109)

Today, "crowds" have been replaced by minority "groups" and these groups as collective formations share a common pattern: a similar failed *jouissance*. It was perhaps also in the name of *jouissance* that in Washington, DC, in October 1996, under waving flags, tens of thousands of Hispanics gathered on "*el día de la Raza*" (the day of "the" race). "Gone are the days when people could talk about Latinos as a mob without ideas and without a political program," declared Juan José Gutiérrez, director of the Coordinadora 96, the group organizing this march. However, the event was portrayed in the *New York Times* (1996) as "the first mass protest organized by Hispanic People in the nation's capital" (p. 26). According to author Steven Homes, "as much as the march and rally reflected anger among Hispanic people, it was an attempt by many participants to display pride in their heritage and to remind the larger society of their presence" (p. 26). The article concluded quoting Juan Martínez, whose great-grandfather was born in San Antonio when it was still part of Mexico. "They hear Spanish spoken at the grocery store or at the Kmart and they say 'My God, we're being invaded.' But if you really look at it, what was the first European language that was spoken in this hemisphere? It wasn't English" (p. 26).

Now that Hispanics have become the "first" minority, in the sense of being the most numerous, they have also organized a first protest, proving that Washington was worth a first mass. Although they are becoming less and less an invisible minority, Hispanics seem to continue to embody the return of the Other in a society that obstinately tries to erase the existence of the unconscious. As I noted earlier, the definition of Puerto Ricans as Hispanic poses problems because Hispanic is a construct overlapping and mixing up categories of race, language, and class. We have seen how in the Hispanic mass/mess, Puerto Ricans are just a subgroup. Is the Hispanic mass/mob the same as the Hispanic group/minority?

LOOKING AT ONESELF THROUGH THE OTHER'S GAZE

Of course not only Hispanics inhabit the ghettos; there are also, for instance, African Americans. Yet, the remarkable feature here is that Hispanics are not segregated by skin color but by the language they speak. Such a divide, observed daily, confirms the definition of the subject in terms of the Lacanian *parlêtre*, that is, a speaking being divided and coming into being as an effect of language. In my personal experience, I often noted how language was racialized and stigmatized. I almost always addressed people in the *barrio*'s streets in my native Spanish, but since I was seen as a white speaker, they would be surprised and would often tell me, "Oh, you don't look Spanish."

According to a segregation machine that runs along such linguistic divides, one of my patients who had dark black skin would complain about the "dirty blacks" that had moved to her block. There was no doubt that her identification was not as black insofar as she spoke Spanish. Assuming herself as part of the amorphous Hispanic crowd, she identified with the Other's discourse and naturalized language as racial difference. Unaware that she was supporting a racist discourse that also segregated her, she became a victim herself of such disparaging remarks. From the Other's perspective, "Hispanic" refers to a language and not a race; what is the race of Hispanics? As we have seen, even the U.S. Census Bureau admits that Hispanics "may be of any race."

We will then explore what the figure of the "Hispanic" may represent in its elusiveness by examining how this signifier may be invested with unconscious desire. If, as we have seen, it is difficult to find a specific trait that makes the Hispanics "Hispanic," we can assume that they might well be "like us." Yet there should be an element at the level of positive reality that is a surplus, an evasive feature that escapes analysis and differentiates them from all other people. That evasive trait, that surplus, is the unitary trait articulated by certain object *petit a*, resulting from a surplus production of enjoyment. If "Hispanic" appears as a signifier connoting a cluster of properties (of Spanish origin, dark skin, living in ghettos, docile, lazy, and so on), this relation is inverted and it is assumed that they are "like that." This inversion is not pure tautology because Hispanic does not mean of Spanish origin, dark skin, living in ghettos, docile, or lazy. Here we see the mechanism of racism at work.[1] Hispanics seem to refer to an unattainable something that is more than Hispanic. That "something" is an impossible-real kernel, a surplus produced by the signifying operation.

In the Real there is no support for a symbolization of the Hispanics. "Hispanic" is a signifier that functions as a signifier without a signified. "Hispanic" operates as a disfigured representation of social contradictions. Only by undoing the network of metaphors and metonymies that fleshes it out can one begin to interpret its meaning. "Hispanic" is a social symptom: a

---

1. For a brilliant analysis of racism in another context and of the political significance of the racist fantasy as a support of reality, see Žižek 1989.

point at which latent social conflicts break up out on the social scene, proving decisively that that society "does not work," that there is "no social rapport." However, from the perspective of the Other, Hispanic identity is clearly structured like a crowd. Hispanics are occupying here a position ascribed to any "other" group (it could be African-American, Jewish, Chinese, and so on)—the power of racism stems out of the primordial fascination each of us experiences facing human counterparts, of the mesmerizing image of the other in the mirror. This fascination for the other paradoxically erases it as such, since one identifies with the other's mirror image while making the other as such disappear. As Philippe Julien (1994) explains:

> With his invention of the mirror stage, Lacan had exposed the very source of racism. . . . Indeed the power of racism is rooted in the primordial fascination of each of us with his or her counterpart, in the captivating vision of the Gestalt of the other's body in the mirror. A specific sort of beauty, silhouette, and muscle tone; the power of the body moving or at rest; the color of the skin, eyes, and hair—all this defines a phenotypic physiognomy productive of kinship along genotypic lines. On the other hand, this vision excludes the stranger, the one with whom I cannot identify lest he break my mirror. [p. 28]

Racism is not simply intolerance of differences but intolerance of excessive sameness. If the characteristics that define Hispanics get blurred, those who identified themselves as non-Hispanics feel their identity threatened. That is to say, the negation of the other is correlative of the self's affirmation. For instance, "something" in the blood of Hispanics makes them lazy and docile as opposed to having dominant, aggressive work-ethics; this is to say, something in their race makes them *other* or *not-me*, and the *I* can be *me* because *I* differentiate myself from the *other*. Fundamentally, here is an *other* that is seen as having access to a *jouissance* from which I am excluded.

To give an illustration, I will recount an uncanny experience I had one morning at the *barrio* clinic. The intake worker at our organization's Center City main office phoned in astonishment. She had received a call from another inner-city branch of our clinic; there was a man requesting services because he was undergoing very stressful circumstances: someone had assumed his identity. Having stolen his wallet, his "double" was obtaining Welfare benefits and health insurance; he used his name, social security number, and, at times, even his address. This markedly distressing situation was indeed complicated: when the new patient started the intake process, a serious problem arose. This new patient could not be accepted for treatment because he was already receiving services at our organization! Someone with his name, his date of birth, his social security number, and his address had already been in therapy with a colleague for at least a year in the unit I was working at. The bureaucratic process insisted upon the fact that if the data matched, then he was that patient. For instance, he could not request a "patient identification number" as the clinic procedures demanded, because he already had one, and so on. In a bizarrely dizzying dialogue, he insisted that he was himself and not the other.

This *méconnaissance* (misrecognition/misconstruction) had challenged the whole computer-system principle of reality, proving that the subject goes well beyond what is experienced "subjectively" by the individual. In the vicissitudes of subjectivity, what the Other sanctions allows the I to come into being. The alienating function/fiction of the I exposes here the passions of the soul, the "Thou art that" that allows the I to be. In this vignette that seems to literalize Freud's Uncanny, the Other sanctions the other patient, the "double," as the one, and leaves the new patient in the fatal limbo of "no identity." The drama of the mirror stage is here parodically precipitated in all its insufficiency and anticipation. The disguise of identity falls, the misrecognition that gives substance to identity dissolves; the decoy does not work, *I* does not equal *I*. Lacking the desire of the Other, one finds the mirror opaque. This is what psychoanalysis shows us about the function of the I, seen as a unity constructed around the image of the proper body in the mirror (an objectified figure) and the perception of one's own reality through this I. No wonder that the new patient's reaction was paranoid: they were stealing his most valued treasure—his legal and institutional identity.

This situation was jeopardizing all the illusions that produce a sense of self. Fortunately, rather than promoting a Hegelian murder, after long deliberations the administration of the organization agreed to provide treatment to both.[2] The assumption of the armor of an alienating, yet pacifying, identity was granted. Professional secret protected the "double," who could continue receiving treatment. The new patient started therapy

---

2. In the "Mirror Stage," Lacan (1977b) talks of "a consciousness of the other that can be satisfied only in a Hegelian murder" (p. 6).

in another branch of our clinic. However, for the Procrustean arbitrariness of the computer system it was never clear who was assuming the identity of whom.

Let us not set aside the geopolitical overdeterminations of this case. The "double" was a citizen from the Dominican Republic, whereas the man whose identity was stolen was from Puerto Rico. The "double" was an illegal immigrant who was therefore having access to medical and social benefits, assuming the prerogatives of his counterpart as a Puerto Rican and U.S. citizen. Not all Hispanics are the same. Yet I would often catch glimpses of the "double" sitting in the clinic's waiting room next to his wife, both dressed exactly the same, producing an uncanny mirror effect. He himself would behave like a crowd, adopting in his persona what the gaze of the Other creates for him—Hispanics are constructed as a crowd of mirror images, in which equality is built obliterating class and cultural, and why not, gender differences, a crowd in which subjective particularities become erased if not impossible.[3]

"OF *LA LA LA RAZA*
PORQUE I LOVE *LA LA RAZA*"[4]

Are we, therefore, better equipped to account for the recurrent appearance of the signifiers *La Raza* in the identificatory strategies of many other members of the Hispanic community? Northern Mexicans, Mexican Americans, Chicanos, greet each other with a *¿qué pasa La Raza?* (what's up, the race?). Puerto Ricans refer to other Puerto Ricans as people of their race, placing *la Raza* as a substitute for nationality as discursive construction. Even I can recall a time when Argentina celebrated *el día de la raza* ("the Race" day) every October 12, marking the anniversary of Christopher Columbus's arrival on this continent, as many other Latin-American countries once did and some still do.

In 1519, Hernán Cortés arrived in Mexico wrapped up in the legend of Quetzalcatl, the feathered Serpent. One year later, in 1520, the Spanish

---

3. The stranger erased in the mirror participates in the *heteros* of woman; the erasure of difference (something akin to the denial of castration) unites those who look alike and creates fraternity and segregation.

4. From "soy un pocho" song by El Vez, in the C.D. "G.I. Ay, Ay! Blues: Soundtrack for the coming 'Revolution'" (1996).

Bishop of Mexico, whose name has been lost in oblivion, burned the codices that contained the clues for understanding the native languages, an equivalent of the Rosetta stone. Millions of Native Americans were killed during the conquest of America. Reclaiming a European heritage, in 1917 the President of Argentina, Hipólito Yrigoyen, declared October 12 a day to commemorate the discovery of America.[5] This decision came after the so-called *Campaña del Desierto* (1879–1882) was completed: the entire native population of the province of Buenos Aires had been exterminated. This wholesale genocide was conducted under the motto of "Civilization or Barbarism." One year later, in 1918, the King of Spain, Alfonso III, resolved to name October 12 the celebration of the day of The Race. Which race is the race that all agree upon seeing as the "one"?

For the Mexicans, *La Raza* is the Chicano, the descendants of Aztlan, proud of their Mexican heritage. But Puerto Ricans are not Aztecs, and 400 years of Spanish domination seems to have erased most of the Taíno presence, romanticizing it at a remove, and excluding any African component.

In Puerto Rico, following the American invasion, the political discourse of the last century invoked *La Raza* in order to sustain a nostalgic view of the colonial Spanish regime. A longing for *la vieja felicidad* (the old collective happiness), condensed in or allegorized by *La Raza*, helped build a sense of national identity around the Hispanic heritage. Mariano Abril— one of the main ideologists of the *Partido Unionista*, according to Mariano Negrón-Portillo (1997)—claimed that Puerto Rico was of "Hispanic origin, and therefore, of Spanish soul," contending that there were few foreigners on the island and that even those Puerto Ricans of African ancestry had Spanish language, customs, and idiosyncrasy. Hispanism also characterized the position of the independentists—Albizu Campos embraced *La Raza* as he reclaimed a Spanish heritage (Negrón-Portillo 1997).

Discussing the experience of Puerto Ricans in New York City, Clara E. Rodríguez (1995) points to the complexity of their racial identification within the U.S. binary black/white system. "Puerto Ricans find themselves caught between two polarities and at a dialectical distance from both. Puerto

---

5. The text of President Yrigoyen's decree portrayed the discovery of America as the most transcendental event in the history of humanity attributed to the "Hispanic geniality and supreme vision of Colombus." The establishment of the festivity honored Spain in "jubilant recognition" of "the magnificent courage of its warriors, the ardor of its explorers, the faith of its priests, the guidance of its wise people, and the labor of its magistrates, spreading their virtues in the Americas."

Ricans are between white and black; Puerto Ricans are neither white nor black" (p. 81). Edwin Torres's character, the street hustler Carlito Brigante, sums it up cogently: "In matters of race, Puerto Ricans was ahead of their time in the forties. We accepted everybody. Nobody accepted us. Since black was not in style in them days, us P.R.'s declared ourselves white. We had a few variations but that didn't bother us none" (Torres quoted in Santiago 1995, p. 200). Consistent with Carlito's observation, Grosfoguel and Georas (2000) note that the racialization of Puerto Ricans as inferior "Others" was initially entangled with the racialization of African Americans. To better illustrate this point, let us take a quick look at a story by Oscar Lewis (1966) that is emblematic of the process of "racialization" experienced in the 1950s by many Puerto Rican migrants in the mainland:

> When I came to New York . . . [I] was asked my nationality and my cousin answered Puerto Rican, but she wrote down Negro. My cousin protested, "No, no, no, not Negro, Puerto Rican." She gave him a look but erased "Negro" and wrote down "Puerto Rican." It was my first experience of that kind up here. [Narrated by Soledad, as quoted by Lewis, p. 227]

According to Grosfoguel and Georas (2000), in the 1950s Puerto Ricans became a newly racialized group different from whites and blacks primarily because they had become an "underclass," "a redundant colonial/racialized labor force." Their conclusion is clear: "Although Puerto Ricans form a phenotypically variable group, they have become a new 'race' in the United States" (p. 24). They argue that since this mass arrival, other immigrants have been subsumed into this "race," which occupies the economic niche of low-wage manufacturing jobs, and quote a Dominican informant who says, "In New York City, if you are not white or black, then you belong to a third racial category called 'Puerto Rican.'" Grosfoguel and Georas note that many multiply efforts to distinguish themselves from the label "Puerto Rican" in order to avoid being associated with the negative symbolic capital that the rubric denotes. Even for those who can "pass," once someone is identified as Puerto Rican he or she enters "the labyrinth of racial Otherness" (p. 24).

Whereas the racialization of dark-skinned Puerto Ricans may be more blatant, even "white" Puerto Ricans are racialized as inferior "others" in the American imaginary. Judith Ortiz Cofer opens her piece "The Story of My Body" with a sentence that illustrates how the gaze of the Other perceives her differently in the mainland and in Puerto Rico: "I was born a white girl in Puerto Rico but became a brown girl when I came to live in the United States" (quoted in Santiago 1995, p. 132). Rodríguez (1995) analyzes recently gathered data on racial classifications in New York and concludes that although for Puerto Ricans "color has never been an issue" . . . "it is possible that they are perceived as darker than they are, when it becomes known that they are Puerto Rican" (p. 87).

SPECIFY RACE: BLACK, WHITE, ASIAN, PUERTO RICAN, ETC.

Recent studies have examined the implications of exposure to U.S. race relations in the construction of Puerto Rican racial and ethnic identities. Landale and Oropesa (2002) surveyed Puerto Rican mothers in the U.S. and Puerto Rico and found out that both mainland and island Puerto Ricans most often designate their "race" as Puerto Rican. However, island women primarily identify themselves as white, black, or trigueña, while mainland women identify themselves as Hispanic/Latina, Hispanic American, or American. The authors argue that these differences between the mainland and the island cannot be explained by parental ethnicity, skin tone, demographic factors, or socioeconomic status. Their findings suggest that mainland Puerto Ricans more strongly reject the conventional U.S. notion of race than do their island counterparts. When Puerto Ricans identify themselves as belonging to the "Puerto Rican race," they may find the answer to the question "What is it to be Puerto Rican?" in the construction of a Puerto Rican race.

Ronald Fernández's *Prisoners of Colonialism* (1994) offers a story that condenses and illustrates the intersection of identity politics, mental health, and war aftermaths in the racialization of Puerto Ricans. Luís is at a Puerto Rico Navy recruiting center and he is filling out a form as a volunteer. He openly dislikes violence and ends his training with a "nervous breakdown"; one may wonder if he also suffered from *ataques*. As in Lewis' interview above, this passage can give an example of how the idea of a Puerto Rican *raza* has been linked to nationality.

> Confronted with a form that asked for his race, "I without thinking, filled in the only race I knew, Puerto Rican." That didn't satisfy the recruiters who, "when they read the form, they called me back and said, 'bullshit, Black,' then they wrote, 'nationality, American, Race, Black.'" . . . If Luís used the word race at all, *la raza* referred to an ethnic group. He didn't recognize differences that stemmed from skin color, and he didn't understand the discrimination that was everyday fare during his basic train-

ing. Puerto Ricans were "spics," and the word was said in a tone of voice that indicated total contempt.

The training transformed Luís. . . . "I had never dreamed such violence could dwell in my being, but this is what happened. . . . The violence that had been implanted in me would not let me live. The contradictions were too great." He had a nervous breakdown and left the Army addicted to heroin. [pp. 134–135]

From a Lacanian point of view, La Raza functions as a fundamental signifier used in the consolidation of a totalizing colonial program; it is a Master signifier (S1) that also exposes the return of the foreclosed Other within the colonial encounter. The signifier's stress is put on "the" Race (La Raza), which presupposes that there is only one or that other races remain in some unnamed outside. La Raza thus underscores an exclusionary discourse. For instance, one often hears the opinion that there are no racial problems among Puerto Ricans. Such a questionable contention surfaces in two books among many. Tomas Blanco's El prejuicio racial en Puerto Rico (Racial prejudice in Puerto Rico) (1948) concludes that "racial prejudice, as it exists in the United States, does not exist" in Puerto Rico (p. 63). S. Arana Soto's Puerto Rico: Sociedad sin raza (Puerto Rico: Society without Race) (1976) opens up by praising how much better slaves were treated on the island (let us not forget that slavery was abolished on the island only in 1873) before concluding with the notion that blacks and whites live together very happily because "in Puerto Rico the black is white, is Spanish" (p. 92).

One may wonder whether a society organized around the concept of La Raza can produce at the same time a society without race. Let us note that the use of the inaugural signifier La Raza allows for this foreclosure because La Raza does not find a second signifier that would be an S2, thus triggering a new chain of signifiers. Stuck in a position of misleading dominance, La Raza underpins a system of unitary identification foreclosing difference. Such an ideology may then assert that it is not racist because it precedes the predication of difference.

LOSING (THE) RACE

Hispanics are losing the race defined by traditional American myths (Get rich quickly in the melting pot) but are winning the race of the race: their birth rate is inversely proportional to their poverty. Hispanics reside at the bottom ladder of the economy and are growing poorer. As we have seen,

Hispanics are not simply those who speak Spanish. Being the emergent of a point of impossibility, they render themselves as witnesses and evidence of the existence of the unconscious that American culture insists on denying. Speaking *Spanglish*, they allow the surfacing of a linguistic failure, of the subversive defile of a language resulting of transliterations that is very close to the Lacanian *lalangue* (thelanguage/language) that in its quality of language traversed by desire, the unconscious, and the impossibility of sexual rapport, marks the lack in the Other. The Lacanian concept of *lalangue* concerns the field of language: insofar as it is "barred," it cannot be a consistent Whole; it is inconsistent, a not-all totality. For Lacan (1990), communication is a way of becoming lacking, in which speech may be talking to oneself or merely the movements of the lips as a level of *lalangue* that makes communication and the existence of others a problem. Where there is only one, there cannot be an other. The idea of completion, of Whole, excludes the possibility of an exception. The paradox of the minorities is that they constitute the exception for the majority in a "united" (whole) state. Hispanics are an exception subtracted as excess.

LIFE IS A DREAM

If we agree that the collective is a formation of the unconscious and that the individual, far from preceding the crowd, is in fact produced by it, as the mirror-stage teaches us, then the unconscious is singular yet traversed by the plural; the unconscious makes of the collective a singular question. The subject, however, is lost in the dream but reappears in the telling of the dream. Freud's originality as a psychoanalyst was in taking the dream in its associations to its forgotten parts. That is to say, Freud takes the dream as the telling of the dream. What is important in clinical practice is that the dream can be told; the dream makes us speak. If the social link materializes the oneiric life, paraphrasing Pommier (1990) one may say that the social link allows us to dream awake.

Freud woke up from his dream of the Hispanic-American War, but the United States is still dreaming this same dream of a Hispanic versus American war, over and over again. I have suggested that the United States constructs itself as an Empire with the Spanish Empire as repressed Other. Therefore, the role of the Hispanics as Spanish Americans becoming the "first" minority is crucial. If Martin Luther King were here with us today, he would not say, "I have a dream" but exclaim, "We are the dream, we are the crowd." Or perhaps he would repeat the memorable words of the main character of Pedro Calderón De La Barca's *Life Is a Dream* (1955). In the play, the imprisoned Polish prince, coincidentally named Segismundo (the Spanish for Sigmund!), was kept in a tower by the king since birth in order to overcome the predictions that his fate was to bring disgrace to the kingdom and downfall to his father. After years of imprisonment, the King has a change of heart and the now young man is brought to court for a trial while in a deep sleep. Awakening to the majestic grandeur of the court, he sees his father, King Basilio, and vengefully tries to attack him. The guards intervene, and Segismundo is returned asleep to his prison. Back in his tower, he believes that everything was just a dream. Nonetheless, when a peasant revolt liberates him, Segismundo is magnanimous with the vanquished king and aware that his new life is but a dream; this time he behaves more prudently. This is what he says:

> I dream that I am here,
> burdened with these prisons,
> and I dreamt that in another,
> I saw myself in a more joyful state,
> What is life? A frenzy,
> What is life? An illusion,
> a shadow, a fiction,
> and the greatest good is small;
> all life is a dream,
> and a dream, is a dream.[6]

In *Life Is a Dream*, the first time that Segismundo is released from his prison, he loses his freedom after trying to attack the king. Back again in the tower, he wakes up still chained and assumes that the day's happenings were just

---

6. Yo sueño que estoy aquí
 destas prisiones cargado,
 y soñé que en otro estado
 más lisonjero me vi.
 ¿Qué es la vida? Un frenesí.
 ¿Qué es la vida? Una ilusión,
 una sombra, una ficción,
 y el mayor bien es pequeño:
 que toda la vida es sueño,
 y los sueños, sueños son.
 (Calderón De La Barca 1955)

a dream. Nonetheless, Segismundo, the prince, learns the lesson that Sigmund, the analyst, could have taught him concerning dreams and attacks: the same fantasy finds different forms of expression both in dreams and attacks. Once he is liberated by the peasant uprising, this second time the prince manages to realize his desire and negotiate a better relation to the object *a*. He dethrones his father but behaves in a dignified way with the defeated monarch, and returns the crown to him, free to leave a loveless marriage arrangement to be with the woman he loves. Thus, the dream substitutes for the attack and realizes desire more successfully.

One of the main lessons of Freud's dream of the Spanish-American War, which we explored in the previous chapter, is how the personal and the collective determinations intersect at an unconscious level. Then, it is not so surprising to see that the solution to the enigma of the *ataque* can be found in a collective dream. Could we rephrase the Puerto Rican syndrome as the Puerto Rican dream? Then, the question one needs to pose becomes: Who is the dreamer? Is there an Other of the dream? The answer may be given by the hysterical mechanism through which Hispanics identify themselves, as we have already seen, when they use the term *La Raza*. Do they then align themselves with the Other's racist assumptions? The *ataque* would appear as the message sent back to the Master so as to write a history that has been repeatedly erased, effaced, and crossed out. As Langston Hughes (1959) writes:

What happens to a dream deferred?
Does it dry up
like a raisin in the sun?
Or fester like a sore—
And then run?
Does it stink like rotten meat?
Or crust and sugar over—
like a syrupy sweet?
Maybe it sags like heavy load.
Or does it explode?

Blocking the Hispanic Unconscious[1]

I have used the Lacanian model to analyze the Puerto Rican syndrome with the understanding that this theory offers a unique insight into the knotting of the political and the individual domains. While I would not want to oppose theory and practice, it is imperative to pose questions about their combined impact when dealing with the complex domain of the clinic.

True, we have seen that one may wonder whether psychoanalytical theory and practice are suitable treatment of poorer patients in inner-city clinics. The relevance of psychoanalysis has often been disregarded when dealing with economically depressed, nonwhite urban populations. Psychoanalysis is derided as a luxury, a therapy of choice applicable to the upper classes for whom it is uniquely available financially. When one presumes that psychoanalysis would not be useful for the "real" problems presented by the poor, one assumes that only the "real" world provides a solution that will have to be found by social, political, or economic means. Rather describing current social realities, this notion condenses a symp-

---

1. Earlier versions of segments of this chapter have been published as "Blocking the Hispanic Unconscious: Subjectivity and Subjection," *Clinical Studies: International Journal of Psychoanalysis* 2(2) (Gherovici 1996c).

tom of our dominant culture, revealing, moreover, the unflattering view practitioners have about the minorities they serve. The purported unsuitability of psychoanalysis for poor minority groups exposes a political conflict with important clinical consequences. The prevailing assumption is that only well-educated, sophisticated, verbal, introspective, and affluent individuals meet the criteria for "analyzability."

The belief that psychoanalysis is inadequate for poor minorities predominates among psychoanalysts, mental health workers, academics, and decision makers in government regardless of their ethnic background, and it simply obliterates the mental health needs of "underserved" ethnic minorities. This situation demands careful examination because of its clinical, ideological, and political effects. The undemocratic character of current mental health practices is more pronounced for Hispanic patients in a situation that ultimately perpetuates marginalization and subjugation.

I contend that the dismissal of psychoanalysis as cost ineffective is fraught with ideological and political reaction. The Lacanian motto, "The unconscious is structured like a language," means that no level of education or sophistication is required in order to sustain an analytic treatment. If the therapist or analyst conducting the treatment wishes to put the patient's subjectivity to work, this can be done even in settings and treatments that may not be explicitly psychoanalytic in orientation or structure. Issues of setting—like the number of weekly sessions—should not define psychoanalysis. That lower income sidetracks the unconscious from therapeutic exploration is, I believe, a grave mistake. Contrary to the tradition of successful psychoanalytic clinical work done in public settings at very low costs met with in France and Latin America, in the United States psychoanalysis has been practiced almost exclusively in a classical milieu, which has meant so far in its most upper-class realm. In the United States rigid class boundaries have prevented experiments like those conducted in other countries like France or Italy. In light of this oversight, can one plausibly make sense of the current unwillingness to include psychoanalysis as an option for the impoverished?

IDENTIFICATION WITH THE AGGRESSOR:
RACISM TURNED AGAINST ONESELF

Distinguished and representative Spanish-speaking mental health practitioners such as Salvador Minuchin (Minuchin, Montalvo et al. 1967), Harry

Aponte (1994), and Jaime Inclan (1985) have cast off psychoanalysis as an "elite" treatment and exclusively endorsed family therapy models. Minuchin, who is widely recognized as a leading family therapist, considers that Freud's "great psychoanalytic insights" (p. 35) derived only from studies of the middle-class population, and therefore are not applicable to "the disorganized and disadvantaged family" (p. 192). Minuchin dismisses the fact that Freud practiced psychoanalysis across class boundaries. While one cannot deny that most of Freud's famous cases were upper-class patients, two of Freud's five seminal cases in *Studies on Hysteria* (Freud and Breuer 1895) concern patients outside that class: Katharina, a waitress at a mountain hostel, and Miss Lucy, a governess. Freud treated Katharina with a brief therapy conducted at a height of over 6,000 feet and without a couch. Katharina's words describing her anxiety attacks as "my nerves are bad" (p. 125) could be a verbatim transcription of what I hear today from patients suffering *ataques*.

Clearly, Freud's usual practice of seeing patients five times a week for one hour at a time and for a few very intense months makes for an expensive therapy no matter how generous with her time and money an analyst can be. But following Lacan's refashioning of psychoanalysis and the various institutional models that have been elaborated, one can argue for a more flexible psychoanalytic practice.

In Minuchin's co-authored classic *Families of the Slum* (1967), the requirement of adapting techniques to the needs of the population is strongly granted, but paradoxically this standard seems instead to recommend techniques adapting a population to a situation of need. The low-income population became known in the United States as an "unreachable" group under the assumption that individual psychotherapy requires a permissive environment, a nondirective approach, and a free-associative atmosphere leading to patients remembering past events. Minuchin argues that skills essential to psychoanalysis are underdeveloped in this population. His approach suggests a stubborn wish to take certain psychological attributes like "lack of verbal and conceptual skills, special linguistic code, motoric 'acting out' orientation, nonintrospective approach" (p. 36) that are ascribed to the allegedly "incompetent functioning" (p. 357) or the "heterogenous nature of the poor" (p. 36) as absolute and impassable givens.

Aponte (1976) slightly modifies Minuchin's notion of "disorganization" by proposing "underorganization," in order "to suggest not so much an improper kind of organization, as a deficiency" (p. 433). Aponte (1994) argues that because of this deficient "underorganized" structure, low-income fami-

lies call for "an even more active approach" (p. 154). Thus, he opposes classical psychoanalysis that he pictures as calling for "a detached and passive
stance in therapy, with analysts keeping their feelings private" (p. 154). Is
Aponte's assumption that psychoanalytic neutrality and a right to privacy
are by nature class privileges? He suggests, nevertheless, heeding Freud's
attention to analysts' reactions to the patient's transference. Consequently,
Aponte strongly encourages therapists to analyze their countertransference.
His consideration of "the need of therapists to look at themselves" focuses
more on the fact of transference rather than on its content, however. Then
he does not avoid the imaginary traps set up by a therapist raised to the
position of all-knowing Other who decides what is best for the patient and
imposes his or her idea of reality. His recommendation "to offer palpable
help with organization and communication" seems to replicate the same
position of dependence he identifies as creating the poor population's
underorganization problems.

While he notes that "the poor are dependent upon and vulnerable
to the overreaching power of society" (Aponte 1994, p. 8) and that they
need "to feel control over their own lives" (p. 9), he contradictorily contends that "therapy with the poor is an active, involved affair for therapists." He recommends that therapists "state opinions, give advice, in short
become activists with the families and the whole community" (p. 154).
But how can one integrate political activism with personal change without wholesale social restructuring? The therapist's active advice may not
be imposing social convention, but it undoubtedly replicates an oppressive social power structure. Instead of steering toward the subject's separation from the Other's tyranny, this strategy produces greater dependence. Is a paternalistic attitude—exemplified by the offered solution,
giving advice, and advocating in the name of the poor—the only way to
"empower" poor minority families?

Jaime Inclán has conceded in his argumentation, not tacitly but explicitly, that the inclination in his treatment modality is to maintain subjection as a social condition and relation of power. Inclán (1985) criticizes
psychoanalytic theory for its allegedly "individualist value orientation"
(p. 330). Rather than emphasizing individuation and freedom, he believes
that family therapy should emphasize the value of the family as a matrix of
identity, which for him is syntonic with the values of low-income Puerto
Rican families. Perhaps unaware of the full political implications of his
theses, Inclán writes:

Family therapy is more readily prescribed as treatment of choice for Puerto Ricans, Hispanics, and other minority groups. Although sometimes this choice is based on discriminatory reasons that implicitly propose "second class" treatment to "second class" citizens, the choice seems to be oriented by some level of understanding of the congruence of values between the therapy modality and the patient population. The value orientation of conquering nature—physical, human, supernatural—is a relatively foreign one to poor people in general, and to poor Puerto Ricans in particular. While in the United States a middle-class value of conquering space, cancer, class boundaries, etc., seems to be accepted as the established value norm, poor Puerto Rican people are governed more by a value of subjugation to nature. [p. 330]

While Inclan argues that the "value-orientation framework" allows one to see cultural differences in a less prejudiced way, he acknowledges that some of the "value-orientation differences" that are attributed to race and ethnicity are the result of social class. Unhappily, Inclán posits a model adapted to "poor Puerto Ricans" that replicates the values of a discriminatory class structure that marginalizes the poor. Thus he identifies the lack of class mobility not as an external social condition but as an intrinsic cultural trait. Inclán seems aware that in the United States "a middle-class value of conquering" is not only the value norm but also the key to success in an individualistic society. Yet what he identifies as the poor Puerto Rican's "value of subjugation" is nothing other than the purported "docility" of Puerto Ricans discussed in the previous chapter. This social construction of "docile" Puerto Ricans is not far from that of "unproductive, lazy" Hispanics, which thus appears to be perpetuated even in therapeutic approaches.

This loaded description has obvious "othering" functions. Such a drift was already visible more than a century ago in Albert Robinson's (1899) book *The Porto Rico of Today*, when he stated, "There is little to encourage a belief that the native people will be disposed to make a radical change in their nature and habits, and transform themselves from a lazy, easygoing, and in the main, idle people, into active and energetic workers" (quoted in Santiago-Valles 1994, p. 19). Robinson's perception of the natives as "unproductive and lazy" who cannot transform themselves is thus not far from the "value of subjugation to nature" ascribed to poor Puerto Ricans by Inclán.

Inclán's refusal to apply psychoanalysis is grounded in its alleged irrelevance as he prefers "second class" models of therapy "congruent" with "values of subjugation" deemed more suitable for those who are described as "second-class citizens." While presenting a portrait of class determination as an "essential" cultural feature, the gesture aims at adapting therapy itself so as to maintain the original unfavorable conditions—therapy carries directly the imprint of an oppressive economic and political system. This position endorses the fact that some people will not be as upwardly mobile as the American Dream of the self-made individual promises. Poverty is understood as the result of personal or racial defects, echoing ominously with statements like "The poor are poor because they are lazy," if not with "They are poor because they are Puerto Rican" (see Sennett and Cobb 1972). An insidious colonial exclusion has therefore been fully internalized and has found an adequate expression in the therapist's ideological biases.

When the alleged unanalyzability of low-income patients is based on stereotypes that describe poverty as either a psychic problem or a "natural" cultural value, we meet prejudices that encroach on therapeutic models. What is at stake in these assertions of mental disorganization of the poor is the implication of some form of psychic inferiority. We see the strange spectacle of practitioners recommending therapeutic interventions that they themselves call "second class." The issues revolving around race, class, language, and culture that arise in these settings tend on the whole to exclude a consideration of the effects of the unconscious. Even when Hispanic therapists are committed to their practice and devoted to the population they serve and also represent, they betray the subtle workings of the logic of exclusion by which prejudice accompanies the vindication of difference. The tenacious infiltration of racism and its irrational nature are no news. Following Lacan's notion of an always precarious identity, we can be made aware of how the self is fundamentally constructed in and by alienation, that is, projected as "other." A psychoanalytic understanding of the logic fantasy and the identifications such a logic underpins will be indispensable if we wish to explain the pervasive inner and outer conflicts inherent to racism.

THE UNCONSCIOUS UNBOUND AND CLASS BOUNDARIES

Why has American psychoanalysis been unable to undertake the task of fostering the integration of the people marginalized by society at large? Besides the purported class bias in Freud's clinical models, the wider political and social relevance of psychoanalysis has been disregarded since here psychoanalysis and the establishment have converged or overlapped. Historically, psychoanalysis in the United States has developed as a medical subspecialty by trying to present itself as apolitical.

One could argue that it was the medicalization of American psychoanalysis that brought along a cleansing of ideology and political content. Its seeming neutrality is obviously political and ideologically loaded, but reveals not just ideological naiveté but also something that runs against the grain of the Freudian experience. Since Freud had posited an unavoidable antagonism between the individual and society, "adaptation" never was a key word for psychoanalysis. Freud condensed his ideas regarding the irremediable suffering that the social order imposes on individuals in a book whose original title was *Das Unglück in der Kultur*, literally *Unhappiness in Culture/Civilization*. "*Unglück*" also calls up accident, disaster, tragedy. The word was later changed to "*Unbehagen*," a term for which it is difficult to find an English equivalent, though *malaise* comes quite close. In a letter to Joan Riviere, his translator, Freud suggested *Man's Discomfort in Civilization*. Riviere came up with the final title: *Civilization and Its Discontents*. The word *Unbehagen* calls up the irremediable antagonism between subjects and the demands of civilization. The subversive impact of psychoanalysis lies not only in asserting the radical discontinuity between the demands of society and the individual's wishes, but in refusing to domesticate unconscious desire so as to conform to the imperatives of the social world.

The nuances of the German *Unbehagen*, lost in translation, reappear in Lacan's seminar *Ou Pire* (1971), when he plays on *Unbehagen* as *malaise* and remarks that the relationship of the subject to civilization is structurally disharmonious. We are ill at ease in culture; civilization never frees us from discontent. The imperatives of so-called "mental health" themselves cause some *malaise*. Thus, in what is not such a paradox, "health" itself can be sickening. Lacan (1977c) also takes the double meaning of "culture" in French as a pretext to pun on culture as a linguistic culture medium full of microbes, a *bouillon de culture* in which humans are simmering.

Freud's thesis is sweeping: civilization leads to neurosis just because it asks too much of the subject. Acknowledging this structural imbalance, he claimed that a successful psychoanalysis can rescue an analysand from neurotic misery but only to restore a state of health that he calls "common unhappiness" (Freud and Breuer 1895, p. 305). No wonder that in a country in which the pursuit of happiness is a fundamental tenet of the Declaration of Independence, Freud has become a *malaise*, an affliction. The civilized uneasiness revealed by psychoanalysis has turned into cultural unrest.[2] The numerous controversies around Freud's legacy have raged with increasing bitterness in recent years. Why is psychoanalysis still creating such tenacious resistance?

I am not advocating that psychoanalysis provide a universal panacea for all evils but cannot help wondering why past efforts to take into account class, culture, and race have produced and added discrimination. The discrimination has been double, first against psychoanalysis as luxury treatment and then against all those who are "different," not fully included in American mainstream society. "Culture" sends us on the trail of multiple class biases. Is the exclusion of psychoanalysis a class prejudice? The National Council of La Raza, in a paper on "Cultural Relevance: An Anglo's Guide to Working Effectively with Hispanics" (McKay 1985), states, "Some characteristics considered to be 'typical' of Hispanics are actually typical of low-income Hispanics" (p. 3). Most authors agree that richer Hispanics once away from the ghetto will lose most of the characteristics associated with being Hispanic. Ultimately, the consequence of a position that excludes the access to psychoanalysis for poor Hispanics would be that a poor Hispanic's unconscious is out of reach.

We have seen how intelligent people end up supporting such irrational racist, classicist, ethnocentric, ultimately impossible assumptions, in spite of all their good will. This happens because the malaise of civilization has remained the same: In the text I quoted above, Freud opposes the biblical injuction of "Loving thy neighbor as thyself" to the more cynical motto of "*Homo homini lupus*" (Man is wolf to man). The two collapse when racism returns to stress difference in the presupposed ideal identity of all. As Christopher Lane (1998) has contended, one observes how racism resurfaces despite an awareness of its irrationality. One possible explanation would be to see it derive from nationalist politics and colonial history, from capitalist greed and massive unemployment, and from poverty and global uncertainty. Lane adds one more twist to these reasons when he asserts that such "prejudice is cogent and palpable today *because it has never left us*" (p. 3). Even when the manifestations of racism can be understood historically, racism expresses a deeper psychic determination that is common to all subjects and that civilization tries to control with more or less success.

---

2. Alleged Freudian ideas have encouraged such abominations as the imprisonment of innocent parents on the basis of "repressed memories" of abuse solicited from young children by overeager therapists.

What happens then, when Lacanian psychoanalysis is taken to the margins and is actually practiced among marginalized people? Is it a transgression or a challenge of the boundaries of traditional psychoanalytic practice? As we have seen before, the reigning assumption shared by analysts and nonanalysts is that among low income populations, psychoanalysis is trivial, costly, and impractical. This unrelenting exclusion of psychoanalysis mobilizes the connection between the unconscious, class, race, and language, but also interrogates the relationship between the ethics of psychoanalysis and wider political concerns.

While most of the literature on psychotherapy with the Hispanic population often addresses the issues of culture, what has been left unexplored is how class permeates the psychotherapeutic situation. Within the American psychoanalytical field, apart from very rare exceptions, the issue of social class has been completely ignored. The dominant assumption is that this is not even an issue since both patients and therapists come from the same class. As Neil Altman (1995) has perceptively noted, the social location of the practitioners (psychologists or psychoanalysts) is usually within the "professional-managerial" class (p. 80). This dominant class is described by Altman as very insecure: ". . . they have nothing more tangible by way of capital to hold onto than their knowledge and expertise" (p. 81). I will argue that precisely this "capital" that places the analyst in a position of domination is what the analyst gives up in order to assure the progress of the cure. Thus, the injuries inflicted by the current social structure, and the interpersonal conflict and alienation that are its derivatives, will be *de facto* transformed by the nature of the Lacanian analytic relationship. As Raul Moncayo (1998) points out, the Lacanian analytic relationship overcomes the model of interactive domination because it "neutralizes" the class-bound "Master" position by offering a different mode of social link—analytic discourse. Moncayo argues that the Lacanian analyst's work progresses because it assumes that the symptom is something uncontrolled by the subject and to which certain knowledge is attributed (for example, a patient who complains of insomnia and does not know why he cannot sleep often believes that the practitioner will know why). These two factors, which are at the basis for the establishment of any transferential relationship, allow the treatment to start. The knowledge that the analysand will attribute to the analyst what Altman calls "capital" dissolves from the Lacanian perspective that describes the role of the analytst as shaped by an *ignorantia docta* or a "wise ignorance," as systematized by German Renaissance philosopher Nicholas Cusanus (Lacan 1998a). While the analyst operates in a place of wise ignorance, the supposed knowledge (or capital) is transferred to the side of the patient. The analysand's initial idealization because of her or his transference to the analyst, which is a precondition to the progress of the treatment, will eventually let the analyst fall from the position of subject-supposed-to-know; then the knowledge contained in the symptom will emerge not from the analyst's expertise or knowledge but from the analysand's unconscious. This shift requires that the analysand direct the cure toward the supersession of illusions, among which the illusion of the analyst's capital will also be given up.

This experience has transformative effects that introduce a new social link. This social link, rather than be regulated by a Master's model to which one is supposed to adapt or subject oneself, is regulated by the analyst's desire for pure difference. This social link acknowledges and accepts difference, meanwhile offering not only a new relation to one's unconscious but also a restitution of the "capital" of knowledge from which the analysand had been alienated. In the process, what is provided is the experience of a new model of social rules that is of particular importance for oppressed minorities.

Lacan adamantly contested the emphasis American ego psychology places on adaptation and opposed the functionally adapted subject required by the American free enterprise system. He rejected the idea of therapeutic improvement in terms of "better, more functional" adaptations to reality (which can be pathological) and believed that "adaptation" and "reality" are concepts determined by cultural values. Rather than reforming patients' behaviors with adaptational techniques or modifying patients' life performances with emotional reeducation, Lacan advocated listening to them while insisting that the unconscious is intractable. At the opposite end of the spectrum, most therapeutic approaches aim at changing behavior and domesticating via persuasion. As we will see in the next chapter, persuasion temporarily eliminates symptoms only to see them reappear, displaced in new formations. There is something that irreducibly haunts the subject and needs to be dealt with. Psychoanalysis should thus offer an ethics acknowledging the discontents of modern subjectivity. In Lacan's view, there is no need to advocate adaptation and happiness as defined by utilitarianism. Obedience to altruistic notions of duty only hides a perverse narcissism not unrelated to mechanisms such as found in Sade's libertine philosophy. The psychoanalytic subject is immersed in a universe ruled by desire and determined by a social order ushered in by language acquisition. This is why psychoanalytic practice gives priority to the speaking subject while accounting as well for the interaction of cultural determinations and class differences in each individual's fate. When this fate is construed as calling up the spirits of the dead, it becomes crucial to address the delineation of an overarching "spiritism" as the site that traditional culture had prepared in advance.

13

The Phenomenology of Espiritismo

Locating the source of an illness is an important first step because it will determine the treatment sought after. In an influential anthropological study about Puerto Ricans living in New York, Elena Padilla (1958) observes that this community believes in "natural" and "supernatural" causation for illnesses. Padilla notes that Puerto Ricans will consult physicians for those illnesses considered as having a "natural" causation, and *espiritistas* or spiritualists for those illnesses seen as caused "supernaturally" (p. 289). Since they firmly believe that spirits have the power to cause and prevent supernatural illnesses, to cure supernatural illnesses one will need supernatural treatments.

Melvin Delgado (1977) argues that Puerto Rican *Espiritismo* is a widespread form of indigenous therapy, noting that Puerto Ricans generally have negative attitudes toward social workers and other mental health professionals who are often seen as punitive authorities. Not only are social workers seen as oppressive figures, they also "lack the prestige given to spiritualists whose roles are sanctioned by the entire society to which they and their clients belong" (p. 453). Delgado sums it up: "If a Puerto Rican in need of assistance is offered a choice between a [spiritualist] medium and a social worker, he will probably choose a medium" (p. 453).

Indeed, all throughout the bibliography on *ataques*, the same pattern has been observed: often those Latinos suffering from *ataques* consult first a folk healer (*espiritista, curandero,* or *santero*) (Abad et al. 1974). Only when the folk healers do not solve or alleviate the problem will a mental health center or hospital emergency room be approached. Usually, by this time, the situation has reached critical proportions (Wallen 1992). Is therapy seen as no more than a last resort, when all other prospects have been exhausted?

THE FREUDIAN SPIRIT

Joan Koss (1975, 1987), Alan Harwood (1977), Melvin Delgado (1977), and Lillian Comas-Díaz (1981) praise the therapeutic aspects of *Espiritismo* and propose it as an effective alternative approach for the *ataque*. Harwood, however, argues that usually *ataques* do not require spiritual treatment since they are expectable, everyday cultural occurrences.

> Culturally appropriate times and places for seizures [of the *ataque* kind] include occasions when a show of grief is called for (such as funerals) or when one has witnessed or received news of a shocking event, particularly one affecting a loved one. While not necessarily approved, seizures are also expected from some women when they do not get their own way. Seizures of this kind, which occur under culturally predictable circumstances, are not referred to a spiritist for treatment. [p. 75]

For those who decide to look for help, choosing a psychoanalyst or an *espiritista* would not make any difference since, according to Garrison (1975, 1977) and Lubchansky and colleagues (1970), there is considerable similarity between psychoanalysis and *Espiritismo* not only on the practical but also on the theoretical level to claim an equivalence between the approaches of an *espiritista* and an analyst. Lubchansky and colleagues call the spiritualist healer a "paraprofessional."

Vicente Abad, Juan Ramos, and Elizabeth Boyce (1974) advise that the mental health worker serving Spanish speakers collaborate with the folk faith healer, and recommend the systematic inclusion of a folk healer in all mental health clinics for the Spanish-speaking. Their model of intervention, along with psychiatrists and social workers, includes individuals related to Puerto Rican clergymen and *espiritistas*.

When Delgado (1977) compares the roles of the Puerto Rican medium and the social work professional, he concludes that "both have a propensity toward task-oriented therapy, place heavy emphasis upon recognizing the impact of environmental factors upon psychic functioning, and utilize similar treatment modalities (individual, family, group)" (p. 456). Emelicia Mizio (1977), like Delgado, sees parallelisms in the theories of illness and healing and the healing method itself of social work therapy and *Espiritismo*. Mizio reaches conclusions similar to Delgado's and recommends that in order to increase efficacy, the social work profession should try to imitate the work of *espiritista* mediums. Mizio observes in *espiritistas* a "know how" that social workers do not seem to possess.

> Therapists have much to learn from the practices of spiritualists. . . . They know how to work with the extended family and call upon the support of the spiritual community, which militates against that sense of aloneness and alienation so typical to mental illness. Also, there is no stigma as the cause is externalized to spirits. They utilize suggestion, persuasion, and manipulation techniques which Lincoln Hospital psychiatrists in the South Bronx in New York City, one of the largest and most depressed Puerto Rican ghettos, are becoming skilled in applying. [p. 471]

It is true that there is a striking similarity between the strategies of folk healing and current mental health practices. From a structural perspective, psychoanalysts occupy a function and place quite homologous with that of the *espiritista* or the social worker—this is the place of the shaman or *griot* in other cultures. One finds an end to the similarities, however, when one explores not only the techniques but also the conception of cure and its ethical implications. To further explore the parallels between the spiritualist's and social worker's techniques and how they would differ from those of psychoanalysis, let us take a look at an example quoted by Mizio (1977):

> The woman was having great marital difficulties and was upset by her husband's affair with another woman. Upon visiting one day, the [social] worker was delighted to find the client was smiling and looking pretty. The [social] worker believed the treatment was finally working, only to learn that the woman had been to a spiritualist. The spiritualist had told the woman to purchase a male and female doll and to stick pins in them. Each day she was to chant one hundred times while looking at the dolls *Cayte muerte, Cayte muerte*—"Drop Dead," "Drop Dead."

> Before her husband's return from work each night, she was instructed
> to bathe and perfume herself and be sweet and loving. The client looked
> much happier. The hostility was being released and her changed be-
> havior was achieving a new positive response from her husband. The
> support the social worker gave her throughout may have been very sig-
> nificant, but so was the spiritualist's intervention. [pp. 471–472]

Although it cannot be said that this kind of intervention has not been extremely effective in modifying behaviors, one is left wondering about its ideological implications. George Devereux (1958) claims that indigenous therapy
does not provide a cure but rather a "corrective emotional experience." Symptom relief is its primary goal. This is accomplished by way of what Devereux
describes as "remission without insight, while not a 'cure' because the patient remains vulnerable, is nevertheless a 'social remission' and therefore
sufficiently valuable to the patient and the community" (p. 360).

Delgado (1977) describes *Espiritismo* as an institutionalized outlet for
the discharge of frustration and aggression. It is interesting, however, to
situate our example in the broader context of women's status in Latino
culture. Repeating a mantra such as "Drop Dead, Drop Dead" a hundred
times a day and using hypnotic devices (the prescription of perfumed lo-
tions to get rid of spirits), this woman achieves a "social remission" of symptoms—she manages to keep smiling, looking pretty, *looking* happy even in
an "upsetting" marital situation. By way of the "corrective emotional experience" she is able to comply with the request of being "sweet and loving"
with her husband. The nonexistent complementary between the sexes finds
a supplement to conceal an irremediable discontent: the pinned male and
female dolls get to exorcise the demons of the nonexistence of sexual rapport. It is not obvious that this "magic cure" successfully provides a direct
expression of anger, or whether it perpetuates women's dependency by
denying assertiveness in women by stressing an ideal of female coopera-
tion and compliance.

EXORCISING THE UNCONSCIOUS

Regardless of whether one may agree with the politics and ethical implications of magical cures, it is quite clear that the "improvements" are due
primarily to suggestion. The hypnotic effect of *Espiritismo* was identified
already more than a century ago, at a time when hypnotism was a serious
scientific enterprise. Joseph Bram (1958) mentions that at a spiritualist

convention held in Mayagüez, Puerto Rico, in April 1903, one of the speakers advocated for the inclusion of spiritualism in psychiatry, arguing that since at the time hypnosis had been validated and incorporated into medical therapy, so should the spiritual hypnotic power. Like Delgado and Mizio more recently, the conventioneer of the last century saw spiritualism as an extension of psychiatry and believed that exorcistic rituals should join psychotherapy.

With or without dolls and needles, contemporary psychotherapy still works at the level of suggestion. Given that, on the one hand, today there is growing skepticism about the powers of most forms of psychotherapy, and, on the other hand, Puerto Ricans are more culturally prone to accept the suggestions of an *espiritista*, it is clear that the folk healer with his or her "aura" of supernatural powers will be more likely to create magic, "miracle cures" for *ataques*. Let us not forget, however, that the results of suggestion are usually short term—patients' symptoms are improved by a "placebo effect." Over time, the healer is forced to repeat the same suggestions again and again, at regular intervals. I maintain that the existing parallel between folk-healing practices and therapy does not extend to psychoanalysis because of the radical difference between psychoanalysis and practices that rely on suggestion.

To better understand this difference between psychoanalysis and psychotherapies, let us then explore how the *espiritista* healer may approach a case of *ataque* in order to see how the modality of treatment of an *espiritista*—which will be compared to the psychiatric and psychotherapeutic approach—differs from that of a psychoanalyst. Thus, I will first analyze a case of spirit possession observed by Vivian Garrison, an anthropologist. Garrison (1977) describes this case study—one among 150 researched—as unique and inconsistent although she labels it "a 'typical' illustrative example of the '*ataque de nervios*'" (p. 384). However so, "unique" and "inconsistent" seem to be typical features of the *ataque*. Here is María's *ataque*:

> One hot Friday afternoon . . . María, an attractive, 39-year-old, married Puerto Rican woman, was sitting at a bench in a handbag factory in New York's garment district, where she had worked for four years. Suddenly, to the surprise of those around her, she began to scream and tear her clothes from her chest. She ran to the window, apparently trying to throw herself through it. When restrained, she fell to the floor in an unconscious or semiconscious state, with her whole body twitching. [p. 383]

Garrison notes that the *ataque* triggered a chain of events that engaged family, several physicians, the working place, a few psychiatrists, an anthropologist—Garrison herself—and one *espiritista*. The various specialists saw María's strange manifestations in diverse and contradictory ways: from malingering immature behavior to spirit possession, from neurotic reaction to paranoid schizophrenia. All this because she was just undergoing a well-known Puerto Rican experience—an *ataque de nervios*. Garrison notes:

> Psychiatrically she presents herself alternatively as hysterical, possibly psychotic, hypomanic, phobic, hypochondriacal, and as a relatively mature, self-assertive, and competent, although manipulative woman who uses hysterical mechanisms provided by the culture as an acceptable way of coping. Her premorbid or basic personality structure is not yet clear despite approximately thirty hours of observation and formal and informal interviewing. [p. 385]

Thus, as with any hysteria, María's manifestations seem to cover the entire field of pathology. Even after *thirty hours* of observation and thorough interviewing, María's symptoms manage to elude an accurate definition. Once more we are reminded that 4,000 years of failed interpretations reveal the tenacity and elusiveness of hysteria.

If María's symptoms may strike us as extravagant, esoteric, and old-fashioned, let us recall that Freud contends that we do not need to be surprised to see current mental disorders masquerading as neuroses of olden times. Freud (1959), in his 1923 piece "A Neurosis of Demoniac Possession in the Seventeenth Century," follows Charcot and identifes states of demoniacal possession and ecstasy as manifestations of hysteria. Freud argues that in his time, which he describes as the "present unpsychological epoch," an era in which the "somatic ideology of 'exact' science" prevails, neuroses appear under a hypochondriacal guise, masked as organic diseases" (p. 436). His observation remains even more current today, almost a hundred years later. Is not depression these days, for example, "unpsychologically" understood when it is considered to be a mere "chemical imbalance" that simply needs to be treated medically with "vitamin P"?[1] At a time when it seems normal that children grow up

---

1. "Vitamin P" is one of the names used colloquially for the antidepressant Prozac.

taking amphetamine-like stimulants (Ritalin) and graduate to antidepressants, when even shyness is treated with pharmaceuticals, Freud's views still appear up-to-date and are worth revisiting. "Demonic possession" seems an ideal venue in which to do so.

Both in today's somatic neurosis and demoniacal possessions of olden times, Freud goes on to say that there is common content. It is interesting to note, indeed, that María herself would have agreed with Freud's contention about the medicalization of the psychic realm by a "somatic ideology of 'exact' science." After the *ataque* described above, the factory foreman called María's family, and although both she and her relatives thought that she was "all right then," they took her to a nearby clinic "because she had to go anyway" (Garrison 1977, p. 391). At the clinic she was diagnosed as psychotic, possibly with paranoid schizophrenia, and was referred for immediate hospitalization at Bellevue Hospital in New York City. She could not agree less with the clinic's recommendation. María thought that although the doctor could not find anything medically wrong in her body, he still wanted her to be treated medically at a hospital. For María, although the problems engaged her body, the causation resided elsewhere. And thus she went to see an *espiritista*.

THE CURE

Already this clash between value systems seems to have a sickening, iatrogenic effect—Garrison notes that when María reached the *espiritista*, her "main complaint" was that she "had been referred to Bellevue" (p. 392). According to Rosa, the *espiritista* medium to whom María arrived by "chance" or "divine guidance," the *ataque* had been caused by three misguided spirits sent by witchcraft to work against Maria. Thus, during her first *consulta*, María knew that she was possessed by evil spirits because she was in the process of "developing spiritual faculties." The spiritual diagnosis was *obsesión*, literally meaning obsession but conveying spirit possession.

Rosa, the leader of one healing-cult center, administered the treatment. At the *centro*, two kinds of services were performed: the *reunión*, or public meeting, and the *consulta*, or private consultation. Rosa calls herself *espiritista*, *santera*, and "Apostolic Catholic." Let us note that *Espiritismo* and *Santería* are healing practices and not religions; thus they co-exist with Roman Catholicism. *Santería* is an Afro-American syncretic cult that evolved in Cuba and spread among Puerto Ricans and African Americans in the Northeastern United States. *Espiritismo* can be traced back to the nineteenth-century Allan Kardec, whose writings argue that the world is populated by spirits that surround the visible world and can penetrate it by attaching themselves to human beings. These spirits can at times incarnate themselves as human beings. Disembodied spirits may influence negatively or positively the existence of the incarnated spirits. The disembodied spirits can hold communication with the embodied spirits through "fully developed mediums" who have perfected their spiritual faculties. All spirits are subjected to a law of spiritual evolution. This law states that all spirits are created ignorant by nature but with the potential of achieving full light and understanding. They eventually can become pure spirits. Kardec's system considers that spirits must pass through three levels and ten grades of development of moral perfection— higher levels are purer and more spiritual. The lower levels are inhabited by uneducated spirits misled by "material" impulses. The so-called *espíritus intranquilos*, disquiet spirits, belong to the lower level. These spirits are just a few inches above earth and fail to fulfill their spiritual mission, ending bounded to earth as a result of a special attachment such as an unpaid debt, a premature death, and so on.

María's treatment took place in the saints' room, *cuarto de los santos*. There María sat opposite an altar while Rosa placed a piece of paper on which "María" was written under a fishbowl of water. Rosa then lit a cigar to invoke her Congo protections, breathed deeply, and with jerking movements of her body indicated the presence of spirits. Then she began offering María a series of statements about her symptoms and complaints. Rosa divined that María "had not slept for many nights," "she felt very nervous and did not know why," "she felt something in her head," "her mind goes blind," and that "she was afraid she was going to become *loca* (crazy)" (Garrison 1975, p. 396). Rosa also foretold María's major somatic complaints: "*dolor de cerebro*," or pain in the brain/mind, and "*dolor de cabeza*," or headache. Rosa concluded that what "she had" was simply "spiritual," not "material." To María's relief, Rosa reassured her that she did not need to go to the hospital—the cause of her *ataque* was definitely supernatural, thus meriting a supernatural approach.

In her short treatment at the *centro espiritista*, María underwent six seances with "developed" mediums. In a trance, the mediums threw themselves on the floor in a state that resembled *ataque de nervios* so as to express the messages of the *causas* or "bring them to light."

"WHO IS BRINGING THINGS TO LIGHT?"

María complained of being possessed by restless spirits. Following Freud and Lacan, we read this as a manifestation of hysteria in which we can identify the typical *jouissance* of the hysteric determined to "bring things to light" at any cost. This creates a situation in which the revelation of a truth exposes the desire of a disembodied spirit incarnated in the hysteric as a "foreign body." Several mediums attend the spiritualist séance; they may voice the *evidencia*, a vision to account for the possessed person's misery. Only under a state of trance will the possessed person utter the *evidencia*. Garrison (1975) observes that the trance state resembles *ataque de nervios*:

> The person staggers around the room arms flailing, body jerking, and voice wailing until he or she ends up on the floor quivering and silent, or beating the floor with fists and crying in what looks like either an infant's or a child's temper tantrum. These trances may look more or less sexual but they are more aggressive than sexual. [p. 438]

This is, as Joan Koss (1975) describes, a true cathartic experience. During the trance, "aggressive and unusual sexual behavior not sanctioned in other social contexts" (p. 160) can find expression. The relief brought about by these experiences is undoubted. What is interesting to note, however, is that this form of healing maintains the belief that the cause of the mental distress is external. The source of the problem is not considered part of the patient but rather something foreign—a deranged spirit possessing the patient's body and soul. In his *Studies on Hysteria*, Freud (Freud and Breuer 1895) describes the *cause* of Elisabeth's hysteria—her love for her brother-in-law—as being present in her consciousness like a foreign body [*Fremdkorper*] isolated from the rest of her ideational life. As with *Espiritismo*'s understanding of possession, in Elisabeth's hysteria the foreign body is radically heterogeneous and seemingly unrelated to the sufferer. This dissociation illustrates the classic hysterical position of the Hegelian "beautiful soul." Lacan (1977b) notes that "the *belle âme* . . . does not recognize her very own *raison d'être* in the disorder she denounces in the world" (p. 70). From a Lacanian perspective one may say that *Espiritismo* practices see the cause being always external and unrelated to the sufferer, that is, Other. This belief, on the one hand, exposes the subject's alienation to the Other, while on the other hand it helps maintain a position of "beautiful soul." This may help elude issues of subjective responsibility. Then, we may pose the question: Do *Espiritismo* healing practices empower or promote dependency? Victor De La Cancela and Iris Zavala (1983) contend:

> Folk healing . . . may function to placate the action potential of angry and frustrated individuals by offering mystical and magical explanations and solutions to what are long-standing consequences of structural inequities within our society. [p. 267]

Psychoanalysis is not a form of faith healing—it does not rely on the analysand's beliefs in the analyst's curative "powers" based on knowledge, experience, or reputation. Rather than the person of the analyst, what is important in psychoanalysis is the unconscious of the analysand. An analytic cure takes as its point of departure the structural splitting of the speaking subject who is "possessed" by the order of language that produces the unconscious. One of the aims of analytic treatment is to direct patients into what Lacan (1977b) calls the "discourse of the Other," that is, the dimension of unconscious desire that makes patients aware that no soul is ever "beautiful," because the discourse of the Other always, unavoidably, implicates them.

DeLaCancela and Zavala's observation about the potentially oppressive features of *Espiritismo* is pertinent. The adaptive, placating effect of folk healing should be opposed to the subjective transformation entailed by psychoanalysis, which, as Lacan (1977b) contends, opens a "little freedom" (p. 48) for the subject. Psychoanalysis breaks with the prevalent ideology of traditional healing systems by helping analysands review their positions facing the Other's desire. Free association allows the analysand to further articulate his or her relation to the Other while the analyst's interventions (through punctuation or scansion) let the analysand separate from the discourse he or she has been forging. Diana Rabinovich (1988) summarizes Lacan's clinical practice as aiming to allow the subject to acquire a margin of freedom in the relation he or she occupies as object of the Other's desire. To achieve this, it is necessary that the analyst take into account his or her desire, a desire to search for that absolute difference without which it will be impossible to achieve that separation that the subject experiences as a consequence of the analytic cure.

ENVY AND THE EVIL EYE

Ultimately, Rosa determined that a *trabajo de brujería*, a witchcraft work literally, a spell, had been launched against María to make her go crazy. Someone had *envidia*, was envious of her. By witchcraft, someone had "hired" obsessional spirits (*espíritus obsesores*) to work against María. These low, undeveloped, disembodied spirits, "spirits of darkness that fill your mind with base, material, ignorant thoughts, and impulses that you can't get rid of," had been "sent against her" (Garrison 1977, p. 423). The fact that the witchcraft against María was done by someone who was envious, is quite evocative.

Let us here take a detour into some useful Lacanian ideas. As Lacan notes in Seminar 11, the power attributed to envy to bring disease or discomfort relates to the powers of an evil eye, of vision, of the gaze. The word envy comes from the Latin *invidia*, which derives, as Lacan points out, from *videre*, to see. Precisely in his 1938 entry on the family for the *Encyclopédie Française*, Lacan talks about a first experience equivalent to "castration," using the example of the "bitter look"—St. Augustine's illustration of envy— a little child seeing his brother at his mother's breast. This is a "bitter look" that has on the child the effect of a poison. Lacan (1978) explains, "Such is true envy—the envy that makes the subject pale before the image of a completeness closed upon itself, before the idea that the *petit a*, the separated *a* from which he is hanging, may be for another the possession that gives satisfaction, *Befriedigung*" (p. 116). It is interesting to note that this reference to envy appears in a seminar session devoted to the object cause of desire, the object *petit a*, in the field of the visible, that is, the gaze.

Immediately following a modification to formula of desire as desire of the Other, Lacan proposes "a sort of desire *on the part of* the Other, at the end of which is the *showing (le donner-à-voir)*" (p. 115). Lacan is here referring to the "appetite of the eye on the part of the person looking" and mentions that the eye is endowed with "the power to separate." This endowment of the eye with "the power to separate" refers us back to a reformulation of the above-referred dictum involving human desire as the desire to be desired by the Other, which reveals the Other's desire as object.

In Augustine's example, an image to which Lacan often returns to evoke the object *a*, the child is no longer the sole object of the mother's love. Not only there is a rift between child and mother—the dream of a perfect completeness of mother and child is lost—but another child occupies the place this child would like to have in relation to the mother. As noted before, the Name-of-the-Father intervenes as a signifier of the mother's desire beyond the child, which breaks the *jouissance* of completeness. The child's envious eyes see a rift in the subject–Other completeness and the presence of a detachable object that permits the articulation of a fantasy relation with the Other. It is the separation from this *jouissance* before the letter that will allow the child to become a desiring being, or better said, desire's subject. Of this operation there is left over—a fantasmatic partner—the object *petit a*. This residue, the object *petit a*, is the object that will arouse desire in the fantasy. The Other, no longer complete, is split into a lacking Other and the object *petit a*. Lacan stressed the importance of his theory on the object *petit a*, which he regarded as one of his most important discoveries. The object *petit a* is one of the four symbols occupying different positions in each of the four discourses' algebra he puts forward in his 1969 seminar *L'envers de la psychanalyse* (1991d). Fink (1995) notes an interesting precursor to the theory of the "four discourses" that create specific forms of social bond, at the end of Lacan's 1965 "Science and Truth" (n. 14, p. 199). There, Lacan associates four other discourses with the four Aristotelian causes—Science: Formal Cause; Religion: Final Cause; Magic: Efficient Cause; Psychoanalysis: Material Cause.[2]

THE CAUSE AND THE CAUSES

Rosa guaranteed María that she was going to free her from the effects of the spirits; she was going to *despojarla*, to relieve her, which also suggested literally stripping her of property. María was to pray and wear a special perfume to repel the evil spirits. Rosa would help her to have her

---

2. "Science and Truth" (Lacan 1989) was the first session of the 1965–1966 Seminar 13, *The Object of Psychoanalysis*, in which Lacan situated the object *a* on four sides: the demand of the Other (object *a* is feces); the demand on the part of the Other (object *a* is the breast); the desire on the part of the Other (object *a* is the gaze); and the desire of the Other (object *a* is the voice).

causas, causes, "worked" or "lifted." *Causas* are ignorant spirits who harass the living. They are divided into "material" (natural) or "spiritual" (supernatural). The working to lift her *causas* involved several tasks. In a *consulta*, a medium aided by *guías*—spirit guides who protect from the influence of ignorant spirits—identifies the *causas* of a client in order to *despojar* and *limpiar*, clean a person's spirit by interrogating the causes. In trance, the medium will speak the message of the spirit and give reasons for harming the affected person. Then, "giving light" will proceed. The ignorant spirit will be educated, or "given light." If the spirit decides to accept the medium's advice to stop hurting the possessed person, the *causa* will be considered lifted. At times a series of tasks and rituals needs to be performed by the affected person in order to complete the education process of the ignorant spirit.

If one sets a parallel between the way magic is used and psychoanalysis, one may note that the curing method of *Espiritismo* combines hypnotic strategies with education, relying on the *espiritista*'s charisma: the possessed persons are influenced by the "powers" attributed to the *espiritista*—they will follow the given advice and show "improvements" by turning into what they believe this Other wants. This strategy may produce "miracles" but instead of leading to a separation from the Other, it increases dependence, subordinating their desire to the *espiritista*'s. At the opposite end, the psychoanalyst operates as pure "desiring substance" so as to lead to an empty space whose function is structural. In Seminar 13 Lacan (1964–1965) describes psychoanalysis as having the effect of separating us from the herd. We have seen how the crowd is kept together by a hypnotic "glue." Psychoanalysis separates us from the herd because it is positioned beyond hypnosis and underscores subjectivity, rather than sending patients back to a collective myth of shared identifications.

By now, we can agree that *Espiritismo* practices are effective at the level of suggestion. One should notice that suggestion becomes effective because the faith healer is directly placed in the position of the absolute Other, thus duplicating the structure that underpins the alienation that creates symptoms like María's. The effects of suggestion are short lived; they require that it be repeated again and again over time because the object *a* cannot be reduced to the Demand of the Other. For example, the faith healer told María that in six sessions she would feel well. Although this may bring some improvement to the possessed person who possibly will be changed for the better, it is evident that this change is not due to a permanent betterment. Rather, the possessed person improves because of what has been glimpsed of the function of the Other's desire. The charismatic healer *wanted* María to feel better after six sessions. When the "possessed" one sets out to satisfy the Other's Demand, he or she subordinates his or her own desire to this request. The actual causes of the "possession" remain untouched while the "cure" becomes a new instance of "possession." Thus, the mechanism producing the neurosis is as functional as before; it is in fact repeated by the "cure"—it lingers more or less dormant until it reappears. Therefore, the alienated position of the subject remains untouched since the "miracle cure" follows the lethal process of *alienation* and prevents the emergence of the subject's own desire.

One may argue that the speaking subject is always alienated in language. The process of subjectivation takes place in the field of the Other where one signifier is missing—the Other is lacking. The verbal becoming in which subjectivation is constituted splits the subject. The result of the operation of division of the subject produces a remainder—the object *a*, an object that takes the position of cause of the Other's desire. Since for Lacan desire is desire for the Other's desire, to desire for the other is to desire the object *a*. Often the divided subject facing the unspeakable dimension of the Other's desire procures an answer by taking the demand of the Other for the Other's desire. This process is called by Lacan *alienation*—there is no desire of one's own, the subject "fades" under the signifiers of the Other's Demand. However, the lack insists because the object *a* cannot be reduced to the demand of the Other. With the intervention of the Name-of-the-Father a second operation takes place, a *separation* between the subject and the object *a*. The child no longer needs to fulfill the desire of the Other; symbolic castration allows the child to respond to the Other's lack with his or her own lack.

RESISTANCE AND ALIENATION

According to *Espiritismo* beliefs, all of María's troubles were produced by disquiet *causas*. Are these *causas* operating as a Lacanian object-cause-of-desire? Perhaps, but María remains trapped in *alienation*; she is fully occupied, "possessed" by the consuming task of completing the Other rather than questioning her own desire and its causes.

What kind of sacrificial self-abnegation may be at stake? She was able to show herself through symptoms that staged a spectacle, but then renounced her own desire. Her body was touched—transformed—by the speech of a medium in trance who evoked half-dead spirits talking in the irrational manner of dream language. *Espiritismo*'s way of suggestion rapidly lifts symptoms but fails to offer a path to the recognition of desire. In order to let symptoms *speak*, Freud always recommended that it was unwise to get rid of them too soon.

Garrison (1977) maintains that María's *causas* "come expressing anger, hatred, and 'resistance to light'" (p. 436). At the very point when one can move beyond the symptom's alienation and truly begin, the *Espiritismo* treatment ends—the symptoms disappear but unless a separation from that which caused the symptom occurs, they will usually come back. María's position as a "beautiful soul" remains untouched. This is due to the issue of subjective responsibility, that is, María does not separate from the position of object *a*; the implication that she was the subject of *her* unconscious has been avoided.

The terminology of *Espiritismo* rituals of "working the *causas*" may suggest an overlapping with the Lacanian conception of the role of the analysts in the analyses, as object *cause* of desire.[3] For a psychoanalysis to progress, the analyst should avoid being seen as an imaginary object or as the symbolic Other to be placed instead by the analysand in the position of object cause of desire. Once in that position, the analyst will *cause* things to happen—the analysands will believe that they dream for the analyst, they will believe that previously neglectible events like a slip of the tongue, a joke, or a parapraxis will no longer be overlooked since they have acquired an Other meaning. Thus, formations of the unconscious that before would be passed over as incidental can have another reading than what they consciously mean; they become interpretable, sending us on the royal path to the Other's discourse. Often they are seen as produced *for* the analyst, who will help decode this Other dimension.

The analyst is situated in a position that differs radically from that of the *espiritista*. With the progression of the treatment, the psychoanalyst will have to be discarded by the patient and thus will fulfill the fate of any object that stands for the object *petit a*. The *espiritista*, on the other hand, remains

---

3. For Lacan, the object *petit a* plays a crucial role in the progress of an analysis since the analyst should position herself as the semblance of the object *petit a*, the cause of the analysand's desire.

as the ideal with whom the patient identifies and whom she introjects (the patient will appropriate the image of the *espiritista* and will as a rule become one herself by developing her *facultades* to communicate with the spirits).[4] The analyst will skirt the traps of becoming a mentor, an educator, or guru (as Lacan notes, even though the analyst intially plays the role described as "subject *supposed* to know," the analyst's knowledge is limited—the important knowledge in psychoanalysis is to be found in the analysand's unconscious). Apart from the fact that the analyst is in no position to educate or coach an analysand, such a stance would be in disagreement with the objectives of the analytic cure. Lacan strongly opposed analysts like Balint who argued that the identification with the analyst is the end of analysis. Lacan considered the end of analysis as a process where the subject's identifications are questioned; they will no longer be the same after analysis. The Lacanian analyst does not aim at helping the analysand embrace the analyst's values or ideals (be it happiness, improvement, or even getting cured); the analyst's desire is defined by Lacan (1978) as the opposite of identification, as a desire for "absolute difference" (p. 271).

There are equally fundamental discrepancies in the way the "possession" will be seen in the two systems. In the spiritist system, María's treatment will be a process to develop into a medium learning how to interrogate the spirits. It is quite positive that her symptoms will not be pathologized but rather taken as a sign of her developing *facultades*; any subjective meaning they may carry, however, will be supressed. For a psychoanalyst, María's possession will have a completely different logic: María's body is marked by inexplicable, mysterious symptoms. These symptoms will be taken as questions addressed to the Other—What do you want? Who am I?—questions for which she demanded a response. María had been *enferma de los nervios*, sick in her nerves, for *one* year before the *ataque*; the *ataque* that Garrison (1977) describes took place when her father fell ill and was sent to a hospital. There is a chronological correlation between her problems with her "nerves" and periods of illness suffered by her husband. During a psychoanalysis María could reconsider her relationship with her husband, her father, and beyond them, with the Father. The illnesses of these men in her life forced María to

---

4. *Facultades* (faculties) is the ability to hear or see spirits, to enter trance, to have inspirations.

become a nurse. Like Anna O., Dora, and Elisabeth, she was forced by the tasks of nursing the sick to suspend her own desires. Freud notes that being in a position of service, in which one's own desires are subordinated to the other's demand, has a hystericizing effect. One should reverse cause and effect and see this relation of causality differently. As Serge André (1999) remarks, it is not because of the nursing and the restrictions it imposes that someone becomes hysteric, but rather that the hysteric is particularly well suited for this task because the restrictions nursing imposes are an extension of the structure of hysteria. The self-sacrifice and abnegation before the demand of the Other required by sick-nursing actualizes the suspension of desire characteristic of the hysteric position. This situation allows the hysteric to mistake demand for desire and suspend her own desire that is subordinated to the desire of the other.

According to the *espiritista*, María was vulnerable to bad spirits because she was in the process of developing *facultades* (powers). Let us note that the resolution of her symptoms is based on the premise that María can become a spiritualist medium; it means that by devoting herself to an Other, she will inherit the phallus, the *facultades*. When Garrison met with María five years after her *espiritista* treatment, she found her still "very nervous." Garrison concludes that any improvement "was, at best, only temporary" (p. 416).

In analysis, rather than letting María be identified to the object *a*, the analyst does not respond to the demand (since the analyst functions as the object *a* that provokes the speech of the analysand to produce knowledge and truth). The analyst places herself or himself in a position to break up the trap where her paradoxical *jouissance* confines her. María appeared to have been turned into a passive object of enjoyment that completed the Other. Then, the Other appears as not lacking, and María accessed the Other through the object *a* to which she was identified. She has identified with the object *a*, which she interpreted as the answer to what the Other wanted. María turned herself into that which guaranteed the Other's wholeness. The outcome of this self-abnegation is not surprising. Like Dora, Anna O., and Elisabeth, María's wish to be ready to satisfy the implacable Other's demand led to exhaustion and depression. She felt "too nervous" (p. 416). Anxiety was the price she paid. It is precisely for this alienation that the work of a psychoanalyst could offer a more freeing treatment.

WHAT KIND OF SPEAKING BODY WITHOUT BODY IS EMBODIED IN A POSSESSED PERSON?

Garrison (1977) argues that states of possession appear to be what Breuer and Freud called "hysterical attacks" (p. 416). She notices an interesting overlapping: both spiritists and Western physicians treat those hysterical manifestations as ailments. For psychoanalysis, however, symptoms are not seen as "illnesses"; conversely, normality could be a symptom. In any case the elimination of symptoms is not at all the sole objective of the treatment. Although symptoms may disappear during the cure, the most important issue is that symptoms are signifying—symptoms speak. A psychoanalyst will try to decipher what any "symptomatic" condition—attacks, trances, depression—is saying. But first let us pose two questions raised by María's case: Who is speaking in the trance? What kind of speaking body without a body is embodied in a possessed person? María believed that it was not her possessed body that was the problem, but her soul: "Physically I don't have anything wrong, nothing, nothing, nothing. They have checked my heart, lungs . . . (she named every organ system) and they don't find anything wrong" (p. 417). María had seen a great number of doctors and they all told her that there was nothing wrong. Finding the Other of medical knowledge lacking, she did not accept the idea of a deceived Other and indicated, "My disease is so very, very, very rare that I can't explain it" (p. 417). The explanation for her "disease" was to be sought somewhere else.

Levi-Strauss (1958) compares the work of the psychoanalyst to that of the shaman: he says that they are both "talking cures," stressing their "symbolic function." He argues that the analyst manipulates the "psychic organ" while the shaman involves the "physiological organ." Such an opposition that seems to follow the old nature/culture distinction is problematic, especially when hysteria twists the old scheme of dualism body-soul. From its very early days psychoanalysis has dealt with the visible features of hysterical symptoms that do not correspond to any known or knowable organic cause. The "somatic" problems affecting a hysterical body were found by Janet (1901) and Freud not to be faithful to anatomy but to everyday language. As we have seen, Freud (1893) noted that hysteria "takes the organs in the ordinary, popular sense of the names they bear" (p. 169). The hysteric body shows how determining is language—the organ, be it physiological or psychic, is made up of words, of signifying connections. We have seen that the hysteric body is body more faithful to common speech than to anatomy. The body of hysteria breaks with the physiological body; it is a desiring body produced by signifying elaboration, by the surreptitious language of *jouissance*. The spirits are speaking through María's body; María's body becomes an echo chamber for the voice expressing the message of the half-dead. What are these lost impure souls, these ignorant spirits bounded to earth, doing to a body like María's?

Can one say that the body/soul split, the material/spiritual division, is resolved in a case of spirit possession? María's possessed body renders testimony to the disharmony of thought and soul: "[W]hen I am with people, I am fine. It is when I am alone that I feel badly, and I don't think about anything" (p. 417). María's mind is blank; she can neither think nor clearly articulate what is "possessing" her. During the possession trance paroxysms, the *Espiritismo* mediums allow the ignorant spirits to express themselves; the spirit speaks though the hysterical body suggesting that the hysteric thinks with the soul, but this is the soul of the other. If the hysteric takes the other as her soul, does she (mis)take the other for her soul? One may see how María's identification process with the spirits ("*obsesados*") bears witness to her subjective alienation in her relation to the desire of the Other. The Other is embodied in her, she cannot think, her body is taken over by foreign souls, by *causas* that think for her and use (enjoy) her body. If the unconscious is the discourse of the Other, are these souls embodied in María speaking in the name of the unconscious?

The subject of the unconscious touches the soul through the body. Lacan (1990) states that language carves up the body: when speech cuts through the body, it produces a body that has nothing to do with anatomy and maps out erogenous zones.[5] In María's case, the spirits are "parasites" causing body illnesses that follow language and not anatomy. In the bodies possessed by spirits there is a gap; this is a gap inscribed in the status of *jouissance* in the *dit*-mension of the body. Speech emerges from it, since the possessed body speaks where it enjoys.

To conclude, let us complete the answer to the question: What does the body without a body of *Espiritismo* embody? It embodies a defense against desire. María is possessed. What does this mean? If she is possessed,

---

5. Lacan contradicts Aristotle when, in *Television* (1990), he says that the subject of the unconscious is only in touch with the soul through the body, by introducing thought to it. Lacan's analytic hypothesis is that human beings do not think with the soul. For him there is not such an instrument to think *with*; the soul is not the mechanism on which the body is based. Lacan also mentions that thought is not in harmony with the soul.

it means that someone *possesses her, has her*; she *being* the phallus, that which could fulfill the other's desire. She enjoys vicariously that someone is *having it*. In analysis, María may come to admit that the Other desires, but does not ask her to embody the lost primal cause of his desire. She may entertain the fantasy of the supposed possession of the phallus, which implies that in fact although nobody has it, one can make semblance. Accepting her castration, she can find a desire that she recognizes as hers, and in her desire find the causes for her actions.

María finds herself in the position of being sacrificed for the Other's enjoyment. Her possessed body speaks where it enjoys. A psychoanalytic treatment would let her speak and it is hoped that she would make her own something that remains foreign to her. To understand the dynamic that leads from subjection to subjectivity, let us vary Lacan's rendering of his favorite Freudian dictum: "*Wo Es war, soll Ich werden*" (Where id was, there ego shall be). Let us then read, "Where the Other possesses me, acts as my cause, I must come into being as my own cause." But to let these contentions come alive, I will offer three examples of clinical work. That is the main topic of the following chapter.

14

The North Philadelphia Story

On July 25, 1898, U.S. troops landed in Puerto Rico. More than a hundred years later, the political status of the island remains problematic. Every four years, when Puerto Ricans elect their governor, mayors, and legislators, the same heated debate over the present political arrangement with the United States is reopened. Unlike many other countries, in Puerto Rico the population is massively involved in the democratic process and roughly 80 percent of the people vote. As we have seen, the equivocal in-between status of the island—which is qualitatively different in Spanish and English (*Estado Libre Asociado*, or Free Associated State, and Commonwealth)—creates an uncertainty that calls for a resolution. Each of the three major political forces in the national political arena offers a different interpretation of the current status of Puerto Rico. These interpretations of a few signifiers condense each party's ideological stand and play an important role in the island's political struggles.

Besides a minority pro-independence party (PIP), which advocates for Puerto Rico's self-determination as an independent nation, a great part of the political debate is centered about the degree of sovereignty granted by the state of union with the U.S. The two main Puerto Rican political parties campaign either for statehood or for association with increased benefits. The party called the New Progressive Party (PNP) is in favor of making Puerto Rico another state of the Union. The other party, the Popular Democratic Party (PPD), supports the current "free association" (even though it used to be called *autonomistas* and is now the PPD). Alfredo Carrasquillo, in his paper "The Logic of Permanent Union or the Structuring Fantasy of the Free Associated State" (1994), has noted a striking fact: in the discursive strategies of these two main parties, the idea of a "permanent union" is equally used to characterize Puerto Rico's relation to the United States. While the PPD contends that Free Associated State is a permanent union with the United States that offers an advantageous association avoiding complete assimilation, the pro-statehood PNP claims that statehood is the logical course in order to be in permanent union with the United States. Carrasquillo argues that "permanent union" functions as what Lacan calls a nodal or quilting point (*point de capiton*) that not only holds together the discursive logic of the actual status of Puerto Rico but is also a structuring fantasy that masks the traumatic origin of Puerto Rico's relation with the United States. According to him, the phrase "permanent union" functions as an ideological fantasy that structures a relation to the Other's desire (Carrasquillo 2000). "Permanent union" would be the colonial answer to the Other's imperial desire that conceals the antagonistic and traumatic origin of the Free Associated State while creating an illusion of permanence. Carrasquillo argues that this illusion needs to be maintained "because juridically the *Free Associated State* is a political status that can be amended unilaterally by the Congress of the United States and confirm to us that there is not such a thing as *permanent union*" (1994). He suggests that Puerto Ricans as a colonized nationality place themselves in the position of the hysteric in relation to the imperial Other (Carrasquillo 2000).

Freud's ideas about the hysterical attack—an unrestrained motor activity, the "minor epilepsy" interpreted as a pantomime of and equivalent of coitus—can thus let us see the *ataque* as a parody of the fantasy of *permanent union*, a union which, as Carrasquillo argues, is the unconscious structuring fantasy of the Free Associated State. This brings to mind Seamus Heaney's "Act of Union," a poem using the same sexual image in the context of the forced links between Britain and Ireland.

Assessing the political implications of such core fantasy, one can see "permanent union" function like a slogan, a magical formula that promises to produce what it names while in fact it conceals a precarious and traumatic situation that cannot be symbolized—the island's "union" is fractured into three separate political ideologies—the status of "permanent

union" has not been definitely resolved internally, and although "permanent" it still can be changed at any time by the U.S. Congress. It is exactly
as if one of the master signifiers contained in "*United* States" was being sent
back by hysterical discourse rebounding to the Master. Let us not forget
that the United States engaged in a more ambitious imperialist program
just after having been "united" by the Civil War; one might even say that
it was this imperialism that made the state of the Union "permanent."

Although Puerto Ricans became U.S. citizens in 1917, their relationship to the mainland significantly changed in 1952 when Puerto Rico
adopted its constitution and became an *Estado Libre Asociado*. In all the political discussions of the 1950s that led to the creation of the Free Associated
State of Puerto Rico, the key signifiers that were constantly transmogrified
were those of "permanent union." For Puerto Rico it was not enough to be
freely associated, one had to be "permanently" united, which betrays an
anxious need of reassurance that seems to hesitate between tragedy and
comedy. The idea of union sends us back to any situation of long-term
commitment, a little as if a wife were to say: "Oh, you know, I am *permanently* married to my husband." Then, one might look somewhat suspi-
ciously at the nature of this union.

In a contribution to the debate on the status of Puerto Rico, an expert
echoes some of these terms. Maurice Ferré, several times mayor of Miami,
opposes the material success and the important gains in terms of well-being for the inhabitants of the island with what he calls the roots of "happiness." He writes:

> Whether *de juris* or *de facto*, Puerto Rico remains a colony. The tragedy
> of Puerto Rico is that although Puerto Ricans have improved the mate-
> rial quality of their lives since they were given United States citizenship,
> Puerto Rican dignity has not been sufficiently realized. Therefore the
> pursuit of happiness of Puerto Ricans is found wanting by most.
>
> Happiness cannot be achieved without dignity, and dignity can-
> not exist so long as the political status of Puerto Rico remains in limbo.[1]

These very terms call up the concepts developed by a contemporary philosopher who has meditated on the issue of "unions"—whether they be

---

1. Ferré, M. "The Importance of Puerto Rico in National Politics: Commentary,"
quoted in Falk 1986, pp. 83–84.

marriages or political formations—that have been questioned by doubt and reproach and then reaffirmed as deserving to be seen as "permanent." Stanley Cavell (1981) takes as his point of departure a particular genre of Hollywood comedy that he calls the "comedy of remarriage." In *Pursuits of Happiness: The Hollywood Comedy of Remarriage*, Cavell shows how a number of films made between 1934 and 1949 have a similar logic—their heroine is a married woman, the marriage is subjected to the fact or the threat of divorce, and the plot is driven by one motivation: getting the initial couple back together. Cavell examines these comedies of remarriage in order to look at underlying fantasies "that express the inner agenda of a nation that conceives Utopian longings and commitments for itself" (p. 18).

In his brilliant analysis of a slightly atypical comedy of remarriage, *The Philadelphia Story* (1940), Cavell identifies dreams of perfect union and domestic tranquility deferred by class tensions. The story evolves during the weekend-long festivities leading to the second marriage of the aristocratic Tracy Lord to George Kittredge. The new couple looks like an odd match—he is a vulgar "new-rich" lumber producer while she is a distant upper-class goddess. The tension in the narrative is introduced by the presence of two leading male heroes who are equally desirable candidates to make the heroine happy—both are good, nice, and handsome. In the end, the ex-husband turns out to be a fitter candidate for the hand of the spoiled Philadelphia divorcée. Not only is the other suitor of a lower social class but the divorced partners "have grown up together." Cavell notes that although those words are meant ironically to refer to their marriage and divorce, they also refer to a common past that in the universe of comedies of remarriage is the best recipe for connubial happiness. As expected, the movie closes with the ex-married pair refinding the promise of happiness in a second union.

Cavell (1981) argues that *The Philadelphia Story* tackles national questions: "whether America has achieved its new human being, its more perfect union and its domestic tranquility, its new birth of freedom, whether it has been successful in securing the pursuit of happiness" (p. 152) and whether these issues are being discussed in a proper language. How can the private dilemmas in the love lives of Hollywood characters become affairs of national importance? One cannot deny that these characters assume their ethical responsibility in acting in conformity with their desires, but it may be hard to see how their personal choices are raised to the status of events of national importance. Cavell's thesis is tantamount to justifying in social terms the significance of the Lacanian motto "do not yield on your desire." To do so he needs to make a detour via Milton's tract on divorce. For Milton, private unhappiness is a matter of public importance with national consequences.

> He who marries, intends as little to conspire his own ruin as he that swears allegiance; and as a whole people is in proportion to an ill government, so is one man to an ill marriage. If they, against any authority, covenant of statute, may by the sovereign edict of charity save not only their lives but honest liberties from unworthy bondage, as well may he against any private covenant, which he never entered to his mischief, redeem himself from unsupportable disturbances to honest peace and just contentment. And much the rather. . . . For no effect of tyranny can sit more heavy on the commonwealth than this household unhappiness on the family. And farewell all hope of true reformation in the state, while such an evil as this lies undiscerned or unregarded in the house: on the redress whereof depends not only the spiritful and orderly life of our grown men, but the willing and careful education of our children. [quoted in Cavell 1981, pp. 150–151]

If we follow Milton's argument, we see how an unhappy marriage makes the whole commonwealth suffer in ways similar to those of the individual. The commonwealth grants the individual divorce in order to preserve the commonwealth's happiness and combat the tyranny of an unhappy bondage. Then, marriage appears as a duplication of the covenant of the commonwealth.

With Milton one understands the legitimacy of divorce—social or individual. This leads Cavell to speculate about the legitimacy of marriage, especially for the couples who seem unable to *feel* divorced and appear trapped in the unhappiness of a union that is destined to remain permanent. Can we say that they declare their "union" to be "permanent" despite their efforts at dissolving it? Cavell points out that in comedies of remarriage one finds an isolating happiness or a shared imagination of happiness that produces insufficient actual satisfaction rather than an isolating unhappiness. Even though *The Philadelphia Story* closes with the wedding, the "happy ending" is subtly twisted out of its usual course. The last picture of the couple kissing appears in what could be a wedding album or even a tabloid magazine. Is the couple going to be happy ever after? If that is the case, why would their picture be printed in a magazine dedicated to jagged gossip? Even the mood conveyed by the photograph indicates that the film's ending remains uncertain in its pursuit of happiness.

One may wonder if this "happy uncertainty" is not much closer to the "common unhappiness" Freud promised as the purpose and end of analysis than to the American-style ideal of unattainable happiness that Lacan so relentlessly attacked. Of all the guiding principles that rule our life as divided subjects, that of "happiness" seems to be one of the most alienating. Psychoanalysis helps us understand how we fall into the trap of believing that one should find "happiness," that is, the pursuit of a return to a mythical, fully satisfying fusion with the mother. Although we are always inevitably pursuing it, happiness is in fact found in a restrained satisfaction that is obtained with limited means. Any other form of satisfaction beyond these constraints would fall within what Lacan calls "Other's *jouissance*"—that is, a form of satisfaction that if realized would put in danger the subject's whole being. This is why Lacan takes hysterical desire as the model of human desire. Let us recall Freud's interpretation of the dream of smoked salmon: the hysteric creates an unfulfilled wish; her dream represented this renunciation put into effect. The beautiful butcher's wife, although she craves caviar, wants not to be given any. In order to maintain her desire for caviar eternally alive, she limits her satisfaction and purposely avoids finding an object for her desire. The resulting dissatisfaction re-sends her desire in an aspiration toward a removed ideal of being. Lacan suggests that in the human economy of desire what lies behind the pursuit of a perpetually fleeting ideal object is, above all, the desire of an unsatisfied desire.

Against the Anglo-Saxon pursuit of adaptative "success" or "happiness," he assigns to psychoanalysis not simply the cure of symptoms but the creation of a passageway to truth and ethics. Consistently, one should then stress the incontrovertible singularity of each treatment. Lacan (1992) states that rather than happiness it is tragedy that is in the forefront of our experiences as analysts. For Lacan, analysis ultimately brings the analysand to face the question of human existence as it is posed ("What am I there?") in that space of Law and buried *jouissance* called the Other. Thus, the analysand resembles the quest of a tragic hero to the extent that the analysand should go beyond the anxiety characteristic of the ego functions, slowly reaching a passage to the primordial horror caused by the mysteries of procreation and death. Psychoanalysis's goal is located beyond the pursuit of happiness. As Peter Kerr notes, like tragedy, analysis points to an ethical field beyond pleasure, beyond any concern for utility or consequent focus on instrumentality, beyond even the desire for an identifiable object—to an ethical field, in short, beyond all utilitarianisms.[2]

From an ethical perspective, psychoanalysis can be subversive because it acknowledges that the Sovereign Good is an ideal that can only be pursued in the concrete reality of a reduced satisfaction, thus refusing a boundless *jouissance*. For the neurotic, satisfaction can be experienced as an absolute peril. Desire is a safeguard against a limitless *jouissance*. Accepting that there is no perfect solution to the nonexistence of sexual rapport can be profoundly liberating—and paradoxically, make us happier in our dissatisfaction by renouncing *jouissance*.

At the end of *The Philadelphia Story* we face the dilemma of holding onto the fantasy of completion or accepting a measure of lack and unfulfillment. Is the second marriage going to last? Will the couple manage to resolve the problems that made their first marriage fail? Will this second union be a more perfect union? Is the movie promising the realization of a utopian dream? The narrative device used to reframe the film's ending is a series of photographs. They not only leave the ending open but force the movie's viewers to put into question their position: Who is supposed to have taken those photographs? And what are we likely to see in them? Are they *paparazzi*-style shots of startled society figures? Wedding pictures? Or stills of the film that betray that the movie itself is made of pictures in motion? According to Cavell, the impromptu photographs that close *The Philadelphia Story* direct the viewers to reconsider the ontological status of what they have seen and hence question their perception. This questioning can take place because the photographs take the viewers back to their position of externality in the visual field—like the voyeur who is reminded of his act of seeing when finding another eye already staring on the other side of the keyhole.[3] The surprise that the photographs produce at the end of the film indicates that the viewer feels "caught" seeing. The spectator's shock expresses that he or she "does not want to know" that he or she is looking at a fiction. We do not like to be moved from the position of illusory participants to that of passive spectators and experience uneasiness when taken outside the frame of our fantasy and reminded of the precariousness of our voyeuristic position.

---

2. Kerr, P. "The Tragic Ear of the Intellectual," posted on http://www.usc.edu/dept/comp-lit/tympanum/1/starr1.html

3. Following Lacan's theory of the gaze, the visible does not simply depend on the eye of the seer—his theory of the visual field concerns a split between vision and gaze. Even while looking, the subject is seen but this gaze is excluded from the field of vision.

The movie's ending also makes us rediscover depth in the very image while confronting the limits of representation. We may wonder, What are we really seeing? This reversal in the visual narrative allows us to start questioning the relation between the image and the word. Tracy Lord, our heroine, stages her desire to attract the gaze of her suitors and of ourselves, the bewitched admirers of a luminous movie star—pretty much like the hysteric, who stages her desire by constructing a scene to appeal to the gaze of the Other as represented by the priest, the doctor, or the Army psychiatrist. Anna O.'s evocative phrase "private theater" conveys the fascinating power of hysteria as spectacle. But "theater" implies a performer and an audience. As we have seen, Freud's originality in his treatments of hysteria was to break radically with a long tradition of careful medical observation that was mainly visual, what we may call a "clinic of the gaze." Freud's approach to hysteria was effective because he *listened* to the symptoms rather than looking at them. He was neither a *visuel*, a "seer" like Charcot, nor had he enough imaginary appeal to become a successful hypnotizer. Let us recall that Charcot constructed an iconography of hysteria based on photographic representations: with vision-based empiricism he tried to fulfill his fantasy of a coherent language of images that would fully explain the pathology. Freud produced an epistemological break when he stopped taking visible bodily signs as reliable clinical indicators. Psychoanalysis was invented because Freud was not captivated by the visual luster of the hysteric syndrome; he confined hysteria to an act of saying and focused on what was said—speech became the key. We have seen how hysterical symptoms result from signifying substitutions like those at work in dream production and how this discovery was instrumental in offering a form of treatment that would not just eliminate symptoms (which is probably easier to achieve by a purely suggestive appeal) but using what we may call a linguistic procedure, address the desire that symptoms express and handle. As Lacan (1977b) emphasized, in the analytic experience speech is the instrument, context, and material. It is even the background noise of the analyst's uncertainties—one can discover in the unconscious the whole structure of language.[4] The experience of analysis teaches us that symptoms are legible and they can be resolved when deciphered.

---

4. "The Agency of the Letter in the Unconscious or Reason Since Freud," in *Ecrits*, p. 157.

Now, the scene still takes place in Philadelphia, but in the dismal avenues over which the elevated subway throws its dark shadow, in a neighborhood whose boundaries are drawn by the language one speaks. This time we are in the heart of Kensington next to the *Bloque de oro*, the ghetto's Golden Block, the main street with sidewalks painted yellow in remembrance of the American dream of finding gold-paved streets. In the Golden Block, a bustling shopping strip and the busiest commercial location in the *barrio*, almost every available surface has been covered with graffiti: the store-fronts, walls, signs, trucks. The scribbles spread over the small churches, hairdressers, a *cocina criolla* butcher, hardware stores, two *botánicas*, a few *bodegas*, a Puerto Rican bakery, and the clothing stores that stand amidst burned-down houses, abandoned empty lots, and heavy drug traffic.

The utopia of a prosperous neighborhood whose streets are paved with gold has been replaced by the drab reality of an urban decay that Hollywood has used as post-apocalyptic science-fiction movie scenery. It seems almost preposterous to wonder whether the *Bloque de oro* might prove to be more than a symptom, more than a monument to American social dysfunctions, and whether it might not turn into a gateway, a royal road to the unconscious. And yet this is the difficult path I will follow.

15

Socorro, María, Consuelo: Women on the Verge of *an* ataque de nervios

By way of a clinical example, the first of three Philadelphia stories, I will both address the internal limits of psychoanalysis and challenge the external obstacles that the cultural context presents to a population that is marginalized and segregated, haunted by all the factors I have already mentioned (race and class problems, colonialist legacies, urban poverty, violence, pressure to acculturate, and language barriers). This is a case story that gathers all elements that are the outcome of an impossible situation that cannot be symbolized, and that finds an answer in hysteric discourse.

SOCORRO

The patient I will call Socorro became the victim of a violent crime and almost died during that experience.[1] Initially, she presented neither any indication of hysteria nor any symptom in the "classic" psychoanalytic manner. I approached her, keeping in mind Freud's recommendation that

---

1. My choice of a pseudonym is not arbitrary; *Socorro* in Spanish means help.

one should listen to every analysand as if he or she was the first psycho-analytic patient. At times, the analyst's knowledge can become a form of resistance: one aims at finding what one is already looking for. That is how Jungian analysts have Jungian patients, classic Freudians have classic Freudian analysands, and some Lacanians have only Lacanians on the couch. Freud, in the early days of his practice, did not have this problem; he was confronted with inexplicable symptoms that no existing theory could account for. The wonderful hysterics of olden times spoke without knowing and guided Freud toward unconscious knowledge. Their associations revealed a logical scene—they concealed a traumatic event that caused the symptoms. The fragment of the case I am about to share with you, however, runs against the logic of a traditional psychoanalytic cure: it begins with the aftermaths of a violent shock that is no secret at all, follows with a trauma, and ends (or one should say it actually starts) with inexplicable symptoms.

Socorro was 24 years old when she came to her first appointment, referred by her primary physician. Socorro had been the victim of an attack, a very violent crime that took place six months before she started the treatment. It happened one night in the laundromat where she worked. It was late, half an hour before closing. Just a handful of customers were there, drying their laundry. She had finished cleaning up; it was time for her to go home. At the shop with her were her 6-year-old son and her older brother, who had both arrived unusually early to fetch her. Suddenly, a group of three men stormed into the store. They ordered everyone to lie on the floor, face down. Socorro's son, very scared, cried loudly. To calm him down, Socorro covered him with her body, trying to muffle the sound. When the attackers were leaving with the money they had collected from the employee in the back office, they shot at random at the people lying on the store's floor. There was only one person hit—Socorro, who was shot through the head.

The police and the ambulance took a long time to come, since the danger of the area placed it out of reach. During the anxious wait, the situation looked desperate. Socorro's son could not stop screaming next to his wounded mother, while her brother improvised a bandage to stop the hemorrhage. Still semiconscious, Socorro believed that she was going to die. She survived almost by miracle, parts of her brain gone. After three months in the hospital, Socorro recovered somewhat, at least physically. Her friends and family were relieved; everyone insisted that she managed to come home walking. A few bullet splinters were left in her skull; it was too dangerous to try to remove them. She lost some of her vision and had partial hearing. Six months after the event, Socorro told me during her first appointment that she had recurrent nightmares, had trouble falling asleep, could not go out alone, felt uncomfortable in the presence of strangers. She occasionally thought that someone was following her and was afraid of running into the attackers, who had not been arrested; she imagined that they would take revenge against her. Listening to her I felt she initially did not present a main complaint that directly implicated her, as is the case in most neuroses. There was, however, a clue toward where her subjectivity was anchored in the potentially traumatic events: she felt ashamed of the huge scar on her scalp, explaining that "if somebody sees the scar they will think something bad of me, like that I deserve it." Her articulation of shame and guilt betrayed her subjective implication, as if the trace of the wound somehow represented her. I could not stop being reminded of the etymology of the word trauma: *wound*.

In order to conceal the scar she wore a complex head arrangement, a scarf of vibrant color elaborately wrapped around the head. It looked like a small turban; it called up both an adornment and a bandage. I found it interesting because it not only hid but revealed what she wanted to conceal, while calling attention to the area. Socorro seemed to want to hide and at the same time expose her scar. I also thought about the scarf around her head as an element of masquerade; the head arrangement allocated an absence while trying to veil it. It designated the lack while trying to fill the gap. Indeed, her having come so close to the Real had left her deeply marked, with scars more or less visible.

TRAUMA, WOUND, SCAR

This is what I heard: What was unbearable for her was that she had gotten shot for no reason; it was a random event that hurt horribly and from which she almost died. What was intolerable for her was less the physical problems it imposed than the painful arbitrarity, the cruel absurdity of the senselessness of the events.

Socorro spent her first sessions crying inconsolably. In Seminar 24 (*L'Insu que sait de l'une bévue s'aile a mourre*), Lacan (1977c) mentions the "signifiying effects of the Freudian unconscious." There, he argues that the analytic hypothesis consists in "saying," an enunciation that Lacan identifies with "truth." For Lacan, psychoanalysis opens the possibility of a "saying that helps": Help comes when one takes advantage of a truth offered by speech. Lacan plays on the homophony between *discours* (discourse) and *dire qui secourt* (a speech that helps). The French pun works in English if we accept hearing "succor" scrambled in "discourse." *Secours* calls up aid, help, a meaning that is also to be found in the Spanish *socorre*. Socorro cried but she also spoke. I listened to Socorro to help her hear what truth was produced in her own sayings about that incoherent realm that is the Real.

Socorro communicated in English. She was born in Puerto Rico but had moved to the mainland while still a toddler. Even if her mother and grandmother spoke only Spanish to her, which she understood quite well, English was the language in which the treatment was conducted. Socorro talked about the terrible events with an understatement by only alluding to "what happened." In a first stage of her treatment she described how difficult her life had become after "what happened." For instance, there were problems brought about by her diminished vision: "I can't see well." After some sessions in which she explored her associations about what it was that she couldn't "see well," she noted that when she was discharged from the hospital everyone insisted that "she managed to come home walking." She stressed that her attackers "walked," that is, they had committed a terrible crime and were not punished while she had to undergo a long recovery. She did not feel as well as those around her believed: "I am not well and they can't see it." How could they *see her well* while she was still in so much pain? She "couldn't see[m] well." She then decided to get glasses and was able to read again and watch TV. "Seeing better," she felt less insecure and more autonomous. She also managed to overcome her reluctance to use a hearing aid. Gradually, she talked more and more about her anger at the perpetrators of the attack who "walked" while she could "have ended unable to walk" (alone). Her almost miraculous survival made her feel guilty as if she had "walked" away from the grasp of death. The exploration of these signifying permutations around the signifiers "walk" and "see well" produced some effects. Soon her fears diminished and she was able to come to the clinic on her own—walking.

Above all, what I found startling in this case was Socorro's insistence on her feelings of shame and guilt. She was ashamed about the scar: it was ugly and visible. One could read her shame as an indicator that not only were the events precariously represented in her fantasy but that she felt represented by them—she wanted to conceal the scar with the idea that it exposed events that were "bad." Above all, this showed that she was "bad" for having caused them. Her inextricable enmeshing in the bewildering sequence of traumatic events seemed to define her. Could Socorro's guilt speak of an unconscious complicity in the traumatic scene? Or were her self-reproaches in fact addressed to someone else?

Socorro's discomfort diminished when she started talking about her fantasies. She insisted that "whoever saw such an ugly scar would think that something bad happened to me" and would assume that she was responsible for it. This elaboration took place in the treatment during a stage at which Socorro was looking for anyone who could be found guilty. Searching for the guilty party, she was really searching for a reason. She felt guilty for working in a laundromat late at night; she thought that her boyfriend was guilty because he was unemployed and did not bring any money home, which forced her to accept a bad job. Or it was her son's fault because he started screaming. Or it was the laundromat store's fault because they did not have a better security system.

Lacan (1977c) contends that there is no truth about the Real, because the Real appears to exclude meaning. He argues that one would be going too far when asserting that there is a real, because saying supposes meaning. The word *real*, however, in itself has a meaning that Lacan makes resonate with echoes of the Latin word *reus*, (guilty party, culprit) and notes that one is more or less guilty of the real. Why was Socorro shot, and not the person at her side? Why was she shot at all? Any explanation could fall into the category of paranoid speculation. It is impossible to know certainly. The temptation of playing the role of prophet or of Master of truth and closing up the anxious uncertainty with an answer, thus imposing meaning, would slide dangerously onto the treacherous slope of deception and would have put a stop to Socorro's associative work in her sessions. Socorro was trying to produce meaning and reproached herself or accused others trying to find a reason in randomness. In order to make sense of circumstances beyond symbolization, she reckoned with the impossible.

One could, however, identify economical determinations both for the robbery of the laundromat and for her working in a dangerous neighborhood where crime is rampant. But to produce a subjective inscription of the events, Socorro searched for words to write what never ceased to be written. Up to that moment, the events were "what happened." Let us note that this phrase lacks a subjective core; it is an impersonal and abstract description. Socorro was bordering on a treacherous field—what we may call an impossible realm—in order to create an aftermath for the trauma. She reached something new when she started talking about "the accident."

But was this an accidental event? How was it an "accident," as opposed to, for instance, an "attack"? Can a random shooting be seen on a par with a car crash on a highway? In the context of psychoanalysis, however, the term "accident" sounded quite evocative: "accident" derives from the Latin *accidere* (to happen) and is etymologically akin to *cadere* (fall). This "fall" (*cadere*) is also present in the root of the word "chance," and in the root of the word *symptom*, which in Greek literally means "to fall together" (*syn*, with, together + *piptein*, to fall). This new verbal production corresponded to a moment in the treatment during which Socorro was suddenly able to let "fall" the idea of finding a guilty party, of blaming it all on "somebody's fault." After this semantic fall, she proceeded to talk about her separation from her boyfriend, her conflicts with her son, and focused especially on her relationship with her mother. Thus she had moved around the polysemy of the phrase "It's my fault." Although this phrase initially responded to the question, "Whose fault was it?" and originally meant the guilty party in the shooting, it could still acquire new meaning. For trauma fractures meaning—it resists symbolization. Socorro, however, found an inscription for the trauma by relating it to other "faults." In the formation of symptoms, an event literally "falls together." The issue of trauma looms large in Socorro's case and we will have to return to it later. For now, let us concentrate on specific subjective dialectics and only state that for trauma to be constructed as such, it needs "to fall" and meet a preexisting "chance" occurrence: the "fracture" of castration that raises all events to the status of trauma but *nachträglich*, afterward.

From arbitrary events that had occurred without necessity, from this *tyche*, Socorro could then construct a symptom that fell along the lines predetermined by her fundamental fantasy. Since two scenes are necessary to construct the trauma the symptom conceals (a first moment when the event occurs and the second occurrence that retroactively signifies the first), one may wonder what makes an event rise in importance in order to become "first" and thus start the series. In his latest work, Freud noted that in the progression of a psychoanalytic treatment, termination implies paradoxically a regression: the encounter with the *Ur*-trauma—castration. This trauma conditions subjectivity and forces the neurotic to invent a fantasy to organize the world.

For Socorro the developments that followed her having been shot challenged her place in her fantasy of the Other. Recall that for Freud, the mother, this primordial Other, is the child's first seducer. Since tender childhood, when the child's crying is heard as language, another register is entered that changes the logic of the subject. This new life of symbolic communication brings about a loss of *jouissance*. This is why Socorro's mother was to play a key role in Socorro's trauma. Shortly before she started her treatment, Socorro had just separated from her boyfriend, whom she described as "abusive." The horrid circumstances of the robbery had a dramatic impact on her relationship with her mother and ended up changing things radically between them. This is a complex case not devoid of tragedy, and the abuse she experienced at the hands of her boyfriend is less central to our understanding of Socorro (it is simply a return of the same) than the new evolution with her mother in the aftermath of the shooting. The latter functioned as a fragile inscription that allowed her and her mother to restore a relationship, albeit a precarious one.

Socorro's mother was touched by the event: it allowed her for the first time to relate to her daughter from whom she had been distanced since her early childhood. Socorro had been raised by her grandmother because her single mother had run away with a boyfriend. Socorro had little contact with her mother during her childhood and adolescence and was totally estranged from her at the time of the shooting. But as soon as she heard the news, Socorro's mother, who was at the time living with her own mother in Chicago, moved back to Philadelphia and devoted herself to the care of her daughter. She sat beside her every day at the hospital, ardently praying. After that, they became inseparable. The highly traumatic occurrence had allowed mother and daughter to reestablish a relationship. The real trauma, the partially unspeakable, had paradoxically re-created a connection between the two women—a consuming, devouring rapport. This situation touched the fantasmatic core of Socorro's being. Earning the mother's devotion after almost being killed seemed tantamount to a desperate gesture, as if Socorro had done anything to recuperate her. Getting her mother back was for Socorro the "good" thing obtained by going through something "bad" that she believed she had partly created herself. To understand this better, we need to go back in time to the conditions under which Socorro was born.

Her mother was a late-teenager when she got pregnant with Socorro. The father (also very young) did not recognize her as his child. Socorro was born into a place that was a "no" place. Her mother complained that Socorro should have never been born—she used to say "I was a kid having a kid." Did Socorro's birth represent the transgression to a prohibition, the rebellion of a teenager? Or was Socorro a parting gift offered by the mother to the grandmother?

Socorro was raised by the maternal grandmother who took to her more and more lovingly. The mother lived elsewhere. When Socorro was a child, her mother would be contacted only when something "bad" happened. If the girl was sick, which happened quite often, the mother would talk to her over the phone and occasionally visit. Expectably, recurrent asthma attacks, bronchitis, digestive problems, inexplicable fevers, eczema became the means to connect with her mother. It was as if the mother could only recognize Socorro as a sick child ready to die. Paradoxically, Socorro is reborn for her mother after having almost died.

The situation of psychotherapy offered Socorro a space in which she spoke and produced knowledge about the trauma and asked, by the pure effect of speech, what it was that she wanted. Since speaking is always speaking to someone, and since one always receives one's own message from the Other in an inverted form, by questioning the Other's desire she asked what it was that she wanted from herself.

Since Socorro had constructed the symptom within transference, the symptom could be interpreted. She started having headaches that her physician related to either her "head trauma" or stress. According to the numerous medical exams she underwent, the headaches did not have an identifiable organic origin. Her most recent CAT scans confirmed that the bullet splinters had not moved. The trauma had left a mark; the trauma had scarred her body, leaving traces of knowledge of an occurrence that had shattered the barrier of meaning. Trauma appears as the paradoxical inscription of something that exceeds meaning. It is made of bits and pieces: fragmentary memories, overheard words, secrets, gazes (Socorro's impaired vision and hearing as well as her complaint of "I can't see well" point the way to two embodiments of the object *a*: the gaze and the voice, and with them one can address the drive or the closure of the "life" cycle in the death drive). These fragments that together make up the trauma also indicate the places where the signifier had failed in stopping the Other's *jouissance*.

One could sum up the concept of trauma as the subject's confrontation with the lack in the Other: it is that which puts the subject in touch with a foreboding *jouissance*. Such *jouissance* is extremely threatening because usually language prevents direct access to its frightening real. We must speak our needs and rely on the Other for their satisfaction. Let us recall that pleasure means enjoying as little as possible. Trauma is the return of this forbidden, excessive *jouissance*, which traverses limits and breaches the law. Socorro's life-threatening experience gives vivid meaning to the traumatic fact that the subject's whole being is endangered when a failure in the signifier, a crack in meaning, allows the Other's *jouissance* to claim the subject's being as object.

Previously, Socorro had been relatively well integrated in the world of signifiers: she was able to work and to love. Neither signifiers nor law shielded her from the violent attack. Socorro broke free from the *jouissance* of the Other and thus escaped the trauma's domination when she let herself to be guided by the knowledge inferred from the wound. She could then put the trauma at some distance. At that time, Socorro was able to question what place she occupied in the Other's desire as object of the desire of the Other's desire, and tried to separate from it.

Socorro went from being an "atypical analytic patient," someone in a state of shock, to her construction of what Lacan (1979) calls the "neurotic's individual myth." Her elaboration of trauma, and ultimately the formation of a symptom, shows us how psychoanalysis allows for the construction of a logical scene in which trauma permits a more freeing constitution of knowledge that makes room for desire. Jean-Pierre Winter (1998) succinctly expounds how a psychoanalytic cure overcomes the Real of trauma: "Between reminiscence and memory, psychoanalysis offers a symbolic inscription that allows one to forget that of which it is impossible not to be reminded" (p. 100).

Finally, a very determining shift took place when Socorro started talking about "*when I was shot*": the phrase retained in its passive voice a fragment of the Real, but included a subject that could articulate itself in the first person singular. This subjectivity inscribed a hitherto "impossible" accident that had now become a symptom. It was precisely because of its connection with the real, of the *tyche* it represented, functioning as a mark of and for death, that the scar started to heal just at that point in the treatment. Socorro decided to stop hiding it and somehow it seemed to be less conspicuous: she had accepted it as a mark of the inevitable. She no longer had recurring nightmares. Now she took delight in talking about her dreams, which up to this point she could never recall.

From a psychoanalytically oriented psychotherapy that lasted one year and a half, I would like to underline one element: Socorro was trying to make sense of the impossible and thus generate a trauma. We have said that she did not present a case of hysteria, although Freud (1910) describes hysteria as the consequence of having "been subjected to violent emotional shocks" (p. 10). According to this contention, hysteria would be a "post-traumatic stress disorder." If hysteria is caused by trauma, should hysteria be distinguished from other neuroses caused by the special circumstances brought about by terrifying experiences? There should not be such a distinction. When Freud observes the role of trauma in transference neurosis (hysteria) and compares it to traumatic or war neurosis, he argues that ultimately war neurosis is to be regarded as traumatic neurosis because in both the psyche is defending itself against what is seen as threatening its life. Freud also notes that in traumatic and war neurosis the violent danger threatens from without or is embodied by the ego itself, while in transference neurosis the danger is caused by an internal enemy, concluding that at the basis of *all* neuroses there is repression, that is, the most elementary reaction to trauma. Once more, hysteria shows us the structure governing all neuroses, which is why Lacan called it the paradigm of neurosis.

Hysteria involves trauma, but does trauma necessarily involve hysteria? This relates back to the moment when early in his career Freud believed that the hysterics had been victims of an actual seduction. The violence of the trauma emerged delayed. In a later elaboration, *Beyond the Pleasure Principle* (1920), Freud returns to the topic of "traumatic neurosis" and makes a subtle differentiation between fear (*Furcht*), anxiety (*Angst*), and fright (*Schreck*) according to their relationship to danger. Anxiety is a state in which the danger is awaited, anticipated, even when the danger could be unknown. In this text Freud is quite Lacanian and does not hesitate to contradict an earlier thesis and claims that anxiety *has* an object. Fright is described as a sudden state of shock that takes by surprise—one did not expect it and is not ready for it. Trauma is not so much the result of violence as it is of surprise and fear of death. Here the etymology of "shock" is helpful: "shock" means to strike against; likewise, trauma strikes against an old inscription that offers its content to the second scene while revealing that prior moment as one beyond symbolization. In opposition, Freud argues that anxiety cannot cause a traumatic neurosis—for in fact anxiety protects against it. The trauma arises because the anxiety that should have protected the psyche against fright did not rise.

Freud's (1895) first etiology of hysteria (seduction theory) implied the alienation of the patient in the inescapable fate of the trauma. Hysteria as "posttraumatic disorder" set up a relationship with the past that left both patient and analyst with little they could do about it. "This is all perfectly correct and true, isn't it? What do you want to change in it now that I've told you?" (Freud 1905, p. 44). If all is "perfectly correct and true," what can the analyst change about it? "Abreaction" of the psychic trauma was not sufficient—the careful reconstitution of the past was not enough to transfigure the trauma. A more revolutionary transformation needed to happen to effect a cure. Thus, the patient needed to become more actively involved in the trauma that has been passively suffered. The hysterics were to become the subject of their traumas. Not only would the hysteric be understood as an actor in an incidental trauma, but also as the scriptwriter of the scene. To make this transformation happen, Freud invented the Oedipus complex, a structural model for the understanding of human nature. This is how, in an often quoted letter to Fliess, Freud explained his theoretical turn:

> I no longer believe in my *neurotica*. This is probably not intelligible without an explanation; after all, you yourself found credible what I was able to tell you. So I will begin historically [and tell you] where the reason for the disbelief came from.

Freud continues, giving three sources, namely:

> The continual disappointment in my efforts to bring a single analysis to a real conclusion. . . . Then the surprise that in all cases, the *father*, not excluding my own, had to be accused of being perverse. . . . Then, third, the certain insight that there are no indications of reality in the unconscious, so that one cannot distinguish between truth and fiction that has been cathected with affect. (Accordingly, there would remain the solution that the sexual fantasy invariably seizes upon the theme of the parents.) [Moussaieff Masson, p. 264][2]

This letter is followed by the almost simultaneous unearthing of the Oedipus complex in Freud's self-analysis. Freud abandoned the traumatic theory to sustain the oedipal complex, the germ of "the theme of the parents"; this solution finally brought his analyses to a "real conclusion." This operation, contends Millot (1988), implies a grammatical inversion: the desire of the father continues as a capital pathogenic agent, but the change takes place from the subjective to the objective genitive. The source of hysteria is now the repressed desire *for* the father and not the sexual assault he may have committed (the desire *of* the father, his "assault," becomes a secondary elaboration in the fantasy). In Millot's rendition, one sees the guilt for having the desire return to its sender. This new trajectory

---

2. Here I use *The Complete Letters of Sigmund Freud to Wilheim Fliess 1887–1904*, for the careful attention paid by Moussaieff Masson to the rendering of an exact translation into English.

has aroused the well-known controversy in which Freud is accused of conspiring and betraying truth, and of blaming the victim (see Moussaieff Masson 1984). We should keep in mind that Freud's theoretical turn was imposed by a clinical need: *analyzability*. According to Millot, the real trauma is a limit for psychoanalysis. Facing the real of the trauma, the analyst is reduced to a position of impotence. If Freud had opted to denounce the seductions, and thus called into question the integrity of so many fathers, he would have restored the father to an ideal status. As Millot (1988) notes, however, rather than falling into the trap of denouncing fathers that also betrays and sustains a belief in the existence of an Ideal Father, "Freud substitutes the real of the trauma for its fantasy, that is, for the truth of fiction, the truth of the subject. The advancements offered by this operation are on the side of psychoanalysis and its therapeutic direction" (p. 17).

This transformation of an actual trauma into a fantasy has nothing to do with protecting fathers from the consequences of their transgressions or making them look innocent. Freud's change in position is not a desertion but a substitution that allows progression. Freud no longer believes in his *neurotica* in order to engage the *neurotica* in the truth of her own unconscious. Freud's realization that there is no "indication of reality" in the unconscious gave rise to the idea of "psychic reality"; this position is that of neither a historian nor a police officer. For Freud, in a psychoanalytic treatment the objective material reality may be eclipsed by a reality of a different nature—the subjective reality of fantasy and desire. Thus, his interest shifted from the symptoms themselves as repetitions of the actual trauma, to the fantasy that originated them. The past as such cannot be changed; yet is the past as such ever recovered? The subject already creates a fiction about it in his or her own unconscious. What Freud identified as seduction is, in fact, already the early traumatic experience of the subject when he or she encounters the desire of the Other. This encounter is traumatic because the subject is in a defenseless, helpless position in regard to the Other's desire. In this encounter, the being of the subject can be affirmed, disavowed, or rejected. What is it that returns again and again in the subjects' compulsion to repeatedly expose themselves to distressing situations? It is precisely this encounter with the Other's desire, with profound psychic consequences, which was "forgotten" and then "returns" in the basic compulsion to repeat the trauma. The return of the repressed presents a temporal paradox. Because the return of the repressed takes its value only in the future, through its integration into the history of the subject, it is something that at a given moment of its occurrence "will have been" (Lacan 1991a, p. 205). Trauma no longer refers to an external event, but rather to the encounter with the inaccessible that has been processed with the fabrication of a traumatic scene (a fantasy, that is). This is why Freud could write, "I no longer believe in my *neurotica*."

He could no longer believe in his *neurotica* because patients speak, and like anyone and everyone who speaks, patients can lie in telling the truth, or tell the truth with a lie, as we shall soon see in another clinical example. Yet hysteria presented Freud with truth in speech; this truth revealed to him the reality of what is neither true nor false. In analysis the relation to the past is ambiguous. The past reveals itself in repetition. As Lacan (1977b) noted, speech testifies to the power of the past, yet it is *present* speech "that bears witness to the truth of this revelation in present reality" (p. 47).

In psychoanalysis one deals not with memories but with recollections, that is, with constructions. Psychic reality is dominated by the primacy of sexuality and unconscious fantasy and desire, which puts aside the problem of evidence, a problem that concerns the "authorities" but not the analyst. To accomplish an analytic cure the analyst stresses the truth of psychic reality, perhaps even to the detriment of material reality, granting to the unconscious a primal role. It is from fantasies, not reminiscences, that hysterics suffer the most. This by no means implies that all traumas are fantasies, but that all real traumas undergo a particular subjective inscription called unconscious fantasy. It is upon the truth of this inscription that the analyst can operate. This is further specified by Lacan (1977b): in psychoanalysis what is at stake is

> history, a balancing of scales, in which conjectures about the past are balanced against promises of the future, upon the single knife-edge or fulcrum of chronological certainties. I might as well be categorical: in psychoanalytic anamnesis, it is not a question of reality, but of truth, because the effect of full speech is to reorder past contingencies by conferring on them the sense of necessities to come, such as they are constituted by the little freedom through which the subject makes them present. [p. 48]

Hysterics are famously described as those who "suffer from reminiscences." They may consciously "forget" but their symptoms are repetitions of memories that are kept alive in act. Trauma victims like Socorro cannot forget either: when they experience flashbacks they are caught in the eternal present tense of a compulsive repetition of the dreadful event. Once the trauma is constructed as a carrier of meaning, metaphorized, "hystericized," then the victim may forget but keep a leftover—a "frozen" memory. That memory is a scene that reorganizes the scenes and triggers occasional returns to the same place. This repetition compulsion is addressed by Freud when he explores the desire realized in the dreams that reenact trauma. The so-called traumatic dreams led Freud to speculate on the existence of a principle beyond pleasure. Thus, trauma is the inscription of Freud's death drive—an excessive *jouissance*, an intolerable amalgam of pain and pleasure.

As we have seen, the ghetto provides a strong example of the complex dialectics of *jouissance*—understanding *jouissance* as that which goes against life.The denegation of the death drive is not restricted to American psychoanalysis, or limited to the frontiers of the ghettos. In the ghettos, however, denial collapses as violence reigns, crack ravages and becomes the base currency of exchange. The reality of ghetto life is constant violence with all its thrills and losses, an intoxicating and terrifying mixture that calls up a war situation. Many of the patients whom I treated included in their free-association the daily report of deaths. Their everyday reality is a battlefront and my analytic listening was constantly pierced by the Real of violent death. Can psychoanalysis as a clinic of the Real sustain itself within a space that seems to exceed the possibility of representation? If psychoanalysis is the clinic of the Real that eventually discloses the impossibility of sexual/social rapport, how do we go from one impossible to the other?

In the seminar *L'envers de la psychanalyse* Lacan (1991d) suggests that one should take psychoanalysis from the inside out, from its underside (*envers*)—its underweave. Like Freud, Lacan believes that governing, educating, analyzing, are three "impossible" professions; he adds to the list a fourth profession that would aim at "making someone desire." This fourth profession would map out the hysteric's discourse. In my clinical examples, one can locate a knotting between hysteric symptoms that seem to create a discourse, a social link, the hysterizing discourse of psychoanalysis, and the traumatic "impossible" effect of the "Real" of life in the ghetto. In Socorro's case, although she had been referred with a dignosis of posttraumatic stress disorder, I provisionally questioned this label because I wanted to see what her subjective positioning in the events had been. I wanted to tackle the foundations of her situation; this could be done by going from the present "post trauma" to whatever makes of any given occurrence a true traumatic situation. In fact, I was returning to issues that decided Freud's controversial abandonment of the seduction theory. Freud's recognition of fantasy implies there is no correct way of perceiving reality and, further, that even reality itself undergoes an inscription, a writing.[3] The particular features of each person's fantasy stage a unique scene in order to stage unconscious desire. Even though fantasy is a *scene*—that is to say, a visual image—fantasy emerges in an analysis, and it emerges by way of the only medium of psychoanalysis—speech. Thus, fantasy presents itself having the structure of a sentence, in a form of writing like ancient Egyptian hieroglyphs or Chinese characters, which reproduce simultaneously phonetic and symbolic uses of signifying elements. The "archaeological" labor of fantasy reconstruction reveals a phrase whose syntax denotes the means by which the subject sustains his or her desire and negotiates with *jouissance*. The fantasy expresses the analysand's position in a symbolic structure. Behind an image, there is always a signifying structure. Retrospectively, this is what Freud noted in hysterical paralyses. The body paralyses follow a map delineated by the common use of a particular word. The word that appears coagulated in the symptom is a writing extracted from a missing text that has to be reconstructed in each treatment, which is why Lacan (1977b) defined the unconscious as "a censored chapter" in one's history:

> The unconscious is that chapter of my history that is marked by a blank or occupied by a falsehood: it is the censored chapter. But the truth can be rediscovered; usually it has already been written down elsewhere. Namely, in monuments in my body. That is to say, the hysterical nucleus of the neurosis in which the hysterical symptom reveals the structure of a language, and it is deciphered like an inscription which, once recovered, can without serious loss be destroyed. [p. 50]

The hysterical symptom reveals the structure of *a* language. This language inscribes itself in the body. The symptom functions like a rebus. This rebus can be deciphered by sticking to its letter in the text of the free association of the analysand, and, thus, once it is decoded, the symptom is destroyed as such.

---

3. Both reality and fantasy are discursively constructed. Freud identified the discursive nature of memory when he noted that memories of past events were distorted according to unconscious desires. He also discovered that unconscious desires were based as much in material facts as they were in fantasies.

Already in the *Studies* (Freud and Breuer 1895), Freud had identified the deadlock presented by the "real" life of a patient: "Why, you tell me yourself that my illness is probably connected with my circumstances and the events of my life. You cannot alter these in any way. How do you propose to help me then?" (p. 393). Let me insist on this crucial point: Freud revised his notion of "reality" and thus reconsidered the reality of trauma. The traumatic experience is necessary logically; whether it occurred certainly or not becomes secondary—the outcome remains the same. Freud introduces the structural function of fantasy in the activation of trauma; trauma explains what eludes symbolization.

Trauma entails its transformation into fantasy. Ultimately, fantasy is an answer to the traumatic experience no human being is spared: that of the early encounter with the desire of the Other. This "shocking" encounter with the Other's desire is "repressed" and "returns" in the basic compulsion to repeat the trauma. Trauma ultimately refers to the encounter with the inaccessible that has been processed with the fabrication of a traumatic scene—a fantasy that enacts a relation between the subject and the Other. The subject is completely defenseless in regard to the Other, who can affirm, disavow, or reject her. Moreover, the subject is traumatized by the frightening desire of the Other. The trauma realizes and designates at the same time a place occupied by the subject in the fantasy of the Other; it spells out some form of *jouissance*.

In Socorro's situation it was crucial to explore what fantasies were realized in her traumatic encounter with the Real. She had a dustuchia, an unhappy encounter with the real that she was trying to integrate into the fabric of repetition by dressing it with guilt. She was trying to master the difficult acceptance of the impossible. It was critical to identify where Socorro was placing herself in the horrendous events she had gone through. One cannot change the past in therapy. But together we could work on how she was conceiving of the past (how she felt it was affecting her in the present time) and revise what role she felt she had played in it—she could transform her fantasy.

Socorro's case did not appear as a case of "Puerto Rican syndrome" but of "posttraumatic stress disorder," although the latter diagnosis is often applied to the cases described in Breuer and Freud's (1895) *Studies on Hysteria* as well as to current cases of *ataque*. Hers is the story of a treatment that succeeds by producing a hysterization that allows for a *construction* of trauma. Without downplaying the role of severe traumatic events, from a Freudo-Lacanian perspective one may question the specificity of the diagnosis of posttraumatic stress disorder since, as we have seen, trauma is structurally part of the human psychic configuration. Although Socorro was referred to me with this diagnosis, it was obvious that the traumatic event was overpowering but not yet operative, that is, it was not constituted as such. According to Freud, trauma requires two logical moments in order to be constituted (the violent trauma needs a second moment that retroactively creates the event afterward, *nachträglich*).

Socorro came to the clinic in a state of shock, unable to speak about what she had gone through. She traversed several stages in her treatment that allowed her to finally articulate the unspeakable; she came to reckon with the limits of symbolization, with the Real, with the "impossible," and thus to constitute the scene as *post*-traumatic. This can take place only when trauma finally assumes a symbolic value, when it has been transformed into a carrier of meaning. In the same way that hysteria has created psychoanalysis, any psychoanalysis creates a hysterization because it questions subjects about their desire and brings the unconscious into motion. Since the process of analysis treats and cures by creating an artificial transference neurosis—hysteria—we may conclude her case by saying that this is the story of a patient who is cured by contracting hysteria.

WHAT MAKES PSYCHOANALYSIS PERTINENT? MARÍA'S CASE

Shattering the placid stillness of a Friday afternoon, María made her entrance to the Kensington *Clínica*, disturbing siesta's legitimate calm and waking everyone in the waiting room. When María stormed through the door screaming as in a scene from a Western, the secretary called me immediately: "Come downstairs, now! We have *una emergencia!*" I could hear uproar in the emergency. The piercing screams reached me over the phone, up the stairs, and through corridors, doors, and walls. I hurried downstairs where I found María covered in tears, rolled in an almost fetal position, shouting in a corner: "*Mis hijos! . . . Oh, Dios, mis hijos!*" (My sons! Oh, God, my sons!) I heard the other patients in the waiting room murmur: "*La pobrecita, le ha dado un ataque.*" (The poor one, she is having an *ataque*.) "*Ay Dios mío, Bendito, está loca!*" (Oh, my God, Blessed one, she is crazy!) Her disheveled looks and dirty old clothes betrayed a homeless existence; her empty gaze and frantic behavior were both frightening and full of fear.

I spoke in Spanish to the distraught woman, suggesting she come into a side office and talk. She managed to relax a little as I asked her why she was there and how she thought we could help her.

María (as I'll continue to call her) continued crying inconsolably. Suddenly, she knelt down and said with the most intense sadness: "*Mis hijos, mis pobres hijos, ayúdame.*" (My children, my poor children, please help me.) "*¿Qué pasa con sus hijos?*" (What is happening with your children?), I asked. "*Los transformaron en perros,*" she responded, explaining tearfully that her sons had been transformed into dogs, and that it was "*horrible.*" I asked her to explain her "horror" and what she meant by her sons being "transformed into dogs." She sobbed: "*No me hubiera importando que los transformaran en patos, pero los transformaron en perros.*" (I would not mind them transforming my sons into ducks [*patos*] but they turned them into dogs [*perros*].) She then asked my name. As soon as I answered, she volunteered her own. After our brief interaction, María left calmer, agreeing to return for a full evaluation two days later.

She failed to keep her scheduled appointment. One month later, however, María showed up at the clinic and asked to talk to "Patricia." Her return provoked many questions. What was the meaning of María's earlier *ataque*? Had her concern with dogs been sheer madness, or had her earlier delusion been a creative attempt to produce an explanation that would bring order to her mental chaos? Why would she not have cared about her sons being turned into *patos* (ducks, but also Puerto Rican slang for gays) yet wept about their becoming *perros* (dogs)? Was my first name, Patricia, for which the nickname in some Spanish-speaking countries is *Pato*, already part of her delirium? Had María been confirming in her hallucinations Freud's early theories of paranoia as a defense against homosexuality? Was her statement about ducks and dogs a true statement, or rather the articulation of something she lacked the means to express?

A first concern was whether I should be raising these questions: Shouldn't I simply trust antipsychotic medications that would silence María's "madness" and make her look "normal" again? Conversely, I wondered if I should see her *ataque* as a culturally accepted expression of distress and rule out a diagnosis of psychosis. And yet, what about her seemingly delusional ideas about ducks and dogs? Was María merely hysteric rather than psychotic? If the latter proved to be the case, should I—an analyst working in a *barrio* clinic—enter the deep waters of psychosis? Is psychoanalytic theory and practice suitable for treating psychotics who also happen to be poor Hispanic patients of inner-city public clinics?

As we have seen in the previous chapter, some people stubbornly believe that the poorer sections of the population are essentially different. This difference would obstinately resist any psychoanalytic treatment. While denying this arbitrary stricture, I do not want to avoid the counterobjection that I may have taken psychoanalysis too far when attempting to treat patients presenting with the Puerto Rican syndrome.

Along with the suffering caused by her "mental" symptoms, María endured several social "illnesses": no medical insurance, no identification of any kind, no recollection of a social security number, and no address— she was homeless at the time. The clinic's administration required a psychiatric evaluation as a first step in the admission process. To accelerate the intake procedure, an appointment with the clinic's psychiatrist was scheduled for the following Monday. Perhaps overwhelmed by the urgency of her delirious production, María could not wait even two days and thus did not return to the clinic for her scheduled appointment. When she walked in one month later, the thoughts and questions that her arrival raised were similar to the thoughts and questions awakened every day by the challenges of clinical work in a social area defined as "marginal" and considered *de facto* beyond the effects of the unconscious. As we have seen, there is a persistent exclusion of psychoanalysis as a therapeutic option to treat Hispanic patients, as if Hispanic patients were without an unconscious. While this clearly absurd thesis is impossible to sustain logically, unfortunately it continues to be affirmed by a tenacious exclusionary discourse. My belief in the pertinence of a psychoanalytic approach marked my clinical practice first as a provider of psychoanalytic psychotherapy and later as clinical director of a bilingual mental health outpatient clinic. Being an analyst in the inner-city clinic implies accepting a big challenge. María's impromptu arrival at the clinic not only shattered the stillness of a Friday's siesta, her dramatic entrance reminds us that clinical practice in the *barrio* poignantly tests and reformulates the foundations of psychoanalysis. María could risk becoming a mere "298.90"—the representative of a codified mental disorder, and thus disappear as an individual person, simply reduced to a universal symptom cluster. Once evaluated, was María going to be given some medications and be sent home? Or was she going to rely exclusively on talk therapy? These initial questions remind us that one cannot disregard the status of the symptoms and much less even forget the diagnostic criteria that qualify María's manifestations as pathology. The diagnosis is crucial because it not only records the signs and predicts the course and outcome of the syndromes patients present with, but also provides a label of pathology that can have stigmatizing effects—it classifies patients rather than pathologies.

Did the clinic offer the best treatment option for María? In the here and now of each case, one can no longer ignore overreaching concerns such as the politics of psychiatric care, the viability and effectiveness of psychotherapy, and the role of the mental health institution in each treatment. As we have seen, administration requirements specified that María should get her psychiatric evaluation first, in order to be able to start her psychotherapy. A simple two-day wait proved too long in this case, which shows how with a very impaired patient, a clinic's policy can jeopardize access to mental health care. Had María been sent to a hospital emergency room, most likely she would have been evaluated; however, since she was not a life threat to herself or others, she would have been placed in observation, been given some medications, and then discharged.

On the other hand, could a person with severe symptoms like María's rely exclusively on outpatient talk therapy? This raises the question of how to listen to a seemingly psychotic production. In most cases, psychotic production is dismissed as purely "nonsensical," which puts aside the crucial factor that the delusion is an attempt to restitute sense in the face of what is experienced as a state of psychic chaos; the psychotic production is filled with meaning and follows a logic, possibly quite idiosyncratic, and is an essential reference point in any psychoanalytic treatment of psychosis.

When one talks of a psychoanalytic treatment in a mental health clinic, other issues are introduced such as the use of interpretation, timing of sessions, frequency, money, face to face versus the couch, and so on. In the forefront of the practice, one is forced by practical concerns to challenge one's technique while probing one's ethical stance. The same claim made about the value of María's construction about dogs and ducks can be made about any other "symptomatic" production, be it a psychotic hallucination or a neurotic symptom. In psychoanalysis, "symptoms" can reveal their meaning through interpretation. There is a content kernel articulated in symptoms but also dissimulated by them. Because of this concealment, symptoms should not be eliminated before their meaning is decoded. Psychoanalysis breaks the belief that a "symptom" is nothing but a simple and meaningless disruption, a disorder caused by psychological processes and as such having nothing whatsoever to do with signification. By means of the translation of the core or content kernel of symptoms, we overcome the illusion that symptoms are pure hazard, an accidental annoyance. Yet, the unmasking of symptoms at an individual level is not sufficient. Symptoms are the evidence of unspoken statements waiting to be read between the lines. The possibility of such reading opens the way to an unconscious discourse that seeks utterance and that the analysand can put into words with the help of the analyst. The formation of symptoms results from the singular structure of the subject's individual and cultural history. Lacanian psychoanalysis is concerned not just with affected parts of the patient's body but with the meaning that the signs betray in connection with the social structure. As Lacan suggests when he talks about James Joyce as the symptom of literature, the analyst will read the symptom as a knot tying together several realms—race, class, and language. From this perspective, following the Freudian idea of *overdetermination*, the symptom has several causes working together to bring about a new concept of causality.

By making symptoms readable, psychoanalysis deciphers rather than suppresses the message of symptoms both at a subjective and societal level. It thus brokers an integration of the social and psychological realms by paying attention to the unconscious interaction of race, class, ethnicity, and language. What could be more appropriate to the treatment of the urban poor? I am not advocating that psychoanalysis become the *only* option for inner-city public clinics. Rather, I strongly oppose the current position of unrelenting exclusion of psychoanalysis from the public inner-city clinics as if class determines the needed treatment.

When María returned, she was seen by the psychiatrist, who started her on a cautious dose of medication that diminished her anxiety and allowed her to talk. As she spoke in our weekly sessions, María's delusional formation yielded some meaning. What initially seemed to be an incoherent construction, a delusion about children, ducks, and dogs, proved later to have a restitutive function.

María's delusion was characterized by the special form of discordance with common language that we often find in the private language of psychotics. Yet her words were not just a paranoid construction but a message expressed in a strange language that could be decoded. She used *pato* with her private meaning, an irreducible meaning not fully shared with others. On the one hand, this private meaning was an effort at explaining a situation that overwhelmed her and produced a paranoid projection: "They transformed my sons into dogs." On the other hand, there was in the very repetition the insinuation of a failed meaning expressed by the stereotyped insistence of her stubborn concern for her sons: "*mis hijos, mis hijos.*" Her delusional symptom had a function: it offered an organization that rendered some coherence and provided a possible answer to an impossible situation (sons turned into either ducks or dogs). The truth of María's symptoms resided not in their universal meaning but in their subjective specificity. I thought if I could listen attentively to María, the nuances of her verbal expressions would reveal the story of her mental illness.

From a psychoanalytic perspective one would address María's delusion not as a behavior to be reeducated but as a construction replete with meaning. Her presenting symptoms contained the code, as it were, that allowed for a productive understanding of the causes of her delusion. María did not have any contact with her father. She was raised by her maternal grandmother whom she called *mami* (mother) and referred to her biological mother, who had a peripheral role in her life, as *titi* (auntie). According to this system of naming, it seemed that her grandmother and her mother were sisters. No father figure was present during her childhood, except for her grandmother's homosexual brother, José, to whom she felt very close. María's Catholic family both condemned and accepted José's homosexuality; her grandmother was intensely ambivalent. If María spent too much time with him, her grandmother would get angry and punish her; however, the grandmother would also get upset if María did not visit him regularly. Sometimes, she would joke that María and José (Mary and Joseph) would one day "have baby Jesus."

The grandmother's dream that María would become a nun collapsed when María got pregnant at the age of 14, leading the enraged grandmother to expel her from her house. After giving birth to a son, María claimed that she heard voices telling her that her son was Jesus. In this delusion, María was fulfilling an incestuous desire for her uncle José, realizing a fantasy of virginal conception, and perhaps repeating literally her grandmother's joke (interpreted verbatim by María as the grandmother's desire). Her second crisis took place weeks after her second son was born. María was found walking aimlessly down a road next to her hometown, holding her baby in her arms.

María's free association gave access to a system of signifying elements: in the peculiar words she was using to describe her illness, María was offering me a key to address her enigmatic condition. To resolve her symptoms, it was crucial to take into account her particular choice of words, usages specific to her. Looking for universal meanings in her symptoms risked missing the specificity of her subjectivity, the particular knowledge about her symptoms she had hidden as a mad truth. My strategy was to listen attentively to María. Indeed, in her choice of verbal expressions, I found the keys to the story of her alienation.

The two signifiers *perro* and *pato* condensed everything that she rejected (pregnancy out of wedlock, homosexuality, and virginal conception); yet at the same time those signifiers represented her. Was she hallucinating them in the Real? By Real, I mean Lacan's sense of a domain outside language, a site in which what is experienced is an impossibly (sur)real hallucination. Was this a strategy to accept homosexuality ("I would not mind if they turned my sons into *patos*.")? María revealed the meaning of "the problem was in her sons turning into *perros*" (dogs) in a session when she described her grandmother's fears that María would turn into a *pata* (Puerto Rican slang for lesbian). Her grandmother used to insist that she should look "more feminine" and forced María to separate from a close adolescent girlfriend. In the grandmother's opinion, María was spending too much time with her girlfriend and looked *enamorada* (in love), instead of staying home learning how to become a good wife.

The perception that her sons had been transformed into dogs was her self-portrait, a visiting card as it were, written in a strange code, as a sentence couched in a foreign idiom for which we have no dictionary. If there was any way to make sense of her puzzling production, the solution was to be found in María's speech. Her associations around the signifier *perro* related to questions of maternity, out of wedlock pregnancy, and fathers neglecting their parental duty: when María's mother got pregnant, her grandmother accused her of being a *perra preñada* (pregnant bitch) who could not identify the father of the child. *Pato* and *perro* both represented María and symbolized her while providing her with a psychic strategy to deal with one of the most fundamental preoccupations of existence, the mysteries of human sexuality: "What does it mean to be a man? What does it mean to be a woman?" For human beings subjective sex is not the transcription of the biological sex or a body image but rather a question to resolve. This problem is not easily solved because there is no such a thing as a natural, instinctive sexuality for speaking beings. When confronted with the problem of sexuality as an enigma, María answered with *pato* and *perro*. Her innovative strategy granted some kind of resolution to the Oedipus complex and thus to the enigma of sexual difference. *Pato* and *perro* introduced a principle of order, a set of norms as it were, a template dictating two very distinct ways of being: *pato* (which she did not mind, thus an acceptable position) and *perro* (which was the unbearable, horrible position that caused her distress). Is this basic principle of difference comparable to the order that the phallus introduces as a mark of difference between signifiers, including those of femininity and masculinity? Usually in psychosis, however, when one finds such supplements, one soon sees that they do not hold very well, and eventually the provisional order collapses before finding a restitutive solution in the delusional production.

As the treatment progressed, there was a marked improvement in María's condition: she was no longer delusional, she was able to find and keep a home, she started to interact with relatives, attend church, and make traditional Puerto Rican paper dolls that she would sell to make money. My experience with María illustrates how patients' symptoms, deeply rooted in their language and culture, can be addressed and deciphered by psychoanalysis. It demonstrates the capacity of a low-income so-called Hispanic with seemingly psychotic manifestations to productively use a psychoanalytic treatment. In view of the outcome of the treatment and the absence of any determining factor for a Lacanian psychosis (there was no linguistic dysfunction, for instance), I came to question my suspicion of a psychosis and had to assume that this had been a case of severe hysteria, an *ataque* with a vengeance.

CLINIC OF THE IMPOSSIBLE

Socorro's treatment shows how in order to recover from an event that breached her protective shield she needed to peer deeply into the specific and subjective effects of ghetto random violence in her life. She needed to put the events in a particular context; she needed to construct a trauma in which to articulate the unconscious consequences of the events—in therapy she was able to explore the unconscious fantasy that turned the dramatic events into an occasion that she could overcome. The potential of psychoanalysis to create hysteria allowed Socorro to move from unspeakable devastation to the inscription of psychic trauma, and finally to a loss that she could articulate.

María's case presents an example of a treatment in which the medical approach (prescription of drugs) could coexist with a psychoanalytic psychotherapy. Unfortunately, these two approaches are not always complementary. For instance, a patient may come to see an analyst and also request a referral to a psychiatrist for medications. The analyst may prefer to follow Freud's advice not to get rid too soon of symptoms before they can speak. A rushed elimination of symptoms often prevents their resolution and thus reinforces the subject's alienation. This ethical attitude necessary for a psychoanalytic cure mandates abstaining from satisfying the demand; yet here one disturbs the delicate balance with what the law prescribes. Here the demand (the referral to a psychiatrist) enters a frangible field. If a patient wants to see a psychiatrist, this is considered a request for medical care that needs to be granted. In this example, even if the analyst in any particular case may not consider medication as the most therapeutic option, the analyst cannot say so; hence here the analyst is reduced to silence. This is not an analytic silence because this kind of silence does not invite free association but a "not saying," which precludes the expression of speech on both sides.

American culture favors a perspective that understands mental health and illness as a purely somatic reality and thus gives to a medical mode of intervention the upper hand. Physicians appear as the undisputed rulers of a field where drug treatment and short-term, "fast-mood," "quick-fix" therapies predominate. As we have seen, since psychoanalysis runs against the grain of the logic of capitalistic consumption it is wrongly seen as a treatment that costs too much and does too little.

The fact that Freud's discoveries are still questioned with relentless fury testifies, over a century after his invention of a revolutionary cure for hysteria, to the currency of psychoanalysis. The seemingly disadvantageous situation faced by psychoanalysis in the United States may end up being beneficial. Obviously, there is a marked difference between societal and individual resistances to psychoanalysis. Whereas within the treatment the resistance can be overcome through interpretation, this device is useless at a societal level. However, both resist the subject of the unconscious. At a clinical level, resistance is both the greatest tool and the greatest enemy of psychoanalysis. Cultural resistances are useful obstacles. Left without resistance, psychoanalysis would probably die. Historically, psychoanalysis has grown stronger in countries where it encountered the biggest resistance—by analysts, by patients, and by the culture at large. This positive sign of resistance can change the fate of psychoanalysis in the U.S.

Following Lacan's idea that there is only *one* resistance, that of the analyst, while we can hold the clinics accountable for a portion of the responsibility in making difficult a psychoanalytic clinical practice with minority groups, ultimately one can see that it is the analyst's desire to sustain a space for the analysand's unconscious to be listened to that makes possible a psychoanalytic cure. Freud believed that any line of therapy that recognizes the unconscious processes of transference and resistance as the starting point can rightfully be called psychoanalytic.

We have already seen the numerous obstacles that the setting of a mental health clinic can present to psychoanalytic work. This said, how do we address transference in a *barrio*'s clinic? Transference is a universal phenomenon of all relationships that has to be both analyzed and resolved in a successful treatment. In the name of strengthening the ego, mental health practices manipulate transference. Transference is the space that speech has to traverse without being reduced; it can be neither disregarded nor manipulated. Yet in current practices transference is instead perpetuated and promoted to reproduce a sibling relationship that becomes impossible to resolve because the therapist occupies the position of role model that the patient will have to mimic. The reigning ethic is that of the conscientious consumer; it is a eudaemonistic morality in which the imperative is the Sovereign Good. This one of the results of the influence and transplantation of the medical model into the field of mental health is the distortion of the Hippocratic Oath: *primun non nocere* (first, no harm). According to this model, the ethical constraint "Do no harm" becomes the moral injunction "Do Good." In the name of an ideal of Supreme Good, the commandment to enforce adaptation ensues. One may rightfully ask: Adaptation to what? To a model of normality that condenses the ideological imperatives of the majority. It perpetuates a colonialist legacy: the Hispanic psyche functioning as the conquered land. Against common sense's belief, one can see that a "normal" person can be very sick. Psychoanalysis reveals that the greatest achievements—in terms of performance sanctioned by the majority as successful—can be directed against the person or be a derivative of psychopathology. Success is expected from a "normal" person, even at the expense of psychopathogy. "Normality" is, indeed, a very equivocal concept. It is full of subjective arbitrariness as well as determined by mainstream social mandates. Normality introduces the social scene: the norm, median, average, the proportion, the medial value. If normality is the lack of difference, only the majority are normal since, by definition, those in the minority are abnormal.

Mental health services become orthopedics of behavior, straightening up, reeducating, persuading, and domesticating. One can pose the question of the desire of the therapist who, unwittingly or not, reproduces the discourse of the Master by becoming what, following Lacan, can be called the *agent of impossibility*. The therapist plays the role of the Master who knows what is better for the patient by giving advice. Rather than having a treatment that brings about the necessary changes allowing the patient's subjectivity to emerge, the therapist seems to be the agent of a paralyzing, disempowering plot that keeps patients in a position of alienation facing their truth. Any demand for treatment may allow truth to emerge (in speech) only if the therapist maintains a position of neutrality. The patient's demand, which is, after all, always a demand for love, should not be satisfied so as to allow the patient's desire to emerge and be put into question.

During my work as Clinical Director of a *barrio* clinic, for example, the apparently insignificant implementation of a minimal copayment per session brought about crucial changes in the handling of the transference. Patients regularized their attendance, and therapists reported in supervision that patients were more actively involved in their treatments. The copayment reinstated agency on the side of the patients. By paying a fee for the treatment, they were freed from building both dependence and an unpayable debt—which was in most cases paid back by never getting cured. The treatment was no longer seemingly free. This change allowed patients to exercise their freedom. Now, they desired to get help and actively sought treatment.

Often in community mental health centers, pressured by ideals of increased productivity and efficiency, the demand is inverted, and it appears in the place of the therapist who phones the clients to remind them about the sessions and who stresses the importance of the continuation of the treatment. The therapist seems more interested in the treatment than the patient. I have seen some mental health clinics in the *barrio* that had a quite oppressive system to regularize attendance—they sent a van to the patients' homes to fetch them and by offering "free" transportation to the clinic, forced them to keep their appointments in a questionable consensual manner.

For the treatment to progress, the patients need to be able to question what they want (rather than what the therapist or the clinic wants, a wanting that should remain enigmatic), and in this way articulate their own desire. When the demand appears on the side of the therapist it sutures, it makes impossible any production of truth for the subject. The neutrality of the analyst, who abstains in front of the patient's demand for love, looks for a revelation of the truth in which the subject can question what she or he wants. This is how analysands end up finding in their desire reasons for actions that will accomplish a significant change.

A clinical practice that would take into account unconscious processes requires many adjustments. The charming chatty style of a receptionist may unwittingly jeopardize the "analytic neutrality" staunchly sustained by the therapists. Administrative personnel need to be made aware of their role in enhancing the therapeutic process and thus avoid indiscretions that may thwart analytic work. Nonetheless, the important fact is that the analyst has to be clear about his or her role in transference and remain vigilant to the interference that the institution may present to the process.

Needed changes in the way therapy is practiced in mental health clinics should address the wide implications of requesting patients to sign a treatment plan that functions like a contract coercing the patient "to comply," that is, to follow specific tasks in order to achieve certain goals established by the therapist. Periodically (usually every 2 or 3 months), the treatment plan is revised, the patient's performance is evaluated, and a new treatment plan contract is written and signed. This commodification of mental health practices has the potential of triggering many negative effects, namely a fetishization of symptom suppression and adaptation to social mandates. I recall the wise comment of a depressed patient who was asked to sign a form that was part of the regular intake procedure in which he was to promise that he was not going to take his own life during the course of the treatment. He told me: "Then I will die a liar." The absurdity and futility of these pedagogical strategies and the implications of such emphasis on adaptation in terms of individual freedom, especially for individuals of a minority culture or a lower socioeconomic class, are too obvious.

Although most current forms of talk therapy derive from Freud's invention, in the United States psychoanalysis developed in a manner adapted to a cultural juncture that emphasized the ego as the agent of adaptation—the unconscious was Americanized. The importance placed on adaptation determined that both American psychoanalysis and other forms of talk therapy move away from the unconscious to stress adaptation and normal development. A type of treatment that focuses on interpreting unconscious desire and undoing repression seems to offer an option that resonates better with the struggles of minority groups.

HYSTERIC LIES, HISTORIC TRUTHS

A last vignette from a case story will demonstrate how the combined insights of Freud and Lacan illuminate the logics of the *ataque*. Let us return to Consuelo, mentioned briefly in Chapter 10, a 43-year-old woman whose readiness to become a caretaker decided her to move from Puerto Rico to Philadelphia's "Hispanic" ghetto in order to take care of a sister who *perdió la mente* (lost her mind). Once in Philadelphia, her own failing health motivated her to stay. She only stated that she had bad, "altered" nerves (*nervios alterados*). Let us recall how she put it:

> I have this inside me. *Me agito* (I'm hurried/stressed) and something goes up to my head. I feel in despair. My head trembles—my head becomes strange as if something would be walking in my head. All my life I've suffered from my nerves.

Nervios is a term I heard quite often; it conveys the idea of a socially acceptable response to high levels of stress. Since *nervios* afflict anyone in a distressing situation, the term lacks specificity; it was important then to explore the particular significance *nervios* had for Consuelo. Although Consuelo argued that *la vida me ha alterado los nervios* (life "altered" my nerves), she ultimately attributed her condition to a current conflict with her husband. She claimed that "he was not behaving well." ("*Conmigo no quiere hacer na'; solo le preocupa mi nena, mas na' le importa.*") She complained that he did not want to do anything with her; she felt that his only concern was her daughter and that nothing else mattered for him. This comment acquired a different connotation when a couple of sessions later Consuelo announced that she needed to confess a secret.

Initially all appeared to be a complaint about her husband's apathy ("*no quiere echar pa'alante,*" meaning "he does not want to progress"). He was unemployed and unwilling to look for a job and since he was not earning any money, the family relied on the welfare income and had to put a halt to the extensive renovations their house required. Consuelo had a hard time making ends meet and was stressed about money. Above all, she felt very frustrated because he did not want to change and he expected her "to do everything." What seemed like a quite traditional presentation of the famous Lacanian dictum "there is no sexual rapport" was brought under new, disturbing light concerning her marital conflict when Consuelo revealed a secret.

"I had a dream," Consuelo announced. "In the dream, my husband married my daughter," she said. Consuelo's anxiety was palpable. "It was a secret but I knew it." What was this startling statement? Consuelo was convinced that the dream was an eye-opener, that it had revealed a dark and hidden truth. She added that she had been suspicious for some time. Her 21-year-old daughter Yamiltza was not her husband's child. Consuelo had been divorced for a short time when she married her second husband, 17 years ago. Was this an accusation with foundations? She described ambiguous scenes between stepfather and daughter: late one night she heard noises and found her husband in her daughter's room sitting on her bed and they acted as if caught red-handed when she entered. Another time she found them in the bathroom. Her daughter was wearing only a towel and again they acted strangely. Consuelo had been observing her husband and felt that he had been acting as if "*enamorado*" (in love) and was suspecting an infidelity. Now her fears were confirmed; she could not feel more in despair: the other woman was her own daughter. Consuelo was denouncing an incestuous situation. Although her husband was not the biological father of Yamiltza, the situation implied what one may call second-degree incest. From the perspective of the child this man was her father (she usually called him *papi*— daddy). Consuelo was jealous, angry, and afraid for her daughter.

I must say that I was also unsettled by her confession. Although her daughter was already 21, I was wondering if I needed to become a prosecutor and report the situation. Nothing could guarantee that the present threat might not relate to events that could have happened in the past when Yamiltza was still a minor, which would have meant child sexual abuse. I asked Consuelo to see me the very next day. She called in the morning to cancel the appointment. She said she was sick. When I inquired further she told me that she had an *ataque* and was now in bed recovering.

Fue esta mañana. Mi marido se estaba yendo temprano todo vestido y perfumado y me dió un temblequeo. Me fuí del mundo, empece a temblar, las manos. . . . Me dió un ahogo, un dolor tan grande, no toleraba que mi hija perdiera esa imagen de padre que tanto necesitaba. Empecé a llorar y gritar. (It was this morning. My husband was leaving early all dressed up and perfumed, and I started shaking. I left the world, I started to shake, my hands . . . I could not breathe, such a big pain, I could not tolerate that my daughter would lose that image of a father that she needed so much. I began to cry and scream.)

Her husband was there with her. "*Hoy no se tira pa' la calle*" ("Today, he is not going out"), said Consuelo bitterly. Her daughter was at her boyfriend's. At her *boyfriend's*? I asked. Yamiltza had been dating for a couple of months a young man from the neighborhood and she was with him when Consuelo had the attack. Someone had contacted Yamiltza on a beeper and she had not yet come back home. I suggested that Consuelo come for a session as soon as possible and I thought that it would help to talk with Yamiltza, so I asked Consuelo to see if her daughter could come with her.

When I saw Consuelo I learned that she had not mentioned that she had been having *ataques* recently. Curiously, what seemed to provoke the paroxysms was her husband leaving the house. "*Se va pa' la calle y vuelve tarde. Me dice que no me puede llevar. Entonces le caigo encima, rompo cosas, me viene el temblequeo, el llanto y me desahogo.*" ("He goes on the street and comes back late. He tells me that he cannot take me along. Then, I attacked him, I break things, the shaking starts, the crying, and I unburden myself.") Her being so upset about her husband leaving the house was mystifying since apparently the danger was at home with the incestuous situation she was denouncing. "*Mi problema es grave y no lo puedo resolver.*" ("I have a serious problem and I can't solve it.") "*Y mire que salimos hablando con mi esposo, porque yo tengo muchas dudas. Si hasta le dije que iba a haber divorcio, y me dió un sentimiento tan grande y empece a gritar y se me iba la voz.*" ("And look, my husband and I got to talk because I am full of doubts. I even said that we would have a divorce, and such a big feeling sunk in me, and I started to cry and lost my voice.")

The unconscious is always strictly logical so it was puzzling that there was something relatively illogical in her concerns: Why would she be upset about her husband leaving the house while her daughter was at her boyfriend's? What did her *ataque* mean and to whom was it addressed?

An important clue came from her daughter, who wanted to talk to me. Yamiltza was very worried; she felt that her mother was angry and hurt because it seemed that *papi* was involved with another woman. Some people had started spreading rumors that he was keeping a "second house." Consuelo's recent *ataques* looked like desperate means to prevent her husband from leaving the house and meeting the other woman while offering a way to express her feelings. Her *ataques* seemed like a voice of resistance, a cry of protest. Yet how was I to make sense of her accusation, "I believe that my husband wants to marry my daughter"?

Talking to both her husband and Yamiltza, the accusation of incest brought echoes of what is known as a hysterical lie or the "first lie," Freud's (1895) concept of the hysterical *proton pseudos*. This is an enigmatic term that Freud uses in the "Project for a Scientific Psychology," and which is erroneously referred to as "hysterical lie," since Freud purposely chooses to keep it in Greek. If he had meant "lie," he could have used the German *Lüge*. *Proton pseudos* is a concept that he borrows from the Aristotelian logic that relates to an error in the reasoning in syllogisms. Enrique Tenenbaum (1996) argues that Aristotle's contentions in the *Organon* differ from what Strachey writes in a footnote to Freud's text; *proton pseudos* is not a false premise but rather a false reasoning that results from a first mistake. Then one understands Freud's use of *proton pseudos* in hysteria as a way of conveying the idea of a first mistake—as he writes, it is a memory that is taken for a perception. This idea of an "error" instead of a lie is quite useful if we wish to think together about hysteria, trauma, and time, issues we have discussed earlier in connection to Socorro's case. Tenenbaum takes Freud's adherence to the Greek term, first spelled in Latin script and then in Greek characters in the next section, as parallel to the encounter with sexuality, which is in fact an encounter with another language; here we have an encounter with a foreign writing, perhaps untranslatable and mystifying. If one then translates *proton pseudos* as first error, as he suggests, one can locate a knotting of symptom, body, and trauma that results from a first mistake, from a missed encounter (an encounter that happens at the wrong time—either too late or too early). This error in reasoning leads to an irremediable failure pointing to what remains outside meaning. Tenenbaum contends that this "error at the origin" is not only the point of departure of the unconscious but also of the constitution of the structure.

Lacan contends in his seminar on *Ethics of Psychoanalysis* (1992) that lies are also a way of saying the truth. This relates to the fact that truth can be articulated only within the structure of fiction. Much has been said about hysteria and lies. For centuries, hysterics have been condemned as simulators, inventors, and pretenders. But let us note that in order to lie one needs to know the truth, otherwise we would be talking about an error and not a lie. Consuelo is lying while she is not fully aware of it—and her mistake is expressing a truth. As Freud demonstrates in his use of parapraxes, truth is best recognized through error. Precisely, *proton pseudos* is a mistaken reasoning that does not prevent the constitution of knowledge but, on the contrary, promotes it.

"I could not tolerate that my daughter would lose that image of a father that she needed so much," complained Consuelo after her *ataque*. Her accusation of an incestuous marriage relegated her husband to the status of being just a man and no longer a father for Yamiltza. Like most hysterics, she tried to demote the father she had found and to reduce him to the status of perverted seducer. This sends us back to the formula of hysterical fantasies that we have discussed in Chapter 8.

$$\frac{a}{-\varphi} \Diamond A$$

While Consuelo was denouncing her own incestuous wishes, her gesture revealed her desire for a father whom she was at once killing as such. For the hysteric the Other is an impotent prohibitor. She might have been searching for a father, but in order to kill him symbolically. This father was necessary because her *ataque* expressed a fantasy; it functioned as an appeal to the Other (recall Freud's discovery, "Attacks . . . are aimed at *another person*—but above all at the prehistoric, unforgettable other person whom no one coming after can equal."). She was trying to reinstitute a father between her and the Other.

The paternal function was revealed by her recurrent use of the signifier *cuatro* (four). She had come to see me for the first time exactly four (*cuatro*) days before the first anniversary of her mother's death. Her father had also died around the same time of the year, four years before. The number four recurred two times more: Consuelo, like her own mother, was the fourth girl in a large family (11 siblings) and her daughter was four years old when she married her second husband. She was not aware of these coincidences that would become quite relevant in connection to a dream. Consuelo dreamed that she was in a car going very fast; in the driver's seat there was a man holding not the wheel but a *cuatro*. *Cuatro*, she recalled, was the name of her father's favorite musical instrument. He was an amateur musician who played an instrument called a *cuatro* (it had originally four strings only and is Puerto Rico's national instrument, like a diminutive version of the Spanish guitar). Consuelo's father was very unfaithful to his wife and would leave for long weekends, *cuatro* in hand, to return late on Sundays. The associations with the dream further clarified Consuelo's initial complaint about her husband, "*solo le preocupa mi nena, mas na' le importa*" (he only cares about my daughter, nothing else matters) related to how much she wished she would have mattered for her father who, in spite of being so devoted to her, left the family behind as if his daughter did not matter. She was calling her father back to occupy his place and drive her way from the siren songs of her mother's desire.

Consuelo became aware in many subtle ways that she had always searched for the love of her father; she adored him and felt that she was his "baby." But her life story seems to offer a contradictory version: an absent father and a mother who was better off without him. After her parents separated she kept writing to him (she was the only one of her siblings who kept in touch with him). Recall that this was a father who "drank his salary" and stopped this addiction only when he developed *delirium tremens*. He died of a stroke, just weeks after a failed suicide attempt.

Consuelo's mother did not seem bitter but talked disrespectfully about him. "*Mejor perderlo que encontrarlo*" (better lost than found) she used to say, leaving Consuelo without a father who could come between her and her mother. Consuelo's mother seemed to be able to survive on her own quite well, managing to take care of her 11 children. According to Consuelo's recollections, the fact that the mother never complained about being alone with such a tremendous responsibility, was understood as evidence that the mother did not really need her husband. Possibly, the mother found a phallic restitution in her children. This was crucial because Consuelo's mother seemed to have been quite identified with her, an identification that had pervasive effects for Consuelo. For Consuelo, who "played/made the man," her main identification was with her father. As it were, for her mother her father was "better lost than found," while for Consuelo it was "better to try to find him than giving him up for lost."

When Consuelo was 21 (her daughter's age) she was finally reunited with him (he had left the family when she was still a child and never came back). The circumstances were tragic. He had tried to commit suicide this time (he made several attempts during his life) by taking pills but was saved by a neighbor. When he met with Consuelo soon after being discharged from the hospital, he expressed his regret for not having thought of his family and apologized for drinking and for having left behind his family, but specifically for abandoning his adored daughter Consuelo. She then felt determined to live with him "to save him from himself," in an arrangement which, in the way Consuelo talked about it, looked a lot like a marriage. This never happened. Many years later, his sudden death after a stroke just weeks after another failed suicidal attempt filled her with regret and triggered an *ataque*. "*Ese día me dió una crisis. No pude ni aguantarme, me*

volví loca, me dió el ataque y desde entonces se me dañaron más los nervios."
("That day I had a crisis. I could not contain it, I got crazy, I had an *ataque*
and ever since my nerves have been even more damaged.")

Consuelo was not in a purely passive position regarding her father but
in an ambiguous complicity with him. Her father may have been a seducer
but Consuelo was placing herself as the father's partner. Unconsciously
Consuelo blamed her mother for her father's abandonment of the family—
she was the Other who forbade her the pleasure of being with her father.
Consuelo talked about her mother, a woman she feared. *"La maldición de la
madre es como la mancha del guineo"* (this is a saying that translates as "the
mother's curse is like a banana stain" and Consuelo explained that like a tough
stain, a mother's curse never goes away).[4] Consuelo felt her mother had been
unfairly severe with her, forcing her to do a lot of work at home. "Women
had to work" while the men in the family were allowed to go out at their
leisure. She even feared that her mother wanted her dead. Consuelo believed
that she would have been better off if she had been a man, much better
equipped to deal with her mother's severity. "My father loved me and I was
devoted to him. But he was never truly there for us. I was all alone and never
dared to stand up against my mother." She could do without "the father"
only under the condition of first making use of his function.

Consuelo's realization of the meaning of her accusations toward her
husband and of their real object was quite fruitful. She became aware that
her marriage was in danger and that she needed to decide what to do about
her husband's infidelity. She noticed that the *ataques* were attempts at re-
shaping her relationship with him, but while ventilating the anger directed
at her mother she also took care of their unconscious destination. Consuelo
explored her feelings of vulnerability—she felt abused, betrayed, victimized. She was able to gradually detach herself from her fantasy of the Other.
She started mourning—she accepted and separated from an Other that was
now seen as neither faulty nor omnipotent. Something corresponding to
what Lacan calls going from father to worst (*du père au pire*) took place.
The worst is here the object *a*, not the phallus that obscures it, but the
object *a*, cause of desire. From there, Consuelo was able to construct a new
fundamental fantasy beyond the father, further away from the trap of her
mother's desire, following a desire of her own.

---

4. This saying could also have other connotations (i.e., interracial) that Consuelo
did not bring up in her associations.

Yamiltza moved away with her boyfriend, leaving her parents alone to resolve their conflict. After a few rocky months, Consuelo and her husband managed to overcome the crisis. They decided to stay together. Her husband left his lover and found a job. Consuelo succinctly conveyed the progress she achieved in the treatment: "*Ahora que sé defenderme no me dan mas ataques.*" ("Now that I know how to defend myself I don't have any more *ataques.*")

SO HAPPY TOGETHER

Cavell's (1981) work on remarriage comedies shows how divorce, union, and disunion operate as powerful metaphors for the rest of society. His analysis illustrates how the mystery of marriage is ineluctable. Neither law nor sexuality can sufficiently ensure true marriage; not even the wish to remarry can provide a guarantee. Cavell notes that the "world in which dreams come true" for our *Philadelphia Story* heroes is refound "apparently in the larger world in which they divorced, literally in the place they grew up together, not in removing themselves to a world apart from the public world" (p. 146). *The Philadelphia Story* is atypical within the genre of remarriage comedies because the couple rediscovers its happiness in the outside world and not in isolation, eloping to a world of their own. The promised happiness was to be found in Philadelphia.

Is the dream of a happy marriage the metaphor for impossibility? In Lacan's algebra, impossibility is a logical category to which we may add that of impotence. The *barrio* exposes and magnifies the Real of discontent in culture, with the "impossibilities" and effects of "impotence" faced by a clinical practice acknowledging the unconscious. Socorro managed to reckon with the impossible and articulate the unspeakable. María was a true martyr (a witness, literally) to the unconscious rendering testimony to meaning in madness. Consuelo showed that in the face of despair the last resource may be an *ataque*. What my three "Philadelphia Stories" have shown, I hope, is that psychoanalysis is not only possible but much needed in the ghetto.

Is the Puerto Rican syndrome a *proton pseudos*, a lost memory of a national ideal that is mistaken for a perception of current injustice? Can we trust Cavell's optimism about remarriages to bring a solution with the dubious sanction of a fake happy ending? Or should we confront what the dream awakes and simply get rid of the whole "sovereign lie" while seeking beyond colonialism and its *proton pseudos*, the true roots of a fruitful first mistake, the *felix culpa* of contemporary history?

Conclusion

From Alaska to Puerto Rico

An animated group scene calling up strong emotions: In the center, a man with a wide-rimmed hat steps down from a noble horse. He opens a large wooden trunk with the inscription *U.S. MAIL*. He is holding a bundle of letters. To the right, four women engage in a strangely tense choreography of happiness, while behind them more raised arms betray the presence of other people. They evoke a Greek chorus but the mood is cheerful. A little girl grabs one of the women's dresses while dropping a piece of paper, a letter perhaps. To the left, one man and two older girls wave at the horseman. Facing us, a bare-chested adolescent sits amid a pile of canvas bags full of mail. Behind the splendid horse with epic bearing, a very large airplane looms against the sky. Three burly men unload more bags of mail. Beyond the plane, the sea is of the bluest blue. Everyone is dressed in white. All but the horseman are black. Just under the capital letters spelling U.S. MAIL in the geometrical center of the composition, an unfolded letter is held by a woman with a white scarf. The letter bears an inscrutable message—an inscription written in a mysterious language: "*Puerto Ricmiunun ilapticnum! Ke Ha Chimmeulakut Engayscaacut, Amna Ketchimmi Attunim Chuyl Waptictum itt/icleoraatigut.*"

This stunning scene—calling up the frescoes of a Diego Rivera or a David Alvaro Siqueiros—was unveiled on September 4, 1937. That day a mural for the federal post office building in Washington, DC, finally met the public eye. The two wide panels showed two contrasting scenes, one in an Arctic setting, the other in the tropics. The Alaskan scene rendered two Eskimo women holding a letter, Eskimo men with dog and reindeer sleighs, and a group of people in the background waving at an airplane. Both paintings capture a very intense mood, conveying drama and spiritual rapport with the place. The double fresco was meant to illustrate the extensive scope of United States mail delivery, but the painter may have had another agenda in mind.

The murals adorned the corridors leading to the Postmaster General's office and the painted message seemed to contain the words "Puerto Rico." After the inauguration ceremony a major political scandal erupted. What did this strange message mean? One Washington-based journalist, Ruby Black, publicized the results of her investigation. She explained that the murals had been commissioned to the painter Rockwell Kent by the Treasury Department's Procurement Division. After they were displayed to the public, the artist could not be reached for comments. Experts were consulted. The Post Office Department, the Smithsonian Institute, the Department of State, the Bureau of Indian Affairs, and the Division of Territories and Island Possessions were contacted to no avail. Finally a famous Arctic explorer, Vilhjamur Steffanson, came up with the answer to the riddle. The message was written in a rare Eskimo dialect—Kuskokwin. When translated into English it read: "To the people of Puerto Rico, our friends. Go ahead, let us change chiefs. That alone can make us equal and free" (Kent 1955, Traxel 1980).[1] The revelation created a stir that then became a scandal of national proportions. In 48 hours, a nation ignorant of Puerto Rico was forced to pay attention to recent and tumultuous events that were taking place on the island. The mural caused headlines across the nation.

The press scandal had been carefully orchestrated by Kent—it was a one-man propaganda campaign. In preparation for the mural, Kent had traveled to Alaska and Puerto Rico. In Puerto Rico he was overwhelmed by the beauty of the island but also shocked by the wide contrast between the extreme poverty of the majority and the opulence of the rich minority. But he was particularly infuriated by the unjust treatment the American

---

1. Traxel has a slightly different translation of the letter. I quote Kent's wording.

authorities gave to the pro-independence Nationalist movement members. Kent's fury was fired up by something he heard at a party given by the governor.

Those were tumultuous times in Puerto Rico. Shortly before Kent's visit in 1936, the chief of insular police had been assassinated in retaliation for the killing of four Nationalists at a demonstration at the Puerto Rico University. In response, two Nationalists, Hiram Rosado and Elias Beauchamp, were captured by the authorities and executed "in self-defense" in the police headquarters of Old San Juan.

At the time of Kent's arrival on the island, Albizu Campos, the leader of the Nationalists, and seven other Nationalists were undergoing a trial accused of conspiring to overthrow the U.S. government. A verdict had not been reached and a second trial was scheduled. At the governor's party Kent met the federal prosecutor on the case and overheard him assure everyone of a guilty verdict on the second trial—he showed a list with the names of the prospective jurors he had handpicked. Kent took immediate action: he sent an affidavit to Washington stating what he had heard. It served no purpose. The Nationalists were sentenced to 10 years in prison. Kent's indignation increased when the following year on Palm Sunday, day of the anniversary of Puerto Rico's abolition of slavery, the insular police killed 21 persons and injured 200 during a Nationalist demonstration in the city of Ponce.[2] The American Civil Liberties Union investigated the incident and concluded that the federal government was guilty of violation of civil rights and of police brutality. Infuriated by how all these events remained ignored in the mainland, Kent devised a scheme to give maximum publicity to the Puerto Rican situation and exploited the media attention with his politically charged witticism.

Immediately after the unveiling of the mural, Puerto Rican politicians reacted. Rafael Martínez Nadal, President of the Puerto Rican Senate, criticized not so much the revolutionary message as the fact that he was offended because the mural showed mostly black people, portraying Puerto Ricans as "a bunch of half-naked African bushmen."[3] Kent responded that he could add portraits of the critics to the mural but alerted that "painting [them] as

---

2. March 21, 1937. This event was later known as the "Ponce Massacre."

3. "Mural Stirs Ire of Puerto Ricans," *New York Times*, September 22, 1937, p. 26, quoted by Carlos Rodriguez Fraticelli in "U.S. Solidarity with Puerto Rico: Rockwell Kent, 1937" (Meléndez and Meléndez 1993, p. 194).

their faces look out at me from a two-page, halftone spread, might with good cause give some offense to those Puerto Ricans who are not politicians" (quoted in Traxel 1980, p.182). Kent's depiction of Puerto Ricans as "bush-men" had far-reaching implications. The pro-statehood *Coalición* politicians could have interpreted the cryptic message as a call to the U.S. to remain true to its democratic tradition and allow the Puerto Rican people to decide its political status. However, while they were lobbying for statehood for Puerto Rico they felt that now they were to face a new resistance to the annexation; Puerto Rico would be perceived as a "black" state. Infuriated, the Puerto Rican legislature offered to pay for a new mural that would be truly representative of Puerto Rican people in order to "disabuse the minds of people who may have been misled to thinking it symbolizes our culture" (Fraticelli 1937, quoted in Meléndez and Meléndez 1993, p. 194).

Asked to alter the mural, Kent offered the U.S. Treasury Department to include the Preamble of the United States Constitution or the words of President Wilson in regard to self-determination of small nations. Later, he proposed to include in the mural portraits of the three daughters of one of his most severe critics, Santiago Iglesias, the Puerto Rican government representative in Washington. Their names were: America, Libertad (Liberty), and Fraternidad (Fraternity). Alaskan delegates to the Congress entered the controversy. The natives of Kuskokwin affirmed their loyalty as United States citizens. A semantic discussion about the specific words of the message ensued: Eskimos did not have any formal government and the Kuskokwin words translated as chief but also meant guide or leader. Kent argued that the mural's message called not for an armed revolution but simply for a change of chiefs—replacing the colonial administrators or ending Puerto Rico's colonial status (Meléndez and Meléndez 1993, p. 196).

Nonetheless, the artist was accused of having threatened the peace of the land by rousing revolution. Kent denied the accusations but still responded to the official request to modify the second part of the "To the people of Puerto Rico, our friends" message with four provocative alternatives: (1) "Let us, in the spirit of America, fight for life, liberty, and the pursuit of happiness"; (2) "We are told you want equality and freedom. We, people of the Far North, wish you success"; (3) "Success to you in your fight for freedom, for freedom is a tradition of our country"; or (4) "May our people win the freedom and equality, in which lies the promise of happiness." When Kent met with the representatives of the Procurement Division, after hours of heated discussion they compromised on a new revised version: "May you persevere and win freedom and equality in which lies the promise of happiness." This version was finally rejected. In the end, the wording of the letter was changed to something bland but Kent still felt victorious—"my simple little trick . . . has given the Nationalist movement more front-page publicity than was accorded to the Ponce Massacre, or the conviction of Albizu Campos. So much for the newspapers" (quoted in Traxel 1980, p. 182).

Kent's media *coup* was obviously a biased move, but even before he came up with his elaborate publicity plan his choice of sceneries for the mural had already been a political decision. The artist wanted to show not only the extent of American territories but also the plight of oppressed colonial populations. But as so often happens, the political denunciation reveals the logic of a symptom. Indeed, Alaska was the place where the first geographically localized mental disorder was identified. In 1913 A. A. Brill published the first account of *plibloktoq* in the psychiatric literature. The descriptions of *plibloktoq* or Arctic hysteria bear a striking, if not identical, resemblance to the Puerto Rican syndrome.

This is Brill's (1913) description of one *plibloktoq* attack:

> Inahloo, a woman of 45 years, was very violent during her attacks. She did not know what she was doing, she appeared crazy and demented, and would bite when an attempt was made to restrain her. . . . Her face was very congested, her eyes were bloodshot during the attack, and . . . she foamed at the mouth. [pp. 515–516]

As it is the case with Puerto Ricans with episodes of *ataque de nervios*, the Eskimo culture regards *plibloktoq* as an acceptable phenomenon that can happen to anyone facing a stressful situation. In one of the earliest observations made by Westerners, they confirm that Eskimos take *plibloktoq*'s seemingly bizarre symptoms quite naturally. Admiral Robert E. Peary (1907) noticed that

> . . . women, more frequently than men, are afflicted. During the spells, the maniac removes all clothing and prances like a broncho. A case of pliblocto lasts from five minutes to half-an-hour or more. When it occurs under a cover of hut, no apparent concern is felt by other inmates, nor is any attention paid to the antics of the mad one. It is only when an attempt is made to run abroad, that the cords of restraint are felt. [pp. 384–385]

It is also a striking coincidence that these two psychiatric diagnoses correspond to two territories the U.S. purchased from two collapsing empires. In 1867 the United States and Russia signed a treaty and Alaska was bought from Russia for $7,000,000. Puerto Rico was ceded in a treaty with Spain in 1898 for $20,000,000. The territory of Alaska was only fully incorporated to the U.S. in 1959 when statehood was proclaimed and Alaska became the 49th state of the Union.

For a Lacanian, Rockwell Kent's gesture cannot but call up Edgar Allan Poe's allegory of the letter, yet with a significant difference. As Lacan (1991b) noted in his seminar on "The Purloined Letter," one can say that letters fly and words stay.

> What, after all, is a letter? How can a letter be purloined [*volée*]?[4] To whom does it belong? To whoever sent it or to whoever is addressed? If you say that it belongs to whoever sent it, what makes a letter a gift? Why does one send a letter? And if you think that it belongs to the recipient, how is that under certain circumstances, you return your letters to the person who, for a period in your life, bombarded you with them?
>
> When one considers one of those proverbs attributed to the wisdom of nations—the wisdom of which is this denominated by antiphrase—one is sure to light upon stupidity. *Verba volant, scripta manent.*[5] Has it occurred to you that a letter is precisely speech that flies [*vole*]? If a stolen [*volée*] letter is possible, it is because a letter is a fly sheet [*feuille volante*]. It is *scripta* which *volant*, whereas speech, alas, remains. It remains even when no one remembers it any more. Just as, after five hundred thousand signs in the series of *pluses* and *minuses*, the appearance of α, β, γ, δ will still be determined by the same laws.
>
> Speech remains. You can't help the play of symbols, and that is why you have to be careful with what you say. But the letter, for its part, that goes away. It wanders by itself. [pp. 197–198].

Kent's mural is a diptych and is structured by a series of simple oppositions. In each painting the same plane asserts the domination of U.S. technology and is contrasted with archaic modes of conveyance—a horse in Puerto Rico, reindeer in Alaska. In both images a male mail-carrier hands letters to a group of women. Thus, it is not true to say, as most commentators have, that we simply follow the circuit of one letter sent from Alaska

---

4. Note the pun on the two meanings of *voler*—to fly and to steal, to purloin.
5. Words fly, writings remain.

to Puerto Rico (see Marin 2000, p. 116; Traxel 1980, p. 182). The parallels suggest the reduction of male postal agents to intermediaries between two communities of women engaged in a constant give and take—the Alaskan women and the Puerto Rican women. While in Poe's story the content of the letter is never revealed, in the Puerto Rican panel the letter is in full view albeit scripted in an incomprehensible language whose message ultimately subverts the male domination of a mail system using the most sophisticated technology of the time. It is as if the U.S. MAIL system remained in the position of the blind and impotent onlooker who merely transmits incitation to his own demise. Finally, going to the end of the explosive and divisive energies contained in the diptych, Kent cleverly opposes U.S. (us, the communities of women planning a change of leaders that will make us free and equal) to MAIL (male, understood as the pure economy of the U.S. system of exploitation and distribution). The real letter for us is not the upper case letters we can see from a distance but a cryptic and almost illegible flying message still to be decoded. It is not coincidence that Kent enlisted a woman journalist (Ruby Black was a willing accomplice and a political friend of his, well acquainted with the situation in Puerto Rico) in this complex game of hermeneutic hide and seek.

In 1993 Dayanara Torres, Miss Puerto Rico, won the Miss Universe Pageant crown competing with other national representatives, among them Miss U.S.A. That same year a referendum was conducted in Puerto Rico. The commonwealth status was reaffirmed by the voters. As a commonwealth, Puerto Rico remained an unincorporated territory and did not have the status of *free association* with the United States as that status was defined under United States law or international practice. It was also in 1993 that the U.S. Postal Service commemorated the 500th anniversary of Columbus' "discovery" of Puerto Rico by issuing a special stamp.

Puerto Rico's 1998 nonbinding referendum (not much more than a suggestion to the U.S. Congress) offered Puerto Rican voters five choices: "remaining a U.S. commonwealth," "entering into a true 'free association' with the United States (somewhere between commonwealth and independence)," "becoming a state," "declaring independence," or "none of the above." Not any of the first four choices offered seem to resolve the unsettled political status; the last option, "none of the above," received the majority of votes. In November 2000, the first female Puerto Rican governor was elected. Again in 2001, Miss Puerto Rico, Denise Quiñónes, won the Miss Universe title. The second runner-up was Kandace Krueger, Miss U.S.A. Ms. Quiñónes became the fourth Puerto Rican to be crowned Miss Universe.

In 2003, Susie Castillo was the third Hispanic ever to become Miss U.S.A. Castillo has Puerto Rican roots. Spanish is her first language and her generation is the first in her family to be born and raised in the United States. She plans to be inspirational; she is quoted as saying: "Hopefully, I can erase some stereotypes about Latinos—that they're not all housekeepers, drug dealers, or hoodlums in the ghetto. Maybe there are some roles out there for a queen."

References

Abad, V., Ramos, J., and Boyce, E. (1974). A model for delivery of mental health services to Spanish-speaking minorities. *American Journal of Orthopsychiatry* 44(4):584–595.

Adams, L. (1953). A new look at Freud's dream "The Breakfast Ship." *American Journal of Psychiatry* 110:381–384.

Altman, N. (1995). *The Analyst in the Inner City: Race, Class and Culture Through a Psychoanalytic Lens.* Hillsdale, NJ, and London: Analytic Press.

American Psychiatric Association. (1952). *Diagnostic and Statistical Manual of Mental Disorders (DSM-1).* Washington, DC: Author.

——— (1994). *Diagnostic and Statistical Manual of Mental Disorders (DSM-IV).* Washington, DC: Author.

——— (2000). *Diagnostic and Statistical Manual of Mental Disorders (DSM-IV-TR).* Washington, DC: Author.

André, S. (1999). *What Does a Woman Want?*, trans. S. Fairfield. New York: Other Press.

Aponte, H. (1976). Underorganization in the poor family. In *Family Therapy: Theory and Practice*, ed. P. Guerin, pp. 432–447. New York: Gardner.

——— (1994). *Bread and Spirit: Therapy with the New Poor.* New York: Norton.

Arana-Soto, S. (1976). *Puerto Rico: Sociedad sin raza.* San Juan, PR: Asociación Médica de Puerto Rico.

Aristotle (1980). *The Nichomachean Ethics*, transl. D. Ross. Oxford and New York: Oxford University Press.

—————— (1991). *On Rhetoric*, transl. and ed. G. Kennedy. Oxford and New York: Oxford University Press.

Badillo Ghali, S. (1977). Culture sensitivity and the Puerto Rican client. *Social Case Work*, October, pp. 459–468.

Bhabha, H. (1994). *The Location of Culture*. New York and London: Routledge.

Blanco, T. (1948). *El prejuicio racial en Puerto Rico*, 2nd ed. San Juan, PR: Biblioteca de Autores Puertorriqueños.

Bram, J. (1958). Spirits, mediums and believers in contemporary Puerto Rico. *Transactions of the New York Academy of Science* 20:344.

Braunstein, N. (1990). *Goce*. México: Siglo XXI Editores.

Brill. A. A. (1913). *Plibloktoq* or hysteria among Peary's Eskimos. *Journal of Nervous and Mental Disease* 40:514–520.

Bronfen, E. (1998). *The Knotted Subject: Hysteria and Its Discontents*. Princeton, NJ: Princeton University Press.

Brown, R., and Yu, H. (2002). Latinos' access to employment-based insurance. In *Latinos Remaking America*. Berkeley, CA: University of California Press and David Rockefeller Center for Latin American Studies, Harvard University.

Bureau of Labor Statistics. (2003). *Geographic Profile of Employment and Unemployment*, available online at http://stats.bls.gov

Calderón De La Barca, P. (1955). *La vida es sueño*. Madrid: Espasa Calpe S.A.

Canetti, E. (1962). *Crowds and Power*. New York: Farrar, Straus, Giroux, 1973.

Caro Costas, A. R. (1977). *Antologia de Lecturas de Historia de Puerto Rico*. San Juan, PR: UPRED.

Carrasquillo Ramírez, A. (1994). The logic of permanent union or the structuring fantasy of free associated state of Puerto Rico. Unpublished paper.

—————— (2000). Puerto Rican *Hystoire*. (a): *a journal of culture and unconscious* 1(1):59–66. A publication of the California Psychoanalytic Circle.

Cavell, S. (1981). *Pursuits of Happiness: The Hollywood Comedy of Remarriage*. Cambridge, MA: Harvard Film Studies.

Charcot, J.-M. (1888). *Clinical Lectures on Certain Diseases of the Nervous System: Lecture VII*, tr. Hurd, R. Detroit, MI: E. P. Davis.

Clark, R. (1980). *Freud: The Man and the Cause: A Biography*. New York: Random House.

Comas-Díaz, L. (1981). Puerto Rican *Espiritismo* and psychotherapy. *American Journal of Orthopsychiatry* 511:636–645.

—————— (1982). Mental health needs of Puerto Rican women in the United States. In *Work, Family and Health: Latina Women in Transition*, ed. R. Zambrana, pp. 1–10. New York: Hispanic Research Center, Fordham University.

Copjec, J. (1994). *Supposing the Subject*. New York: Verso.

Davis, M. (2000). *Magical Urbanism: Latinos Reinvent the U.S. City*. London and New York: Verso, 2001.

De Certeau, M. (1974–1994). *La culture au pluriel*. Paris: Seuil.

———— (1999). *La cultura en plural*. Buenos Aires: Ediciones Nueva Vision.

DeLaCancela, V., Guarnaccia, P. J., and Carrillo, E. (1986). Psychosocial distress among Latinos: a critical analysis of *Ataques de Nervios*. *Humanity and Society* 10(4):431–447.

DeLaCancela, V., and Zavala, I. (1983). An analysis of culturalism in Latino mental health: folk medicine as a case in point. *Hispanic Journal of Behavioral Sciences* 5:267.

Delgado. M. (1977). Puerto Rican spiritualism and the social work profession. *Social Casework*, October, pp. 451–458.

Devereux, G. (1958). Cultural thought models in primitive and modern psychological theories. *Psychiatry* 21:359–374.

Dunk, P. (1989). Greek women and broken nerves in Montreal. *Medical Anthropology* 11:29–45.

Ericksen, E., et al. (1986). *The State of Puerto Rican Philadelphia: Research on Philadelphia and the Greater Delaware Valley Region*. Philadelphia: Institute for Public Policies Studies, Temple University.

Estades Font, M. E. (1988). *La presencia militar de Estados Unidos en Puerto Rico 1898–1918: Intereses estratégicos y dominación colonial*. Río Piedras: Ediciones Huracan.

Estroff, S. (1981). *Making It Crazy: An Ethnography of Psychiatric Clients in an American Community*. Berkeley: University of California Press.

Falk, P. (1986). *The Political Status of Puerto Rico*. Washington, DC: Lexington.

Fernández, R. (1994). *Prisoners of Colonialism: The Struggle for Justice in Puerto Rico*. Monroe, ME: Common Courage Press.

Fernández Marina, R. (1961). The Puerto Rican Syndrome: its dynamics and cultural determinants. *Psychiatry* 24:79–82.

Fernández Olmos, M., and Paravisini-Gebert, L. (2001). *Healing Cultures: Art and Religion as Curative Practices in the Caribbean and Its Disapora*. New York: Palgrave.

Fink, B. (1995). *The Lacanian Subject: Between Language and Jouissance*. Princeton, NJ: Princeton University Press.

———— (2000). The analytic relationship. In *The Subject of Lacan*, ed. K. R. Malone and S. Friedlander, pp. 157–173. New York: SUNY Press.

Flores, J. (1993). *Divided Borders: Essays on Puerto Rican Identity*. Houston, TX: Arte Publico.

Foley, N., ed. (1997). Becoming Hispanic: Mexican Americans and the Faustian pact with whiteness. In *Reflexiones 1997: New Directions in Mexican American Studies*. Austin: Texas University Press.

Forrester, J., and Appignanesi, L. (2000). *Freud's Women*. New York: Other Press.

Foucault, M. (1965). *Madness and Civilization: A History of Insanity in the Age of Reason*. New York: Random House. Also New York: Vintage, 1988.

———— (1972). *The Archeology of Knowledge*, New York: Pantheon, 1982.

———— (1975). *The Birth of the Clinic: An Archeology of the Medical Perception*, trans. A. M. Sheridan Smith. New York: Vintage.

Freeman A., Kaplan, H., and Sadock, B. (1975). *A Comprehensive Textbook on Psychiatry*. Baltimore, MD: Williams & Wilkins.

Freeman, L. (1972). *The Story of Anna O*. New York: Walker.

Freud, S. (1893). Some points for a comparative study of organic and hysterical motor paralyses. *Standard Edition* 1:157–172.

———— (1895). *Project for a scientific psychology. Standard Edition* 1:281–397.

———— (1900). *The interpretation of dreams. Standard Edition* 4–5.

———— (1905). *Dora: An Analysis of a Case of Hysteria*. New York: Touchstone, 1997.

———— (1908). Hysterical phantasies and bisexuality. *Standard Edition* 9.

———— (1909a). Some general remarks on hysterical attacks. *Standard Edition* 9:227–228.

———— (1909b). Notes upon a case of obsessional neurosis. *Standard Edition* 10:153–318.

———— (1910). *Lectures on psychoanalysis. Standard Edition* 11:9–55.

———— (1915). The sense of symptoms. From *Introductory lectures on psychoanalysis. Standard Edition* 16.

———— (1920). Beyond the pleasure principle. *Standard Edition* 18:12–13.

———— (1921). *Group psychology and the analysis of the ego. Standard Edition* 18.

———— (1926). Inhibition, symptom and anxiety. *Standard Edition* 20:75–172.

———— (1930). *Civilization and its discontents. Standard Edition* 21.

———— (1954). *The Origins of Psychoanalysis*, ed. M. Bonaparte, A. Freud, and E. Kris. New York: Basic Books.

———— (1959). *Collected Papers*, ed. E. Jones. New York: Basic Books.

———— (1985). *The Complete Letters of Sigmund Freud to Wilhelm Fliess, 1887–1904*, trans. J. M. Masson. Cambridge, MA: Belknap Press of Harvard University Press.

Freud, S., and Breuer, J. (1895). *Studies on hysteria. Standard Edition* 2.

Fuss, D. (1994). Interior colonies: Frantz Fanon and the politics of identification. *Diacritics* 24:20–42.

Gann, L. H., and Duignan, P. (1986). *The Hispanics in the United States: A History*. Boulder, CO: Westview.

García Passalacqua, J. (1984). *Puerto Rico: Equality and Freedom at Issue*. New York: Praeger.

García-Prieto, N. (1982). Puerto Rican families. In *Ethnicity and Family Therapy*, ed. M. McGoldrick, J. K. Pearce, and J. Giordano. New York: Guilford.

Garrison, V. (1975). Espiritismo: implications for provision of mental health services to Puerto Rican populations. In *Folk Therapy*, ed. H. Hodges and C. Hudson. Miami, FL: University of Miami Press.

———— (1977). The "Puerto Rican Syndrome." In *Psychiatry and Espiritismo, Case Studies in Spirit*, ed. V. Garrison and V. Caprazano, pp. 383–449. New York: Wiley.

Gay, P. (1986). *Freud: A Life for Our Time*. New York: Doubleday.

Gherovici, P. (1995, 1996). The ghetto sublime hysterics. *Bien Dire* 2–3.

———— (1996a). Sigmund dans le *Barrio*. *Scansions: Actualités de l'interrogation freudienne*, no. 6/7, December, Paris.

———— (1996b). The Puerto Rican syndrome. *Journal for the Psychoanalysis of Culture and Society*, no. 2.

———— (1996c). Blocking the Hispanic unconscious: subjectivity and subjection. *Clinical Studies: International Journal of Psychoanalysis*, vol. 2, no. 2.

———— (1996d). Recuerdos del futuro: hysteria, raza y el ghetto hispano. *Estudios sobre la Histeria: Cien años despues*. Buenos Aires: Ediciones Kline.

———— (1997a). The Hispanic La Raza: psychoanalysis and losing (the) race. *Clinical Studies: International Journal of Psychoanalysis*, vol. 3, no. 1.

———— (1997b). Mens Prozac in Corpore Xanax: As hesitações da responsabilidade subjetiva nos E.V.A. hoje. *Estilos da Clinica Revista Sobre a Infancia con Problemas* II 3:15–20. São Paulo: University of São Paulo Press.

———— (1998). Le ghetto contre-attaque: la production histérique dans le barrio portoricain aux Etats-Unis. *La clinique lacanienne. Revue internationale* 3: 135–150. Paris: Eres.

———— (1999a). Mens Prozac in Corpore Xanax. Las vacilaciones de la responsabilidad subjetiva en los Estados Unidos hoy. *Atas da Reunião Lacano-americana de Psicoanalise da Bahia*. Bahia: ELBA, pp. 910–914.

———— (1999b). El discreto encanto del Prozac. *Psicoanálisis del Hospital. Publicación Semestral de Practicantes en Instituciones Hospitalarias*. 8 No, 1999. Buenos Aires. pp. 8–15.

———— (2000). Psychoanalysis: resistible and irresistible. In *Lacan in America*, ed. J. M. Rabaté, pp. 93–106. New York: Other Press.

———— (2000). Why do people take Prozac? Anxiety, symptom, and inhibition of responsibility. In *Looking at Lacan: A Lacanian Reader for Psychologists*, ed. K. Malone and S. Friedlander, pp. 279–295. New York: SUNY Press.

———— (2001). Anger is sexy. In *Erotic Anger: A User's Manual*, ed. G. Pommier. Minneapolis: University of Minnesota Press.

———— (2001). Etre lacanien aux USA. *Hétérité* 2, Paris.

Glazer, N., and Moynihan, D. P. (1986). *Beyond the Melting Pot*, 2nd ed. Cambridge, MA: MIT Press.

Grace, W. (1959). Ataque. *New York Medicine* 15(1):12–13.

Gramsci, A. (1971). *Selections from Prison Notebooks*, trans. G. Smith and Q. Hoare. New York: International Publishers.

Greenberg, R., ed. (1989). *The Limits of Biological Treatments for Psychological Distress: Comparisons with Psychotherapy and Placebo.* Hillsdale, NJ: Lawrence Erlbaum.

────── (1997). *From Placebo to Panacea: Putting Psychiatric Drugs to the Test.* New York: Wiley.

Grosfoguel, R. (1992). *Puerto Rico's exceptionalism: industrialization, migration and housing development, 1950–1970.* Ph.D. dissertation, Temple University, Philadelphia, PA.

Grosfoguel, R., and Georas, C. S. (2000). Coloniality of power and racial dynamics: notes toward a reinterpretation of Latino Caribbeans in New York City. *Identities* 7(1).

Guarnaccia, P., Canino, G., Rubio-Stipec, M., and Bravo, M. (1993). The prevalence of *ataques de nervios* in the Puerto Rico study: the role of culture in psychiatric epidemiology. *Journal of Nervous and Mental Disorders* 181:157–165.

Guarnaccia, P., DeLaCancela, V., and Carrillo, E. (1989). The multiple meaning of *Ataques de Nervios* in the Latino community. *Medical Anthropology* 11(1):47–62.

Guarnaccia, P., Rivera, M., Franco, F., and Neighbors, C. (1996). The experiences of *ataques de nervios*: towards an anthropology of emotions in Puerto Rico. *Culture, Medicine, and Psychiatry* 20:343–367.

Guarnaccia, P., and Rogler, L. (1999). Research on culture bound syndromes: new directions. *American Journal of Psychiatry* 156(9):1322–1327.

Hancock, R. (1960). *Puerto Rico: A Success Story.* Princeton, NJ: Van Nostrand.

Harrington, M. (1963). *The Other America: Poverty in the United States.* Baltimore, MD: Penguin.

Harwood, A. (1977). *Rx: Spiritist as Needed: A Study of a Puerto Rican Community Mental Health Resource.* New York: Wiley.

────── (1981). *Ethnicity and Medical Care.* Cambridge, MA: Harvard University Press.

Hay Group Study (1987–1997). Hay Group report on the erosion of behavioral health care benefits.

────── (1997). http://www.nami.org/pressroom/keyfind.html

Heller, J. (1971). *Catch-22: A Dramatization.* New York: Delacorte.

Hill, R. T. (1899).Porto Rico or Puerto Rico. *National Geographic Magazine* 10(12):516–517.

Hirsh, S. J., and Hollander, M. H. (1968). Hysterical psychosis: clarification of the concept. *American Journal of Psychiatry* 125:909–915.

Hughes, C. C., Simons, R. C., Wintrob, R. M. (1997). The "Culture-Bound Syndromes" and *DSM-IV.* In *DSM-IV Sourcebook, Vol 3,* ed. T. A. Widiger, A. J. Frances, H. A. Pincus, et al. Washington, DC: American Psychiatric Association.

Hughes, L. (1959). *Selected Poems of Langston Hughes.* New York: Knopf.

Hunter, D. (1983). Hysteria, psychoanalysis, and feminism: the case of Anna O. *Feminist Studies* 9(3):464–488.

Hunter, R. J. (1966). Historical survey of the Puerto Rican status question. In *Status of Puerto Rico: Selected Background Studies*. Washington, DC: US Government Printing Office, p. 125.

Hutcheon, L. (1989). *The Politics of Postmodernism*. London: Routledge.

Inclán, J. (1985). Variation in value orientation in mental health work with Puerto Ricans. *Psychotherapy* 22(25):324–334.

Israël, L. (1979). *L'hystérique, le sexe et le médecin*. Paris: Masson.

Janet, P. (1901). *The Mental State of Hystericals: A Study of Mental Stigmata and Mental Accidents*, trans. C. S. Carson. New York: Putnam.

Jewell, D. (1952). A case of a "psychotic" Navaho Indian male. *Human Organization* 11:32–36.

Johnson, R. A. (1980). *Puerto Rico: Commonwealth or Colony?* New York: Praeger.

Jones, F. (1991). Clinical features of young adult Hispanic psychiatric in-patients: the so-called Puerto Rican Syndrome. *Military Medicine* 156(7):351–354.

Julien, P. (1994). *Jacques Lacan's Return to Freud: The Real, the Symbolic, and the Imaginary*. New York: New York University Press.

Kaplan, M. (1984). Anna O. and Bertha Pappenheim: an historical perspective. In *Anna O.: Fourteen Contemporary Reinterpretations*, ed. M. Rosenbaum and M. Muroff. New York: Free Press.

Kent, R. (1955). *It's Me O Lord: The Autobiography of Rockwell Kent*. New York: Dodd, Mead.

Kleinman, A. (1977). Depression, somatization and the "new cross-cultural psychiatry." *Social Science and Medicine* 11:3–10.

———— (1988). *Rethinking Psychiatry: From Cultural Category to Personal Experience*. New York: Free Press.

———— (1996). How is culture important for *DSM-IV*? In *Culture and Psychiatric Diagnosis: A DSM-IV Perspective*, ed. J. Mezzich, A. Kleinman, H. Fabrega, and D. Parron. Washington DC: American Psychiatric Press.

Koptiuch, K. (1997). Third worlding at home. In *Culture, Power, Place: Explorations in Critical Anthropology*, ed. A. Gupta and J. Ferguson, pp. 234–248. Durham, NC and London: Duke University Press.

Koss, J. (1961). *Puerto Rican spiritualism in Philadelphia*. Read at the annual meeting of the American Anthropological Association, Denver, CO, November 18–21.

———— (1975). Therapeutic aspects of Puerto Rican cult practices. *Psychiatry* 38:160–171.

———— (1987). Expectations and outcomes for patients given mental health care or spiritualist healing in Puerto Rico. *American Journal of Psychiatry* 144:1.

Kripke, S. (1982). *Naming and Necessity*. Cambridge, MA: Harvard University Press.

LaBruzza, A., and Mendez-Villarrubia, J. (1994). *Using DSM-IV: A Clinician's Guide to Psychiatric Diagnosis.* Northvale: NJ: Jason Aronson.

Lacan, J. (1961–1962). Seminar 9: *Identification.* Class of January 10, 1962. Unpublished.

———— (1965). Seminar 12: *Crucial Problems for Psychoanalysis.* Class 4, January 6. Unpublished.

———— (1971). Seminar 19: *Ou Pire,* 1971–1972. Class 1, November 4.

———— (1975). Seminar 22: *RSI, 1974–1975.* Class of February 18. Paris: *Ornicar?* 4.

———— (1977a). Propos sur l'hystérie. *Quarto Bruxelles* 26-2-1977. 1981, No. 2, pp. 5–10.

———— (1977b). *Écrits: A Selection,* trans. A. Sheridan. New York: Norton.

———— (1977c). Seminar 24: *L'insu que sait de l'une bévue s'aile a mourre,* 1976–1977. Class 11, April 19.

———— (1978). *The Four Fundamental Concepts of Psychoanalysis,* ed. J. A. Miller, trans. A. Sheridan. New York: Norton, 1981.

———— (1979). The neurotic's individual myth. *Psychoanalytic Quarterly* 48(3):405–425.

———— (1989). Science and truth. *Newsletter of the Freudian Field* Vol. 3, Nos. 1 & 2 Spring/Fall 4-29.

———— (1990). *Television: A Challenge to the Psychoanalytic Establishment.* New York: Norton.

———— (1991a). *The Seminar, Book I, Freud's Papers on Technique 1953–1954,* ed. J. A. Miller, trans. J. Forrester. New York: Norton.

———— (1991b). *The Seminar, Book 2, The Ego in Freud's Theory and in the Technique of Psychoanalysis,1954–1955,* ed. J. A. Miller, trans. S. Tomaselli. New York: Norton.

———— (1991c). *The Seminar, Book 8,* ed. J. A. Miller. Paris: Seuil.

———— (1991d). *The Seminar, Book 17, L'envers de la psychanalyse, 1969–1970,* ed. J. A. Miller. Paris: Seuil.

———— (1992). *The Seminar, Book 7, The Ethics of Psychoanalysis, 1959–60,* ed. J. A. Miller. New York: Norton.

———— (1994). *The Seminar, Book 4, La relation d'objet,* ed. J. A. Miller. Paris: Seuil.

———— (1998a). *The Seminar, Book 5, Les Formations de l' inconscient, 1957–1958,* ed. J. A. Miller. Paris: Seuil.

———— (1998b). *Encore: The Seminar, Book 20, On Feminine Sexuality: The Limits of Love and Knowledge 1972–1973,* ed. J. A. Miller, trans. B. Fink. New York: Norton.

Landale, N. S., and Oropesa, R. S. (2002). White, black, or Puerto Rican? Racial self-identification among mainland and island Puerto Ricans. *Social Forces* 81(1):231–254.

Lane, C., ed. (1998). *The Psychoanalysis of Race.* New York: Columbia University Press.

Langness, L. L. (1967). Hysterical psychosis: the cross cultural evidence. *American Journal of Psychiatry* 124:143–152.

LaRuffa, A. L. (1971). *San Cipriano: Life in a Puerto Rican Community*. New York: Gordon and Breach.

Levi-Strauss, C. (1958). *Anthropologie structurale*. Paris: Plon.

Levy, R. (1996). Hysteria: structure of all dangers. In *Estudios sobre la Histeria: Cien años después*, vol. 1. Buenos Aires: Ediciones Kline.

Lewis, G. (1963). *Puerto Rico: Freedom and Power in the Caribbean*. New York: M. R. Press.

Lewis, O. (1966). *La Vida: A Puerto Rican Family in the Culture of Poverty—San Juan and New York*. New York: Random House.

Lewis-Fernández, R. (1996). Cultural formulation of psychiatric diagnosis. *Culture, Medicine and Psychiatry* 20:155–163.

———— (1998). Eso no estaba en mí . . . no pude controlarme: El control, la identidad y las emociones en las comunidades puertorriqueñas. *Revista de Ciencias Sociales* Nueva Epoca 4:268–299.

Lock, M. (1989). Words of fear, words of power: nerves and the awakening of political consciousness. *Medical Anthropology* 11:79–90.

Low, S. (1981). The meaning of *Nervios*: a sociocultural analysis of symptom presentation in San José, Costa Rica. *Culture, Medicine and Psychiatry* 5:25–47.

———— (1985). Culturally interpreted symptoms or culture-bound syndromes: a cross-cultural review of nerves. *Social Science and Medicine* 21:187–196.

Lubchansky, I., Egri, G., and Stokes, J. (1970). Puerto Rican spiritualists view mental illness: the faith healer as a paraprofessional. *American Journal of Psychiatry* 127(3):312–321.

Luhrmann, T. M. (2001). *Of Two Minds: The Growing Disorder in American Psychiatry*. New York: Vintage.

MacDougall, W. (1920). *The Group Mind: A Sketch of the Principles of Collective Psychology*. New York and London: G. P. Putnam's Sons.

Mahony, P. (1986). *Freud and the Rat Man*. New Haven and London: Yale University Press.

Maldonado-Sierra, E., and Trent, R. (1960). The sibling relationship in group psychotherapy with Puerto Rican schizophrenics. *American Journal of Psychiatry* 117:239–244.

Marano, L. (1982). Windigo psychosis: anatomy of an emic/etic confusion. *Current Anthropology* 23:385–412.

Marcos, L. (1975). Effects of interpreters on the evaluation of psycho-pathology in non-English speaking patients. *American Journal of Psychiatry* 136:171–174.

Marcos, L., Urcuyo, L., and Kesselman, M. (1973). The language barrier in evaluating Spanish-American patients. *Archives of General Psychiatry* 29:655–659.

Marin, C. (2000). *Distant Shores: The Odyssey of Rockwell Kent*. Berkeley, Los Angeles, London: Chameleon Books and University of California Press, in association with the Norman Rockwell Museums.

Marqués, R. (1972). El puertorriqueño dócil. In *Ensayos*. Río Piedras: Editorial Antillana.

Martínez, C., Jr. (1986). Hispanics. In *Ethnic Psychiatry*, ed. C. Wilkinson. New York and London: Plenum Medical Book Co.

McCormick, R. J. (1986). *Personality Concomitants of the Puerto Rican Syndrome as Reflected in the Minnesota Multiphasic Personality Inventory*. New Brunswick, NJ: Rutgers University Microfilms.

McGrath, W. (1986). *Freud's Discovery of Psychoanalysis: The Politics of Hysteria*. Ithaca, NY: Cornell University Press.

McKay, E. G. (1985). Cultural relevance: an Anglo's guide to working effectively with Hispanics. Washington, DC: National Council of La Raza.

Mehlman, Capt. R. D. (1961). The Puerto Rican Syndrome. *American Journal of Psychiatry* 118:328–332.

Meléndez, E., and Meléndez, E., eds. (1993). *Colonial Dilemma: Critical Perspectives on Contemporary Puerto Rico*. Boston: South End Press.

Metzger, D. (1995–1996). A response to Patricia Gherovici's "The Ghetto's Sublime Hysterics." *Bien Dire* 2–3. Norfolk, VA: Old Dominion University Press.

Mezzich, J., Kleinman, A., Fabrega, H., and Parron, D. (1996). *Culture and Psychiatric Diagnosis: A DSM-IV Perspective*. Washington, DC: American Psychiatric Press.

Micale, M. (1995). *Hysteria: Disease and Its Interpretations*. Princeton, NJ: Princeton University Press.

Michels, A. (2001). *Actualite de l'hystérie*. Paris: Eres.

Miles, R. (1993). *Racism After Race Relations*. London: Routledge.

Millot, C. (1988). *Nobodaddy. L'Hystérie dans le siècle*. Paris: Point Hors Ligne; *La Histeria en el Siglio*. Buenos Aires: Ediciones Nueva Vision.

Minuchin, S., Montalvo, B., et al. (1967). *Families of the Slum: An Exploration of Their Structure and Treatment*. New York: Basic Books.

Mitchell, J. (2000). *Mad Men and Medusas: Reclaiming Hysteria*. New York: Basic Books.

Mizio, E. (1977). Commentary: additional thoughts are presented regarding the needs of, knowledge of, and sensitivity to, cultural factors in relation to Puerto Rican clients. *Social Casework*, October, p. 471.

Moncayo, R. (1998). Cultural diversity and the cultural epistemological structure of psychoanalysis: implications for psychotherapy with Latinos and other minorities. *Psychoanalytic Psychology* 15(2).

Montalvo, B. (1974). Home–school conflict and the Puerto Rican child. *Social Casework* 55:100–110.

Morales Carrión, A. (1983). *Puerto Rico: A Political and Cultural History*. New York: Norton.

Morris, C. (1984). *A Time of Passion*. New York: Penguin.

Morris, N. (1995). *Puerto Rico: Culture, Politics, and Identity*. Westport, CT: Praeger.

Moussaieff Masson, J. (1984). *The Assault on Truth: Freud's Suppression of the Seduction Theory.* London: Faber & Faber.

————, ed. (1985). *The Complete Letters of Sigmund Freud to Wilhelm Fliess, 1887–1904.* Cambridge, MA: Belknap Press of Harvard University Press.

Negrón-Muntaner, F., and Grosfoguel, R., eds. (1997). *Puerto Rican Jam: Essays on Culture and Politics.* Minneapolis: University of Minnesota Press.

Negrón-Portillo, M. (1997). Surviving colonialism and nationalism. In *Puerto Rican Jam: Essays on Culture and Politics,* ed. F. Negrón-Muntaner and R. Grosfoguel. Minneapolis: University of Minnesota Press.

New York Times. (1996). Hispanic march draws crowd to capital by S. Homes, October 13.

O.E.D. Second Edition (1989). *Oxford English Dictionary Online.* Oxford University Press.

Padilla, E. (1958). *Up from Puerto Rico.* New York: Columbia University Press.

Pappenheim, B. (1924). *Sisyphus-Arbeit.* Leipzig: Verlag Paul E. Linder.

Peary, R. E. (1907). *Nearest the Pole.* New York: Doubleday.

Pedreira, A. (1934). *Insularismo.* San Juan, P.R.: Biblioteca de Autores Puertorriqueños.

Pennsylvania Governor's Advisory Commission on Latino Affairs (1991). *Latinos in Pennsylvania: Summary and Recommendations,* April.

Philadelphia Commission on Human Relations (1991). *Report to Mayor W. Wilson Goode on Public Hearings Regarding Concerns of the Philadelphia Latino Community,* September.

Picó, F. (1988). *Historia General de Puerto Rico.* Rio Piedras: Ediciones Huracan.

Pies, R. (1994). *The Clinical Manual of Psychiatric Diagnosis and Treatment: A Biopsychosocial Approach.* Washington and London: American Psychiatric Press.

Pommier, G. (1990). *Libido unlimited—Freud apolitique?* Paris: Editions Point Hors Ligne.

———— (2001). *Erotic Anger: A User's Manual,* trans. C. Liu. Minneapolis: University of Minnesota Press.

Rabinovich, D. (1988). *El concepto de objeto en la teoría psicoanalítica: Sus incidencias en la dirección de la cura.* Buenos Aires: Manantial.

Ragland-Sullivan, E. (1988). The limits of discourse structure: obsession and hysteria. *Papers of the Freudian School of Melbourne.* Melbourne: The Freudian School of Melbourne.

Redlich, F. C., and Pepper, M. (1960). Social psychiatry. *Psychiatry* 116:611–616.

Rendón, M. (1984). Myths and stereotypes in minority groups. *International Journal of Social Psychiatry* 30:297–309.

Rennie, T. a C. (1956). Social psychiatry—a definition. *International Journal of Social Psychiatry* 1:5–13

Ribes Tovar, F. (1973). *A Chronological History of Puerto Rico.* New York: Plus Ultra Educational Publishers.

Riley, T., and Roy, A., eds. (1982). *Pseudoseizures.* Baltimore, MD and London: Williams & Wilkins.

Rivera-Arzola, M., and Ramos-Greniers, J. (1997). Anger, *Ataques de Nervios*, and *la mujer puertorriqueña*: sociocultural considerations and treatment implications. In *Psychological Interventions and Research with Latino Populations*, ed. J. Garcia and M. C. Zea. Needham Heights, MA: Allyn & Bacon.

Robert, E. (1937). *Candle in the Sun*. New York: Bobbs-Merrill.

Robert de Ramírez de Arellano, M. I., Ramírez de Arellano, M., García, L., et al. (1954). *"Ataques," hyperkinetic type: the so-called "Puerto Rican Syndrome."* Its *medical, psychological, and social implications*. Paper read at the Annual Meeting of the Puerto Rico Medical Association, December. Unpublished.

Robinson, A. G. (1899). *The Porto Rico of Today*. New York: Charles Scribner's Sons.

Rodriguez, C. E., Sanchez Korrol, V., and Alers, J. O. (1980). *The Puerto Rican Struggle: Essays on Survival*. New York: Puerto Rican Migration Research Consortium. Also published by Waterfront Press, Maplewood, NJ, 1984.

——— (1995). Puerto Ricans: between black and white. In *Boricuas: Influential Puerto Rican Writings: An Anthology*, ed. R. Santiago. New York: Ballantine.

Rosenbaum, M. (1984). Anna O. (Bertha Pappenheim): her history. In *Anna O: Fourteen Contemporary Reinterpretations*, ed. M. Rosenbaum and E. Muroff, pp. 1–25. New York: Free Press.

Rothenberg, A. (1964). Puerto Rico and aggression. *American Journal of Psychiatry* 120:962–970.

Roudinesco, E. (1997). *Jacques Lacan*. New York: Columbia University Press.

Rubio, M., Urdaneta, M., and Doyle, J. (1955). Psychopathological reaction patterns in the Antilles command. *U.S. Armed Forces Medical Journal* 6(12):1767–1772.

Ruiz, P. (1982). The Hispanic patient: sociocultural perspectives. In *Mental Health and Hispanic Americans*, ed. R. Becerra, M. Karno, and J. Escobar. New York: Grune & Stratton.

Salmán, E., et al. (1998). Subtypes of Ataques de nervios: the influence of coexisting psychiatric diagnosis. *Culture, Medicine and Psychiatry* 22:231–244.

Santiago, R., ed. (1995). *Boricuas: Influential Puerto Rican Writings: An Anthology*. New York: Ballantine.

Santiago-Valles, K. (1994). *"Subject People" and Colonial Discourses: Economic Transformation and Social Disorder in Puerto Rico 1898–1947*. Albany, NY: State University of New York Press.

Schneiderman, S. (1986). *Rat Man*. New York: New York University Press.

Sennett, R., and Cobb, J. (1972). *The Hidden Injuries of Class*. New York: Vintage.

Showalter, E. (1993). Hysteria, feminism, and gender. In *Hysteria Beyond Freud*, ed. S. Gilman, H. King, R. Porter, et al. Berkeley: University of California Press.

——— (1997). *Hystories*. New York: Columbia University Press.

Slavney, P. R. (1990). *Perspectives on "Hysteria."* Baltimore, MD: Johns Hopkins University Press.

Slingsby, B. T. (2002). The Prozac boom and its placebogenic counterpart—

a culturally fashioned phenomenon. *Medical Science Monitor* 8(5):389–393.

Spitzer, R., Gibbon, M., Skodol, A., et al. (1989). *The DSM-III-R Casebook: A Learning Companion to the Diagnostic and Statistical Manual of Mental Disorders*, 3rd ed., rev. (*DSM-III-R*). Washington, DC: American Psychiatric Press.

Steinberg, M. (1990). Transcultural issues in psychiatry: the *ataque* and multiple personality disorder. *Dissociation: Progress in the Dissociative Disorder* 3(1):31–33.

Tenenbaum, E. (1996). *Proton pseudos* revisitado. In *Estudios sobre la Histeria: Cien años después*, pp. 26–32. Tomo I. Buenos Aires: Ediciones Kline.

Therrien, M., and Ramírez, R. (2000). *The Hispanic Population in the United States: March 2000*. Current population reports, pp. 20–535. Washington, DC: U.S. Census Bureau.

Torre, C. A., Rodriguez, V., and Burgos, W., eds. (1994). *The Commuter Nation: Perspectives on Puerto Rican Migration*. Río Piedras: Editorial de la Universidad de Puerto Rico.

Torres, E. (1995). Carlito's Way. In *Boricuas: Influential Puerto Rican Writings: An Anthology*, ed. R. Santiago, pp. 189–204. New York: Ballantine.

Torres Matrullo, C. (1976). Acculturation and psychopathology among Puerto Rican women in mainland United States. *American Journal of Orthopsychiatry* 46(4).

Traxel, D. (1980). *An American Saga: The Life and Times of Rockwell Kent*. New York: Harper & Row.

Trillat, E. (1986). *Histoire de l'hystérie*. Paris: Seghers.

Turkle, S. (1992). *Psychoanalytic Politics: Jacques Lacan and the French Revolution*, 2nd ed. New York: Free Association Books.

U.S. Census Bureau. *The Hispanic Population in the United States* U.S.Census Bureau p20-535.pdf

U.S. Census Bureau (2000). Census of Population, Public Law 94–171 Redistricting Data File. Updated every 10 years.

U.S. Census Bureau (2001). *The Hispanic Population in the United States: Population Characteristics* (retrieved March 24, 2003).

Veith, I. (1965). *Hysteria: The History of a Disease*. Chicago: University of Chicago Press.

Verhaeghe, P. (1999). *Does the Woman Exist? From Freud's Hysteric to Lacan's Feminine*, trans. M. du Ry. New York: Other Press.

Wagenheim, K., with Jimenez de Wagenheim, O., eds. (1973). *The Puerto Ricans: A Documentary History*. New York: Praeger.

Wajeman, G. (1986). The hysteric's discourse. In *Hystoria*, ed. H. Schulz-Keil. New York: New York Lacan Study Group.

Wallen, J. (1992). Providing culturally appropriate mental health services for minorities. *Journal of Mental Health Administration* 19(3):288–295.

Westermeyer, J. (1987). Clinical considerations in cross-cultural diagnosis. *Hospital and Community Psychiatry* 38(2):160–165.

Winter, J. P. (1998). *Les errants de la chair: Etudes sur l'hystérie masculine.* Paris: Calmann-Levy.

Wolf, K. (1952). Growing up and its price in three Puerto Rican subcultures. *Psychiatry* 15(4):401–433.

Yap, P. M. (1974). *Comparative Psychiatry: A Theoretical Framework.* Toronto: University of Toronto Press.

Zavala-Martínez, I. (1981). *Mental Health and the Puerto Rican in the United States: A Critical Literature Review and Comprehensive Bibliography.* A Preliminary Comprehensive Examination Project. Unpublished manuscript.

Zinn, H. (1980). *The People's History of the United States.* New York: HarperCollins, 1995.

Žižek, S. (1989). *The Sublime Object of Ideology.* New York: Verso.

Index

Gann, L. H., 21
Garcia Passalacqua, J., 132
Garcia-Prieto, N., 134, 135
Garrison, V., 201–202, 203, 204, 205, 207, 211–214
Gay, P., 163, 168
Georas, C. S., 14, 62, 178
Gherovici, P., 6, 185n1
Ghetto. *See Barrio*
Glazer, N., 21
Grace, W., 27, 35, 56
Gramsci, A., 59
Greenberg, R., 25
Grosfoguel, R., 14, 62, 63
Group psychology. *See* Collective psychology
Guarnaccia, P., 31, 36, 56, 59, 72, 73, 74, 75, 76–77, 127, 135, 139
Gutiérrez, J. J., 172

Hameln, Glukel von, 112
Hancock, R., 156
Happiness, psychoanalysis, 222–223
Harrington, M., 63
Harwood, A., 82, 198
Hay, J., 166
Hay Group Study, 23n8, 24
Heaney, S., 218
Heller, J., 136
Hill, R. T., 140n11, 141
Hirsch, S. J., 30
Hispanic(s)
  demographics, 6, 12–13, 16
  race and, 173
  as signifier, 173–174
  term of, 12–13, 172
Hollander, M. H., 30

Homes, S., 172
Homosexuality, 46
Hughes, C. C., 73
Hughes, L., 183
Hunter, D., 110
Hunter, R. J., 133
Hutcheon, L., 136
Hypnosis
  espiritismo, 200–201
  Freud, 164
Hysteria, xi–xii. *See also* Puerto Rican syndrome
  Anna O. case (Breuer and Freud), 101, 103–120
  Charcot, 28, 29
  community and, 16–17
  culture, 48–51
  diagnostic categories, 51–54, 59–60
  fantasy and, 149–150
  Freudian psychoanalysis, 18, 26, 48, 52–53, 145–149
  history of, 30
  jouissance and, 26, 54, 205
  Lacanian psychoanalysis, 8–9, 17
  politics and, 218
  Puerto Rican syndrome, 8
  trauma, 106, 236

Identification
  with the aggressor, racism, 186–190
  collective psychology, 19
  Puerto Rican syndrome, 42–43
Identity, crowd and, 168–170
Identity theft, Other, 174–176
Ideology, colonialism, 14
Illiteracy, 16